What readers are saying about
Ubuntu Kung Fu

Ubuntu Kung Fu is excellent. The tips are fun and the hope of discovering hidden gems makes it a worthwhile task.

▶ **John Southern**
Former editor of *Linux Magazine*

I enjoyed *Ubuntu Kung Fu* and learned some new things. I would recommend this book—nice tips and a lot of fun to be had.

▶ **Carthik Sharma**
Creator of the Ubuntu Blog (http://ubuntu.wordpress.com)

Wow! There are some great tips here! I have used Ubuntu since April 2005, starting with version 5.04. I found much in this book to inspire me and to teach me, and it answered lingering questions I didn't know I had. The book is a good resource that I will gladly recommend to both newcomers and veteran users.

▶ **Matthew Helmke**
Administrator, Ubuntu Forums

Ubuntu Kung Fu is a fantastic compendium of useful, uncommon Ubuntu knowledge.

▶ **Eric Hewitt**
Consultant, LiveLogic, LLC

Ubuntu Kung Fu

Tips, Tricks, Hints, and Hacks

Ubuntu Kung Fu

Tips, Tricks, Hints, and Hacks

Keir Thomas

The Pragmatic Bookshelf
Raleigh, North Carolina   Dallas, Texas

Many of the designations used by manufacturers and sellers to distinguish their products are claimed as trademarks. Where those designations appear in this book, and The Pragmatic Programmers, LLC was aware of a trademark claim, the designations have been printed in initial capital letters or in all capitals. The Pragmatic Starter Kit, The Pragmatic Programmer, Pragmatic Programming, Pragmatic Bookshelf and the linking *g* device are trademarks of The Pragmatic Programmers, LLC. The Ubuntu logo is a registered trademark of Canonical, Ltd.

Every precaution was taken in the preparation of this book. However, the publisher assumes no responsibility for errors or omissions, or for damages that may result from the use of information (including program listings) contained herein.

Our Pragmatic courses, workshops, and other products can help you and your team create better software and have more fun. For more information, as well as the latest Pragmatic titles, please visit us at

http://www.pragprog.com

ISBN-10: 1-934356-22-0

ISBN-13: 978-1-934356-22-7

Printed on acid-free paper.

P2.0 printing, February 2009

Version: 2009-1-28

Contents

Contents By Topic

General Productivity Tips

GUI Enhancements

Hardware Hacks

Image, Document, and Multimedia Tips

Security Hacks

Miscellaneous

Chapter 1

Introduction

This book was born out of an experiment carried out when Ubuntu 6.06 was released in 2006. Back then, Ubuntu was rougher around the edges than it is today. Getting MP3 files to play took some effort. Only a handful of wifi cards worked out of the box, and the rest had to be wrangled into working.

So, I wrote twenty-five tips to get Ubuntu working the way I thought it should. I also looked at some cool things that could be done with Ubuntu—the kind of things that wowed people passing by your computer. Everything was kept simple because I knew a high proportion of Ubuntu users had switched from Windows, where things were done differently. Many of the tips were pulled from my award-winning book *Beginning Ubuntu Linux.*

I put the tips on my website and then posted a link to the page on the Digg.com social networking website. Within hours it was in the top ten links for that day. My site was actually knocked offline by the sheer volume of visitors.

The popularity of the tips was partly because Ubuntu has always been popular with the Digg.com crowd, but there was a more important reason. People wanted Ubuntu to "just work." They brought with them the expectations of Windows users. They didn't want to make any compromises in terms of either usability or function. And they wanted to learn how Ubuntu worked. They wanted that above all, in fact.

Ubuntu Kung Fu is for those people and others like them. It's an Ubuntu book for the rest of us.

In its pages you'll find more than 300 tips that:

- make Ubuntu more usable for newcomers and experienced users alike,
- point out cool and often extraordinary things that Ubuntu can do, and
- show how Ubuntu can be *fun*.

Along the way, you'll pick up many skills that will make you a more proficient Ubuntu user.

1.1 How to Read This Book

In a nutshell, *Ubuntu Kung Fu* is a big book of tips. As such, I don't recommend any particular way of reading it. You don't need to be sitting beside your computer to do so. The whole point of *Ubuntu Kung Fu* is that you can jump in anywhere. Start at the beginning, or start in the middle. You could even start at the end and work your way to the front. Just start reading. If you find a tip you like, then try it!

Ubuntu Kung Fu expects no prior Linux or Ubuntu experience from its readers. That doesn't mean all the tips are beginner level. Some are more involved than others, and a handful are written for experienced users. But in every tip I walk the reader through each step of the way. I've also provided a crash course in Ubuntu administration skills in the second chapter of the book. This should get even the greenest of newbies up to speed quickly.

Before you dive into the tips, I need to mention some caveats. First, some of the tips affect your system in a profound way. They show how to edit configuration files, for example, and one wrong keystroke could mean disaster (although it's nearly always possible to fix things—this is discussed in Chapter 2, *An Ubuntu Administration Crash Course*, on page 5). Be sure to read through a tip before attempting anything it says. Check what you type or click against what's written.

If you're unsure about what you're doing, then skip that particular tip and perhaps return to it later.

If you spot anything that doesn't seem to work and you think it should, contact http://pragprog.com/titles/ktuk/errata. Provide as many details as possible. If possible, as well as correcting the tip in question, I'll thank you in a future edition of *Ubuntu Kung Fu*.

Additionally, head over to the forums at http://www.ubuntukungfu.org/forum to see whether a member of the *Ubuntu Kung Fu* community can help you figure out what went wrong.

Second, please note that this book was written using Ubuntu 8.04.1 LTS (Hardy Heron) as a base. As with all releases of Ubuntu, this brings a handful of small but important changes in the way system configuration is handled. If you haven't already, I strongly advise you to upgrade to 8.04.1 if you're using an earlier version of Ubuntu. If you're using a later version of Ubuntu, then you might have to occasionally apply some common sense.

Lastly, please note that the tips concentrate on productivity, enhancements, and doing cool stuff. I've deliberately steered clear of providing workarounds for bugs or gotchas. This is because the tips would become dated very quickly as the bugs are fixed or patched or as official workarounds are introduced. If you run up against something in Ubuntu that doesn't work the way it should, you first port of call should be the official Ubuntu forums—http://www.ubuntuforums.org—where it's very likely somebody will have posted a solution.

1.2 Acknowledgments

Thanks go to Pragmatic Programmers for not slamming the door in the face of a crazy guy who suggested a one-chapter book full of things he thinks are cool. Thanks go to Jackie Carter, my editor, plus Pragmatic Programmers overlords Andy and Dave for their patience, guidance, and encouragement. I've never met such switched-on, optimistic, and genuinely agile people in more than a decade of working in publishing. To paraphrase Simon & Garfunkel, they've got a groovy thing going on.

Thanks also to the technical reviewers who put this book through its paces prior to release and often suggested important improvements. My gratitude goes to Matthew Helmke, Eric Hewitt, Carthik Sharma, and John Southern. There's some astonishingly large brains in that list. A zombie would have a feast. I'm honored that they all agreed to give this book the benefit of their experience and knowledge.

Thanks to Microsoft UK, which supplied a copy of Windows Vista for use during testing. Finally, thanks to the beta testers who took a chance on this book before it was officially published. Your errata comments made *Ubuntu Kung Fu* a stronger book.

1.3 Sharing

If you'd like to share some of the tips from this book on your blog, then feel free. I'm not sure my publisher will be too happy if you take liberties, but sharing a handful of tips you've found useful with others can only be a good thing. If you do, it would be great if you could link to the book's official web page—http://pragprog.com/titles/ktuk (and, if you're feeling generous, you might also like to link to http://www.ubuntukungfu. org, the community site that partners this book).

—Keir Thomas, September 2008

## Chapter 2

An Ubuntu Administration Crash Course

There's a time when all of us sit down in front of Ubuntu for the first time. The African drumbeats of the login sound fade away, and we're greeted by the orange and browns of the desktop wallpaper. (Orange and brown? What *were* they thinking?)

What goes through your mind after this probably depends on how busy you are. To quote from *Peter Pan*, Ubuntu can be an "awfully big adventure." But for that to be true, you have to be the kind of person who enjoys adventures. I suspect most people simply want to know what's what and how things work.

That's what this chapter is about. It's a crash course in basic Ubuntu skills and knowledge. It's the mechanic's guide that tells you which end of a screwdriver is the useful one and how to use it. It's necessary because you'll have to get your hands dirty under the hood of Ubuntu, not only to follow the tips in this book but as part of day-to-day life with the operating system.

There are certainly more comprehensive introductory guides to Ubuntu (I recommend *Beginning Ubuntu Linux, Third Edition*, written by myself and Jaime Sicam). However, if you have little time to spare or just a brief attention span, this chapter will give you enough know-how to get by. You might have to read it more than once and maybe come back to it later. That's fine. It isn't going anywhere.

Even if you're an experienced Ubuntu user, it might be worth skimming through this chapter to ensure you know enough to proceed to the tips ahead. I'd ask that you pay particular attention to the section that describes how to use gconf-editor, which is used extensively in some of the tips. This is a lesser-known but very useful configuration tool.

So, let's get to it.

2.1 The Ubuntu Desktop

Before we get down to specifics, let's take an overview of the Ubuntu desktop. If you've already spent time playing around with the desktop, then you can probably skip this part.

You first thing you might notice is that it's virtually icon-free. This is just because the Ubuntu developers don't like clutter. You can drag and drop icons onto the desktop and get it as messy as you want.

At the top and bottom of the screen are the *panels*. These are almost identical to Windows' taskbar except that there are two of them. The one at the top tends to be about running software and presenting information to the user. The one at the bottom is where programs minimize to; it contains a Show Desktop button (left) and Trash icon (right), along with a virtual desktop switcher (far right).

On the top panel there are three menus—Applications, Places, and System. These will always stick around, no matter what. An application's own menus (File, Edit, View, and so on) will appear underneath.

The Applications menu contains the software you use on a day-to-day basis—media players, office applications, a calculator, and so on. However, software used to administrate the software isn't found there. That's on the System menu, which has two submenus—Preferences and Administration. Preferences lists programs that tweak settings specific to your user account, such as changing the desktop wallpaper. Administration lists programs that configure the overall system.

Programs on the System → Administration menu won't run unless you type your login password when prompted. I explain more about this on page 8.

The Places menu provides quick access to the file system or to any other file system that is attached to your computer, such as your Windows partition or USB memory sticks that are plugged in.

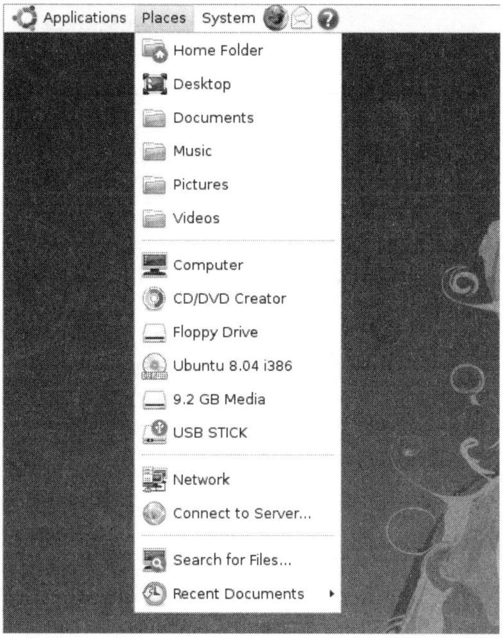

Figure 2.1: UBUNTU'S PLACES MENU

You can see an example in Figure 2.1. The Windows partition will probably be identified as x GB Media, where x is the size of the partition. USB memory sticks will be identified by their name (aka their label). Incidentally, the file browser used in Ubuntu has a name—Nautilus. It's a cool piece of software in its own right, so be sure to explore its functions. Like most applications in Ubuntu, it can be configured by clicking Edit → Preferences on its menu.

Your personal area on the disk is a folder named after your username that can be found the /home folder. Often people simply refer to this as their *home folder*. It's analogous to My Documents under Windows. There are several other subdirectories in your personal /home folder for you to store stuff in—Documents, Music, Pictures, and Videos. There's also the Desktop folder that, like Windows, simply contains any files stored on the desktop.

As mentioned earlier, the Trash icon lives at the bottom right of the desktop. Drag and drop stuff onto it to delete (or just right-click what you want to delete, and select Move to the Deleted Items folder). Click the Trash icon to see its contents and to see a button that lets you empty it.

At the top right of the screen is the notification area, which is just like Windows' system tray. Sometimes icons pop up here to notify you of stuff, such as that there are system updates available or that you have new email. The volume control and clock live here, along with NetworkManager, which lets you configure your wifi/network connection. There's also something called Fast User Switcher. That's why your login name is listed there. Clicking it lets you switch between users on the system. It's useless if there's only one user set up on the system, which is probably the case for 99% of Ubuntu installations. You can get rid of it (or, indeed, anything on the panels) by right-clicking and selecting Remove from panel. You can add it back in again if you want by right-clicking a blank spot on the panels and selecting Add to panel. Then choose it from the list.

If you select Add to panel, you'll also see lots of other handy applets (small programs with a specific function) that can be added to the panel. Some are very useful, so take some time to explore.

Icons can be clicked and dragged from the menus to the desktop for ease of access. In addition, they can be dragged onto blank spots on the panels. The desktop can be used as a semipermanent store area for files, just like with Windows or Macintosh OS X. Just click and drag a file from the file-browsing window. Files are always downloaded to the desktop by the web browser unless you specify otherwise.

Whereas Windows has Internet Explorer, Ubuntu uses Firefox (Applications → Internet → Firefox Web Browser). Outlook is replaced by Evolution (Applications → Internet → Evolution Email). Microsoft Office is replaced by OpenOffice.org (Applications → Office). Pidgin is used for instant messaging (Applications → Internet → Pidgin Internet Messenger). GIMP is used for image editing (Applications → Graphics → GIMP Image Editor). Just have a click around on the menus—it's fairly obvious what everything does, and it's pretty hard to break anything.

Many tips in this book make reference to Gedit, a text editor. This can be found on the Applications → Accessories menu, although you'll nearly always start it from the command line when following the tips.

2.2 Users, Passwords, and Files

When you first installed Ubuntu, you created a user account for yourself. You were allocated a slice of space to save your personal data

Drive Letters and Ubuntu

Ubuntu doesn't use drive letters. The root of the file system, normally indicated by C:\ within Windows, is indicated by a single forward slash (/) in Ubuntu. Thus, you'll see a path like /usr/share/doc/ in Ubuntu, rather than something like C:\Program Files\Microsoft Office within Windows. Whereas Windows uses a backslash (\) to separate directories, Ubuntu uses a forward slash. Other than that, there are no real differences.

But if there are no drive letters, then how are things like additional hard disks or USB key sticks accessed? They're *mounted*. This is the magical process of "plumbing through" the contents of a non-Ubuntu file system to a particular folder. For example, when you click the Windows entry on the Places menu, the contents of the Windows partition will be accessible by browsing the /media/disk/ folder. It's nearly always the case that empty and specifically created directories are used for mounting, but if there is anything already in the /media/disk/ folder, it will temporarily disappear, until the Windows partition is *unmounted*. In theory, any file system you want to access has to be mounted, including things like shared network folders or the CD/DVD-ROM drive. It's nearly always done automatically.

Unmounting is done by right-clicking the desktop icon of the mounted file system and selecting Unmount (or similar—the precise language used varies depending on what you right-click). Rather confusingly, to unmount at the command line, you have to use the umount command—that's unmount without the *n*.

(/home/*username*), and a desktop environment was automatically configured for your use.

Yours is an ordinary, unprivileged user account. You can administer the system, but only if you "borrow" administrative powers. When manually typing commands, this is done by preceding them with either sudo, in the case of command-line programs, or gksu, in the case of GUI programs. You'll then be prompted for your login password. Type it correctly, and the application will run with administrative powers. It's as simple as that.

Some GUI programs on the System → Administration menu automatically request administrator powers by popping up a password request

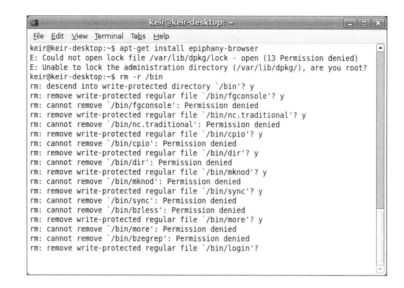

```
keir@keir-desktop: ~
File  Edit  View  Terminal  Tabs  Help
keir@keir-desktop:~$ apt-get install epiphany-browser
E: Could not open lock file /var/lib/dpkg/lock - open (13 Permission denied)
E: Unable to lock the administration directory (/var/lib/dpkg/), are you root?
keir@keir-desktop:~$ rm -r /bin
rm: descend into write-protected directory `/bin'? y
rm: remove write-protected regular file `/bin/fgconsole'? y
rm: cannot remove `/bin/fgconsole': Permission denied
rm: remove write-protected regular file `/bin/nc.traditional'? y
rm: cannot remove `/bin/nc.traditional': Permission denied
rm: remove write-protected regular file `/bin/cpio'? y
rm: cannot remove `/bin/cpio': Permission denied
rm: remove write-protected regular file `/bin/dir'? y
rm: cannot remove `/bin/dir': Permission denied
rm: remove write-protected regular file `/bin/mknod'? y
rm: cannot remove `/bin/mknod': Permission denied
rm: remove write-protected regular file `/bin/sync'? y
rm: cannot remove `/bin/sync': Permission denied
rm: cannot remove `/bin/bzless': Permission denied
rm: remove write-protected regular file `/bin/more'? y
rm: cannot remove `/bin/more': Permission denied
rm: cannot remove `/bin/bzegrep': Permission denied
rm: remove write-protected regular file `/bin/login'?
```

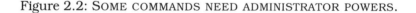

Figure 2.2: SOME COMMANDS NEED ADMINISTRATOR POWERS.

dialog box, while others require you to click the Unlock button some-where within their program window. This will then pop up a similar password request dialog box. An example of such an application is the Users and Groups program on the System → Administration menu.[1]

If you try to run certain commands without borrowing admin powers, you'll see an error message of some kind, as shown in Figure 2.2. The reason you're not allowed to run around the system and do what you want unhindered (like in, say, Windows XP) should be obvious: admin-istering the system brings the possibility of breaking it. The password request also reminds or informs you that the command you want to use has the potential to really mess things up.

What sudo or gksu actually does is borrow the *root user*'s power. Effec-tively, for the short time the command in question is running, you become the root user.

The root user is another type of account. If you were to log in as the root user, you could do anything, unhindered.

---

1. Eventually all the system administration tools will have an Unlock button. This is part of Ubuntu's new *Policy Kit* feature that introduces better security by giving only certain aspects of a program administrator powers, rather than all of it.

But, unlike most versions of Linux, Ubuntu doesn't let you directly log in as the root user. It forces you to use sudo or gksu to borrow root powers. Again, the reasoning behind this should be obvious: there's simply less chance of damage. You can't switch to the root user and then forget you're root, perhaps issuing a drastic command that breaks the system.

The idea of root and ordinary users pervades the entire system. All files—even operating system ones—are "owned" by a user. That user can then set access rights for themselves, their group (all users are also members of a group), and also *anybody* of the system, regardless of what user they are or group they're in. For example, a user could set a file so that it can be read by and written to only by herself. Or she could add the ability for members of the group she's in to read it but not write to it.

All of this might sound strange if there's only one user on the system (yourself!), but it's just how Linux works. There is some logic behind it; it should come as no surprise to learn that most operating system files are owned by root. This is why it's nearly always necessary to borrow root powers when editing configuration files[2] or doing stuff like installing software.

It's not only files that can be owned and have restrictive permissions set on them. Directories can too, and this can be used to stop unauthorized users from even viewing the list of files in some directories.

The end result is that, for many of the tips that make up this book, you'll need to enter your password to carry them out. You'll need to precede commands with either sudo or gksu or just type your password when prompted. I point this out in each tip, so it's not something you need to add yourself. However, it's definitely something you should know about.

2.3 Command Line or GUI?

Ubuntu might be described as an operating system with a dual nature. For many administrative tasks, you can use GUI programs that are

---

2. The configuration files in your /home folder are owned by you, rather than root. This is because they usually relate to your personal settings, such as those for the GNOME desktop. These configuration files are usually hidden, which is to say, their filenames are preceded with a period (.). Most are stored in the .gnome2 folder.

One Giant File System

In many key ways, Linux is one giant file system. If you attach a new piece of hardware to the system, it's made accessible as a virtual file in the /dev folder. The system "talks to you" by providing virtual files in the /proc folder containing information about what it's doing. As a user, even *you* manifest as a handful of files on the system.

Linux is a giant file system because it reduces everything to the same level so things can be accessed and manipulated in a logical and structured way. The concept is one of the fundaments of Unix, which Linux is based on.

That everything really is a file can be demonstrated by opening the file that the mouse is plumbed through to—/dev/psaux. Start by opening a terminal window—click Applications → Accessories → Terminal. Then type sudo cat /dev/psaux. You'll need to type your password when prompted. Then waggle the mouse around a little. The screen will fill up with junk. The computer might beep too. The cat command you issued displays the contents of a file on the screen, and you told it to display the contents of the file that's magically plumbed through to the mouse hardware. So, waggling the mouse causes data to appear onscreen.

When you've finished, just close the program window.

usually provided on the System → Administration menu. Or you can do the same thing by typing at the command prompt. For example, you can install the Epiphany web browser using the Synaptic package manager program. Or you can install it by typing sudo apt-get install epiphany-browser. This applies equally to trivial things such as file management. You can delete that file on your desktop by dragging it to the trash, or you can type rm ~/Desktop/filename.[3]

Which should you use? The choice is yours. The command line is often far more efficient but can be arcane, especially for beginners. Yet it's where the real power lies. GUI tools make things simpler but often at the expense of flexibility in the form of configuration options.

---

3. Note that the command line doesn't have a trash facility. Once a file is deleted, it's gone forever. Tip 36, on page 81, describes a workaround for this.

This book prefers to use the GUI tools whenever possible. It's only when something isn't possible via GUI software that we delve into command-line tools. This is very much in keeping with the spirit of Ubuntu, which is, after all, "Linux for human beings."

But that's no excuse for not having at least some command-line skills. So, how does the command line work? I'm glad you asked....

How the Command Line Works

Let's get one thing straight from the start: the command line is just one more way to administer your system or run software. You don't have to use it if you don't want to, although there are a few tasks where it's unavoidable.

We'd better clear up another misconception too: the command line isn't some ethereal presence, always running in the background.[4] This isn't like Windows 3.1, where everything "sat on top of" DOS, which was always there ready to offer a C:\ prompt. In Ubuntu, everything sits on top of a central program called the *kernel*. If the command line isn't being used, then the command line isn't running.

One last thing—how to refer to the command line in polite conversation. Some folks refer to it as the *shell*. I tend to refer to the *command prompt* or *command line*.

The software that provides the command line is called the Bourne Again Shell, but this is always abbreviated to bash. bash simply lets you enter commands, manipulate files, and see the output once you've done so.

Let's start a command-line session and see what it looks like. There are two ways of doing this—either running a *virtual console* or using GNOME Terminal (usually referred to simply as the *terminal*). Both provide access to the same thing—think of them as doors into the same room.

You can start a virtual console by holding down Ctrl+Alt+F2 (or F3, F4, F5, or F6—there are six in total, corresponding to the first six function keys, and all can be running at the same time, but the first—F1—is used for log/debug output and so is best avoided).

---

4. It isn't *strictly* true that the command prompt isn't always running; the program that provides the command login, getty, is always running, and...what's that? Your head is about to explode? OK. I'll ease off the pedantic explanations.

You'll notice that the desktop and all signs of GUI-ness disappear. Don't worry. You can get it all back by hitting Ctrl+Alt+F7. Give it a try. Then hit Ctrl+Alt+F2 to get back to the virtual console.

What you'll see will be something like this:

```
Ubuntu 8.04.1 keir-desktop tty2

keir-desktop login:
```

You must type your username and then, when prompted, type your password. After some legal boilerplate and some instructions about how to issue administrator commands, you'll then see the command-line prompt, followed by the familiar cursor.

As mentioned, you can also use the terminal program from within the GUI desktop to get a command line. This is far more convenient,[5] so quit your virtual console by typing exit. This will log you out (but only out of that virtual console—you'll still be logged into your desktop). Then switch back to the GUI (Ctrl+Alt+F7), and start GNOME Terminal by clicking Applications → Accessories → Terminal.

No login is needed this time around because you've already logged into the desktop, and the terminal program runs "on top" of that. However, what you see is the same prompt you saw earlier on the virtual console, and you can do the same things.

Let's take a closer look at the prompt. Here's what the one on my test system looks like:

```
keir@keir-desktop:~$
```

It looks complicated but isn't. The first part, before the @ sign, is the username I'm logged in as. My username is keir. The part after the @ sign is the *hostname*, which is to say how the computer refers to itself and is referred to by other computers on a network.

So if we "read" the prompt from left to right, it says that the user keir is logged in at (@) the computer called keir-desktop. If I logged in as the user called jane, the prompt would read jane@keir-desktop:~$.

---

5. So, when should you use a virtual console, and when should you use a GNOME Terminal window? This is answered by situation and circumstance—the only time you *need* to use a virtual console is when you have no choice. For example, if a program crashes and locks up the GUI, you can switch to a virtual console to fix things. However, for some Linux old hands, the virtual console is simply the first port of call when it comes to typing commands. To each their own.

Following this is a colon. That separates what we might call the "location" part of the prompt from the rest of it, which tells us where we currently are in the file system—what folder we're currently browsing. It appears we're browsing the ~ folder. What? Don't worry. The tilde symbol is command-line shorthand. It means you're currently in your /home folder, which is where you'll always be dumped when you start a new command-line prompt. You can confirm the folder you're in by typing pwd, which stands for Print Working Directory (*directory* being another term for *folder*). Give it a try. Type pwd, and hit Enter. Here's what I see on my test PC:

```
$ pwd
/home/keir
```

Finally, at the end of the prompt line, is the dollar sign. This tells us we're logged in as a normal user. If we logged in as root, it would change to a hash (#), but, as mentioned, this is moot as far as we're concerned because Ubuntu doesn't allow root user login (with a notable exception: if you use Ubuntu's rescue mode, you're logged in as root automatically).

Throughout this book all commands I want you to type are listed with a dollar sign before them. Some will be preceded with a hash symbol too if the rescue mode is being used. This is just one of the conventions of computing literature. It doesn't mean you need to type the dollar or hash sign.

Back to the command-line tutorial. If you switch to the Desktop folder by typing the following:[6]

```
$ cd Desktop
```

...you'll see that the prompt changes to something like the following:

```
keir@keir-desktop:~/Desktop$
```

So, we're browsing in our Desktop folder in our personal /home folder (which is represented by a tilde symbol). Again, prove this if you want by typing pwd.

---

6. Capital letters matter under Ubuntu, unlike with DOS/Windows, where they're optional. If a filename, folder, or command has a capital letter in it, then you must type it. You could feasibly have files called Filename.doc, filename.doc, FILEname.doc, and so on, all in the same folder. Virtually all commands are entirely lowercase and should be typed as such. Adding capital letters will mean they won't be recognized.

Navigating Text-Mode Menus

Not all command-line programs provide straight output. Some invoke simple text menus, like you might be used to in any GUI application, but are more primitive. You usually can't use the mouse to click entries and instead must use the keyboard to navigate. The [Tab] key moves the selection highlight from entry to entry, and the spacebar normally confirms the selection of that particular option. Alternatively, you can use the cursor keys to move the selection highlight around. When you've finished selecting the options on any particular screen, you should move the selection to the OK button and hit the spacebar to select it. Alternatively, on some simpler menus, you can move the selection highlight to your choice in the list and just hit [Enter], which will both make the selection and hit the OK button. [Esc] will usually quit the program without making any changes.

Some commands need what are called *arguments*—you need to tell the command what file or folder you want it to work with. We've already seen an example of this when we typed cd Desktop. cd is the command, while Desktop is the argument. Some commands require multiple arguments—if you want to copy a file using cp, for example, you'll need to first specify the file/folder to be copied and then its destination. Here's an example that copies the fstab configuration file in the /etc directory to the Desktop folder: cp /etc/fstab ~/Desktop/.

Some commands also take *options*, which modify how the command works. For example, the ls command (ls being short for "list") will give us a file and folder listing. Let's try this. First, switch back to your /home folder (cd ..—the two periods tells cd to switch back to the parent folder), and type ls. Here's what I saw on my test computer:

```
$ ls
Desktop  Documents  Examples  Music  Pictures  Public  Templates  Videos
```

There isn't any information about file permissions here, and we can make ls provide that by using the -l command option. Command options are usually inserted after the command, so you would type this:

```
$ ls -l
```

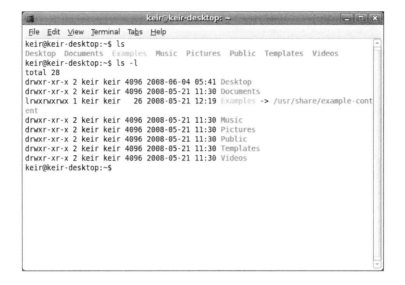

Figure 2.3: USING COMMAND OPTIONS

If you type that, you'll get a long list of filenames/directories on the right, with their permissions and ownership rules on the left. An example from my test PC is shown in Figure 2.3. Often two or more command options are used together—the -a option tells ls to list hidden files too, so a command commonly typed by Linux users is ls -la.

You can usually get a list of a command's most popular options by typing --help after the command (that's two dashes before help). For example, to get a list of the ls command's options, you would type the following:

```
$ ls --help
```

You can see some typical commands in Figure 2.4, on the following page. These make up the meat of day-to-day operations at the command prompt when it comes to handling files. There's lot more to each command, of course, and a good tip is to use the man (manual) command. This provides useful information about what a command does and how to use it. For example, to learn about the ls command, you would type the following:

```
$ man ls
```

ls	Lists files and folders in current folder. -l: Provides long listing, including all details of files -a: Shows all files, including those that are hidden -h: Provides "human-readable" file sizes (KB, MB, GB) *Example:* ls -l
cd	Changes folder; cd .. changes to parent folder. *Example:* cd /home/keir
cp	Copies file and/or folder. First specify the file and then the new location. -r: Copies directories too (otherwise directories will be ignored) *Example:* cp /home/keir/file.doc /home/keir/Desktop/
mv	Moves file and/or folder. First specify the file and then the new location. By specifying a new filename, mv can also be used to rename. Unlike cp, no need for additional -r option for directories. *Example:* mv /home/keir/myfile /home/keir/Desktop/ *Example:* mv oldfilename newfilename
rm	Deletes file and/or folder. -r: Deletes directories too (otherwise directories will be ignored) -f: Doesn't prompt for confirmation *Example:* rm -rf Desktop/newfolder/
mkdir	Creates folder. *Example:* mkdir newfolder
less	Displays text file. Use up/down cursor keys to scroll, and hit Esc to quit. *Example:* less file.txt

Figure 2.4: TYPICAL DAY-TO-DAY FILE MANAGEMENT COMMANDS

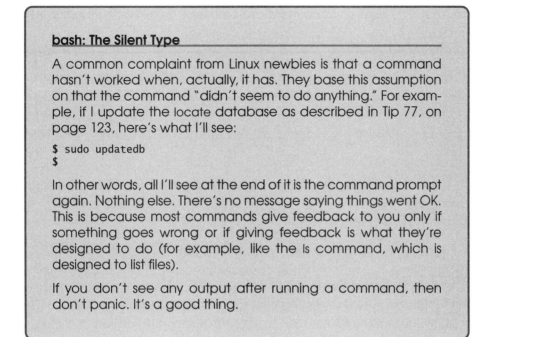

bash: The Silent Type

A common complaint from Linux newbies is that a command hasn't worked when, actually, it has. They base this assumption on that the command "didn't seem to do anything." For example, if I update the locate database as described in Tip 77, on page 123, here's what I'll see:

```
$ sudo updatedb
$
```

In other words, all I'll see at the end of it is the command prompt again. Nothing else. There's no message saying things went OK. This is because most commands give feedback to you only if something goes wrong or if giving feedback is what they're designed to do (for example, like the ls command, which is designed to list files).

If you don't see any output after running a command, then don't panic. It's a good thing.

More Advanced Command-Line Skills

It might sound obvious, but all bash does is take input, usually in the form of commands you type, and then output something. It's like a production-line machine—input goes in at one end, and output comes out at the other end.

Technically speaking, the input of the machine is called *standard input* (*stdin*), while the output is called *standard output* (*stdout*).[7] Stdin is usually your keyboard and stdout your monitor, but that doesn't have to be the case. The rather cool thing about bash is that it doesn't care what stdin and stdout actually are.

Why is this important? Well, the output and input of a command can be *redirected*. A command can be fed the contents of a file instead of what you type. Alternatively, the output of a command can be redirected into a file, rather than sent to the screen. Angle brackets are used for the purpose of redirecting.

---

7. Alongside stdout there's actually a second output—*standard error*, or *stderr*. This is simply the error output of a command (if there is any). It is usually sent to the screen, like stdout, but it too can be redirected. To redirect stderr, use 2>, instead of a single right-facing angle bracket.

Let's say you wanted to create a text file showing a long file listing. All you'd do is type ls -l > listing.txt. Imagine the angle bracket as a funnel—the ls -l command pours its output into the listing.txt file (after first creating the file, of course).

Let's also say you have a shopping list and want to sort it into alphabetical order. bash includes a handy command that can do this—sort—but you have to make it take your file as input. The following will do the trick:

```
$ sort < shoppinglist.txt
```

This is slightly less intuitive because the command comes first, and then the file is "poured into it," courtesy of redirection of input.

If you were to try this, you'd find the shopping list would indeed be sorted, but it would also appear onscreen. This is because sort sends its output to stdout, unless told otherwise. Many commands do this, and it might seem stupid, but it reflects the deliberate simplicity of bash. To get around it, you need to redirect the output of sort into a new file:

```
$ sort < shoppinglist.txt > sortedlist.txt
```

What about if you wanted to create a text file that contained file listings of several different directories? You could create several text files using redirection and combine them manually, but a better plan is to type something similar to the following:

```
$ ls -l > listing.txt
$ ls -l /etc >> listing.txt
$ ls -l /bin >> listing.txt
... etc.
```

Two angle brackets mean that the file is added to, rather than created anew. The first command initially creates our listing.txt file, while the two following commands add their output to the end of it.

The output of one command can also be *piped* into another, which is to say the output of one command can form the input of another. The pipe symbol (|) is used to do this. The most basic example is to pipe the output of the ls command into less, the text viewer:

```
$ ls | less
```

In other words, rather than sending the file listing to the screen, it's piped into the less command and so is then displayed onscreen for leisurely, scroll-through reading. This can be useful when you're working at a virtual console, which lacks those handy scrollbars that GUI programs have.

Figure 2.5: PIPING THE OUTPUT OF A COMMAND INTO GREP

Couldn't we just redirect the output into less—something like ls > less? No. Redirecting is about sending data into (or from) files. With piping, the output is simply transferred from one command to another without creating a file. The ls > less command would create a new file called less, which contains the file listing.

Piping is often used with the grep command, which is able to search through a file for text. For example, say you want to make a list of all the files belonging to a particular project you're working on. The files are in your Documents folder, along with hundreds of others (for the purposes of this demonstration, let's assume you aren't very well organized). One thing is true of all the project files—they have the word *project* in their filename, but that could be at the end, in the middle, or at the front. You could type ls and then scroll through the list of results looking for relevant files, but that's very time-consuming and prone to human error. A better way is to get grep to search for you. We can do this by piping the output of ls straight into it:

```
$ ls | grep -i "project"
```

What you'll see, as shown in Figure 2.5, is the output of grep that has filtered the output of ls to show only the lines that contain the word *project* (the -i command option tells grep to ignore uppercase and lowercase letters when searching).

Dealing with Complex Filenames at the Command Line

The command line interprets a space between two words as an indication that a new command or command option follows. The question therefore arises of how to deal with filenames that have spaces in them. A logical continuation of this thought is how to deal with filenames containing characters that bash would otherwise interpret—symbols such as > or |, for example, which are used in redirection and piping, respectively.

The easiest solution is to simply enclose the filename in quotation marks (either single quotes or double—it doesn't matter). For example, to open the file <keir text file>.txt in less, I'd type less "<keir text file>.txt".

Another method is to *escape* each problematic character (including the spaces). This involves using a backslash (\) before the character to tell bash not to interpret it in the usual way. To view the file <keir text file>.txt in this case, I would type less \<keir\ text\ file\>.txt. Normally it's just easier to use quotes around the filename, but with a minority of commands you must escape instead.

Ubuntu's graphical applications handle filenames containing spaces and strange characters seamlessly. You don't have to escape or use quotes.

2.4 Software Installation and Management

There's a lot of software available for Ubuntu, in addition to what comes installed out of the box, and most of it is not only free but also easily accessible. Because of this, it's possible to suggest that, as far as active and experienced Ubuntu users are concerned, software installation is almost as common as any other activity, such as browsing the Web. Part of the fun of using Ubuntu is exploring what software is available and taking a look at offerings provided by new and interesting software projects that spring up.

Therefore, gaining a good understanding of the software installation subsystem of Ubuntu is vital. Many tips in this book involve adding software to bring new functionality to Ubuntu. How software installation and removal is handled under Ubuntu is radically different compared to Windows or Mac OS X, but it isn't hard to understand.

To install a program, a Windows user will double-click an installation .exe. Ubuntu is different because software installation is automated— even including the download. You literally just choose what you want to install and sit back while Ubuntu takes care of it.

Virtually all Ubuntu software is open source and therefore available for anybody to create their own versions of. So, the Ubuntu developers take the source code for thousands of software projects and compile it themselves, tweaking it to ensure it works correctly on Ubuntu, and put it into large publicly accessible *repositories* (known as *repos* for short).[8] In nearly all cases when you install software, it'll come from these repositories. Manually downloading and installing software is rare, although not unheard of—several tips in this book do just that, in fact.

The second key difference between Ubuntu and other operating systems like Windows and Mac OS X is that Ubuntu lets you install and remove just about everything, including system components that are otherwise invisible but make everything work.

The bits of software that are installed and removed are referred to as *packages*. Packages are nothing more than program and/or system files bundled together in one file, complete with *scripts* (chains of commands) that configure things so that the software works with everything else on the system.

Typically, to install a particular piece of software, it's necessary to install not only the program itself, which is usually provided as a single package, but several other packages containing the background system software it needs to work. You might say that software installation is modular. The software you want to install is said to *depend* on these other packages that provide the system files. As you might be coming to expect, Ubuntu's software install/removal tools automatically take care of installing these dependencies, and because of this, you will often hear people talk of *dependency management* when discussing Ubuntu's software management system.

It isn't just about managing dependencies when software is installed, of course. If you remove some software, you'll be told whether that software is depended upon by any other software. If it is, you might see a suggestion that you remove the other software too. The other software

---

8. Repositories are usually online but not always. The Ubuntu install CD is a small repository containing just what you need to install Ubuntu.

might have *its own* set of dependencies. Sometimes it can be the case that removing a seemingly innocent piece of software can set in motion a cascade where half the system components get removed. (I'm being melodramatic, because this is rare—rarer than it used to be, anyway.)

Dependency management can get fiendishly complicated at times.[9] But no worries. Like a good butler, the Ubuntu software subsystem hides all that from you.

Software can be installed or removed both at the command line and using a GUI tool called Synaptic. Let's start by taking a look at Synaptic.

Using Synaptic

You can find Synaptic on the System → Administration menu. When it starts, you'll need to enter your password when prompted because software administration affects the underlying system. You can see an example of Synaptic's user interface in Figure 2.6, on the next page.

The first thing to do, which you should do always when starting Synaptic, is to hit the Reload button at the left of the toolbar. This grabs the latest list of files from the repository of software on the server so you'll have the latest list of software to choose from. The list changes pretty often, so this is good practice.

The Synaptic program window is split into three parts. On the left is the package category list. This sorts the packages by what they do. On the top right is the package list—the entire list of available software you can install, including software that's already been installed. On the bottom right is where the description of each package will appear when you select one by clicking it.

Typically you'll start by searching for the software you need. This can be done two ways. The first is to click any package in the list in the top right of the screen so that it's highlighted and then just start typing. Say you wanted to install Epiphany, which is an alternative web browser. Just start typing epiphany. Before you've finished typing, the list will have filtered down to a handful of possible results, and more than likely just the one.

---

9. If the dependency management system breaks, it gets really ugly really fast. This is one argument people use if they object to package management systems, such as that used by Ubuntu. However, the counterargument is a good one: it never breaks—unless the user does something stupid, that is.

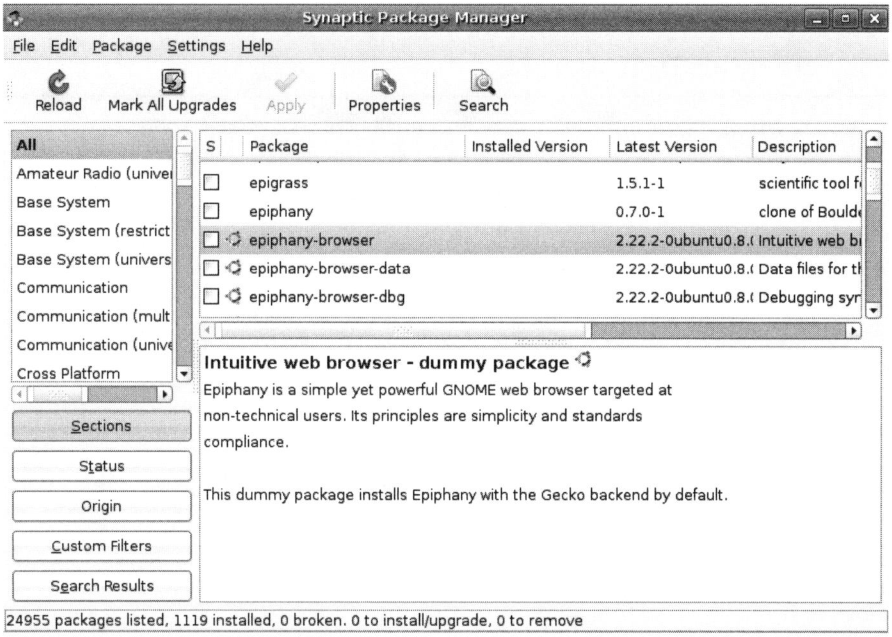

Figure 2.6: SYNAPTIC PACKAGE MANAGER

The second way to search is to hit the Search button, which will open the Search dialog box. This is what I do, because it lets me search not only the package names but also their descriptions. If I were looking for an alternative web browser, for example, I would click Search and then type web browser.

If you want to install a particular software package, click the checkbox that appears on the left alongside it. This will cause a menu to appear, of which one option is usually visible: Mark for Installation. As you might expect, this will mark the package so it can be installed, but installation will happen only after you click the Apply button on the main toolbar. This way you can search for and add several other packages for installation if you want, before starting the installation process.

Immediately after clicking Mark for Installation, you'll be told whether the software has dependencies. A dialog box will pop up asking whether you want to mark additional required changes, as shown in Figure 2.7, on the following page. Normally there's not much to see here, and you can click the Mark button. There are only two things to watch out for.

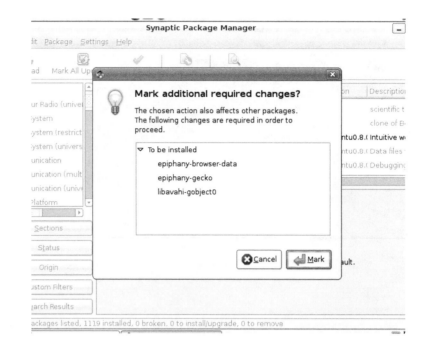

Figure 2.7: Marking additional packages for installation

The first is that, along with software to be installed, Synaptic suggests removing some software (this will appear under the To be removed heading). This is probably because that software is incompatible with what you're about to install.

There's no easy answer in this situation. You can go ahead, or you can click the Cancel button and not install the software. In theory, you can force through the installation, but that would break things and possibly leave the system in an unusable state. Never force, even if you think you know what you're doing. It causes pain.

The second thing to watch out for is if Synaptic wants to install a massive amount of dependency packages. A good example would be if you wanted to install the Konqueror web browser. This requires most of the KDE desktop subsystem to be installed, and therefore marking Konqueror for installation also marks twenty-two other packages for installation. There's no harm installing these packages. The only problem is that they might take a long time to download and possibly weigh in at hundreds of megabytes on your hard disk. However, if you have the bandwidth and cavernous storage, then this obviously isn't an issue.

Once you've marked the software you want to install, hit the Apply button on Synaptic's main toolbar. A dialog box will appear summarizing the selection of packages that are to be installed and informing you of the disk space required. Assuming you're happy with this summary, click the Apply button in the dialog box. This will then download and subsequently install the package(s). When it's finished, another dialog box will appear to tell you so, and you can then quit Synaptic (or install more software if you want).

You might also see some software listed in the summary dialog box under the heading of Unchanged. This is updated versions of software already on your system that Synaptic would like to install. You can mark it for installation by clicking the Mark All Upgrades button on the toolbar in Synaptic's main program window, but it's perhaps better to let the separate Update Manager program handle that kind of thing automatically. It'll probably pop up as soon as Synaptic is closed anyway, having heard about all the updates it can install when you initially updated the list of software by clicking the Reload button.

It's worth noting that only one software installation program can run at one time; you might notice that Update Manager's notification area icon grays out while Synaptic is running because of this.

In Synaptic's main program window, color-coding and icons in the checkbox alongside a package name indicate its status. For example, if the checkbox alongside a package in the package name is dark green, then that software is already installed. If you then click the checkbox, you can select Mark for Removal, which will remove the software but leave behind its configuration files (useful if you want to install it again in the future). Alternatively, you can select Mark for Complete Removal, which will remove both the software and its configuration files.

In a nutshell, that's the basics of software installation using Synaptic. I haven't mentioned filtering search results, reinstalling packages, or lots of other perhaps less vital things. You'll learn about these as time goes on. One handy tip is to click Help → Icon Legend to see what the various checkbox graphics mean.

Software Installation at the Command Line

As with all things command line related, installing software at the command line is where the real power lies. It can also be quicker than using Synaptic, which makes the user jump through several hoops to do even

Software Support

Some software packages have a little Ubuntu logo alongside their checkboxes in Synaptic. This means the software is officially supported and will therefore be updated and maintained for the life of that Ubuntu release (up until 2011 in the case of Ubuntu 8.04, for example). If there's no Ubuntu logo alongside, that means the software simply comes from the Debian repositories and might be updated in the future, although there's no guarantee. The list of officially supported software is proportionally small compared to the massive list of software in the Debian archives. It's a good idea to shy away from unsupported software because of the update issue, but few avoid it completely because there's a lot of good software in its ranks. One or two tips in this book advise you install unsupported software, for example.

simple tasks. Therefore, mastering command-line software administration is a good skill for any Ubuntu user to have. Several tips in this book rely on command-line software installation.

There are essentially two methods of installing software at the command line: using the APT commands, which automate software download and installation just like Synaptic, or using the dpkg command, if you want to download a software package and install it manually.

Using APT

In reality, Synaptic is just a front man for the Advanced Packaging Tool (APT) subsystem. It's actually the APT system that manages access to the software repositories, takes care of package dependencies, and installs or removes stuff. Synaptic just asks it to do things on its behalf and then reports what it says to you.

The APT system comes with several commands, and often using them is simply quicker than using Synaptic.

The first useful command is apt-get. This handles installing and removing software from the repository. apt-get install will install software, while apt-get autoremove will uninstall it.

But before you do that, it's always advisable to get the most up-to-date list from the software repositories. This is the equivalent of hitting the

Reload toolbar button in Synaptic. Type the following, remembering that you shouldn't type the opening dollar sign ($):

```
$ sudo apt-get update
```

You'll notice that we precede the command with sudo. This is because all software management requires root (administrator) powers. There's one exception, as you'll see in a moment: searching.

Back to the apt-get command. The following will install the Abiword word processor:

```
$ sudo apt-get install abiword
```

APT will look up the package, see whether it has any dependencies, and, if it does, add them to the list of software it intends to install. Then it will ask you to read through what it proposes to do and confirm its suggestions, which you can do by typing $\boxed{y}$ for Yes or $\boxed{n}$ for No.

As with Synaptic, sometimes apt-get will need to remove additional software to avoid incompatibilities, and you'll also be told so that you can confirm the choice.

The following will remove Abiword once you've installed it:

```
$ sudo apt-get autoremove abiword
```

This will remove the original software plus any unused dependencies that were installed alongside it (note that, in this way, apt-get offers a function Synaptic doesn't; Synaptic will simply leave any dependencies in place, regardless of whether they're needed by other applications or not). Bear in mind that other applications you've installed since the original application may use these dependencies, in which case they won't be removed. If, for any reason, you want to remove just the original software package and nothing else, use apt-get remove in place of apt-get autoremove.

Searching for files is just as easy, but a different command is used. Let's say you'd heard about the Epiphany web browser from a friend but wanted to find out its actual package name so you could specify it for installation using apt-get. You need to use the apt-cache command, as follows:

```
$ apt-cache search epiphany
```

A list of results will appear, as shown in Figure 2.8, on the next page. The package name is listed on the left, with a brief description of the package following. Included in the results because they also contain

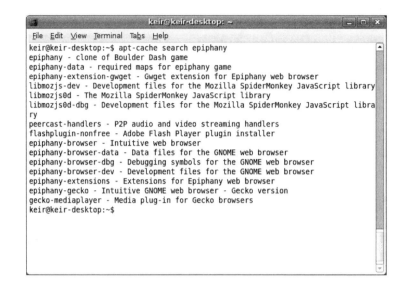

Figure 2.8: SEARCHING FOR SOFTWARE USING APT-GET

the word *epiphany* are several library packages that Epiphany needs to work. These will probably be added as dependencies should we try to install it using apt-get. Also included is a video game called Epiphany, which apparently is a clone of Boulder Dash. However, it should be obvious that the one we want is epiphany-browser.

If we want more information about the package (such as its full description, as appears in Synaptic), we can use the show option:

```
$ apt-cache show epiphany-browser
```

A lot of information is returned, and it tends to flow off the screen, so we can pipe it into the less text reader:

```
$ apt-cache show epiphany-browser | less
```

Using dpkg to Manually Install Packages

Every now and again you might need to download a software package and manually install it. This happens if the software isn't in the Ubuntu repositories, usually because it's very new or because the Ubuntu head honchos have decided not to offer it.

If the software is not in the official software repositories, you might well find that the developers behind the software provide their *own*

Using aptitude to Install Packages at the Command Line

If you browse any of the Ubuntu community websites, you might find that some people ignore apt-get and use aptitude instead. aptitude is used in the same way, with the same commands as apt-get (for example, to install Abiword, you would type sudo aptitude install abiword). The difference is that, alongside updating the system log of installed software, it keeps its own log of installations. This means it can be better at removing software because it is better at tracking dependencies. In addition, packages sometimes come with a list of recommended but nonessential extras, and aptitude will automatically add these to the installation tally, something apt-get can't do. Furthermore, when run without options or arguments, aptitude will start in a semi-GUI mode, with a menu system that lets you administrate software.

Whether you use apt-get or aptitude depends on your personal preference. apt-get has one advantage, which is that it will always be available on any system that is a Debian derivative (for example, Xandros, Mepis, and Freespire). It isn't guaranteed that aptitude will be installed. For this reason alone, you should at least become competent at using apt-get.

APT repository that you can add to your system. This is discussed in Section 2.4, *Adding New Software Repositories*, on page 34, and it is certainly very handy because it means that once the repository has been added, you can use the APT tools and/or Synaptic to install the software.

However, although developers being kind enough to offer their own APT repositories is becoming more and more common, it isn't guaranteed. So, let's assume you have no choice but to download the package and install it manually. This is the case with several tips in this book.

First, let's talk about what you actually need to download. Ubuntu software packages all have the file extension .deb. This stands for *Debian*— the version of Linux that Ubuntu is built upon.

Ideally, you should try to download the .deb package created not only for Ubuntu but also for your version of Ubuntu (that is, 8.04 "Hardy Heron" or 6.06 "Dapper Drake"). This is because the package will be designed to work within the system configuration of your version of

Ubuntu and will also be aware of what dependencies it needs. It will then inform you of its dependency needs when you try to install it. Package names and contents vary between Linux distributions and even between different versions of Ubuntu. So, this can be very handy.

If you can't find a specific Ubuntu package, look for one that works under the most recent release of Debian. Ideally, you want the release of the package made for Debian Sid (Ubuntu is based on Debian Sid[10]), but also look out for releases made for Debian Lenny.

Download the package to your /home folder, and be careful to avoid allowing Firefox to open it automatically with GDebi Package Installer.

Installing the package is then simply a matter of typing the following:

```
$ sudo dpkg -i filename.deb
```

Obviously, you should replace filename.deb with the filename of the package you downloaded.

If you're lucky, everything should work fine. The package will install without error. More likely, however, you'll be told you're missing dependencies. They will be named, so it's simply a matter of installing them.

Until you can install the dependencies, you have a problem on your hands. dpkg is nowhere near as clever as APT and installs the package even if the dependencies aren't met. It just doesn't configure the software for use because of the missing dependencies, so you can't start using it.

This leaves the software installation system in something of a bad state, because it now has a "broken package." You'll be warned about this the next time you run Synaptic, for example, as shown in Figure 2.9, on the next page. Synaptic will still let you attempt to install software, however, and if the missing dependency packages are available in the repository, Synaptic will automatically add them to the list next time you try to install anything. Alternatively, as Synaptic suggests in its error message, you can click the Filter button in the bottom left and then click the Broken link to see what packages are causing the problem and try to enact a manual fix (including, if the dependencies simply aren't available, uninstalling the problematic package).

---

10. Every version of Ubuntu uses as its base the perennial testing release of Debian Linux, known as Debian Unstable or Debian Sid. All Debian releases are named after characters in the movie *Toy Story* (you might remember that the character of Sid was Andy's neighbor in *Toy Story* and was pretty, well, unstable!).

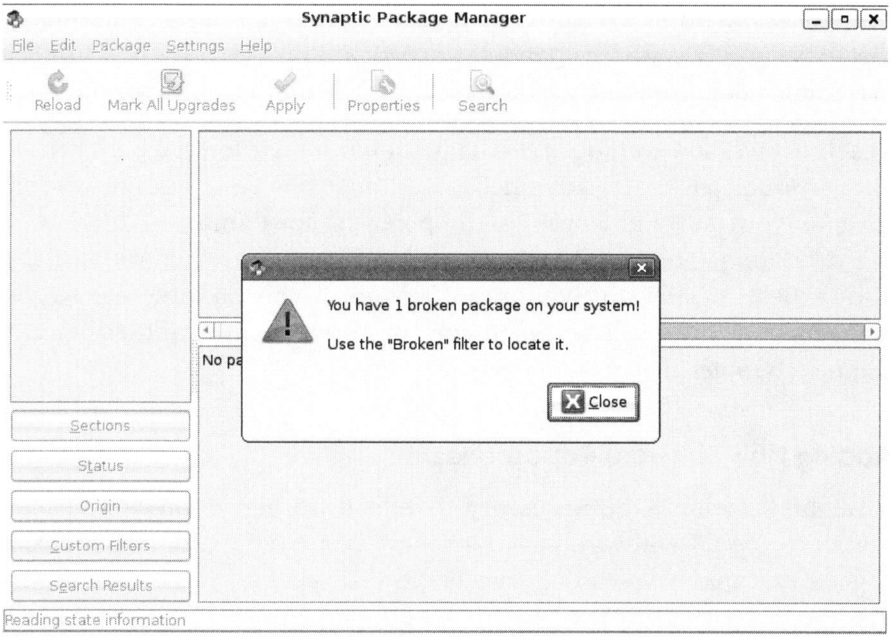

Figure 2.9: SYNAPTIC TELLING OF A BROKEN PACKAGE

apt-get takes a harder line. It will refuse to work until the broken package with its missing dependencies is sorted out. It will suggest the dependency, however, and also suggest you type apt-get -f install, which will attempt to grab any missing dependencies to fix the problem.

dpkg can also remove software too. Say we had installed Epiphany. This will do the trick of removing it:

```
$ sudo dpkg -r epiphany-browser
```

You'll note that, in this case, we don't specify the entire package filename. We refer to the package how it's referred to by the system—within Synaptic, and so on. Usually, this is just the first part of the package filename, sans the stuff afterward, which informs us which hardware platform it works on.

If there are dependency issues (something else depends on what you're trying to remove), then dpkg will tell you and will refuse to remove the file. You can force the removal, but that's an extremely efficient recipe for disaster. Note that, even though a package is manually installed, it will still show up in Synaptic, so it can be removed using Synaptic in the usual way (or via apt-get autoremove). Using Synaptic is infinitely preferable compared to using the basic and rather literal dpkg.

In actual fact, however, dpkg can do just about anything you'd ever need to individual packages. It's one of the most powerful administration tools on your system. However, the potential for damage is high, and you'd be damaging a very important component of your system. It's always best to stick to Synaptic or apt-get if you possibly can. That way, dependencies will be taken care of automatically, and the world will be a happier place.

Adding New Software Repositories

It might sometimes be necessary to add third-party software repositories to install software that isn't supplied by the Ubuntu project. A good example is installing the Skype VoIP package, as explained in Tip 266, on page 295. The people behind Skype provide their own software repository for Ubuntu users. The advantage of signing up to a third-party repository rather than installing by hand using dpkg is that you can then use Synaptic to install the software (it will appear alongside all the other software in the list). Because of this, if the software requires any dependencies, they will be taken care of automatically. Additionally, if a newer version of the software is released, you'll be automatically told about it alongside all the other updated software presented regularly by Update Manager.

Adding a third-party repository is not hard. It takes the form of an address—usually referred to as either an *APT line* or simply a *repository address*[11]—which usually looks something like the following (this example is again taken from Tip 266, on page 295, which explains how to install Skype):

```
deb http://download.skype.com/linux/repos/debian/ stable non-free
```

To add this to the system, start the Software Sources program (System → Administration), and then select the Third-Party Software tab. Then click the Add button, and in the APT Line text field, enter the address, as shown in Figure 2.10, on the facing page. Then click the Add Source

---

11. If, as described in some tips in the book, you install software from the Launchpad.net website, which is a repository for up-and-coming software projects, the APT repository address might be referred to as the *Personal Package Archive*, or PPA.

Figure 2.10: ADDING A NEW REPOSITORY USING SOFTWARE SOURCES

button. Upon clicking Close in the parent dialog box, you'll be told that the list of software needs to be refreshed. Choose to do so.

What Software Sources actually does is update the /etc/apt/sources.list configuration file. You could just as easily open this in a text editor and add the line to the bottom manually. But using Software Sources stops you from making a mistake editing a file without which the software subsystem wouldn't work, so it is perhaps a better choice.

Wherever possible, in addition to adding the repository, you should also import the repository's key file, which Ubuntu can use to work out whether packages are authentic. Some packages are digitally signed, which is a method of protecting the user from fake packages that contain malware. If you should try to install a package that isn't signed, Synaptic or APT will throw up a warning (although you'll still be able to install).

All official Ubuntu packages are protected in this way, and Ubuntu is set up with the relevant key files during initial installation. If the third-party repository uses signing (not all do), a link will probably be provided to the key file on the same page that lists the APT address.

Download the key file to your system, and in Software Sources, click the Authentication tab. Then click the Import Key File button, and navigate to what you downloaded.

Perhaps it goes without saying that key files can be faked, just like packages. You should ensure you download the key file from the official website of the application in question, not from a mirror site.

2.5 Using gconf-editor

Like all versions of Linux, Ubuntu is actually a compilation of many different software projects.

The desktop interface is a modified form of that offered by the GNOME Desktop Project (http://www.gnome.org). Because of this, several tips in this book use a program called gconf-editor, which is designed to change the settings of the GNOME desktop or various GNOME applications. This program doesn't have a menu entry so must be started from either a terminal window or by hitting Alt+F2 and typing gconf-editor. Note that gconf-editor changes your personal GNOME desktop software settings, so it doesn't require root privileges. The configuration files it affects are stored in your /home folder as hidden files, but you'll probably never come into direct contact with them.

If you've ever used regedit under Windows, then you have a head start with gconf-editor. You can see an example in Figure 2.11, on the next page. The purpose of gconf-editor is to let you edit *keys*, which are individual program settings. For ease of access, all the keys are organized by headings, which are listed on the left of the gconf-editor program window. Most applications you use every day can be found under the apps master category.

On the right of the program window is the area where the keys appear. Usually these are either a checkbox or a *value*—a number or text field. The value in a key can usually be changed by either single- or double-clicking it. Beneath the key area is the Key Documentation area where help text sometimes appears describing the key settings.

In several tips within this book, I say something like "Open gconf-editor, head over to /apps/nautilus-cd-burner, and then put a check alongside overburn on the right." By this I mean select /apps and then the nautilus-cd-burner headings on the left, and on the right of the program window, change the overburn key to a different setting, in this case by putting

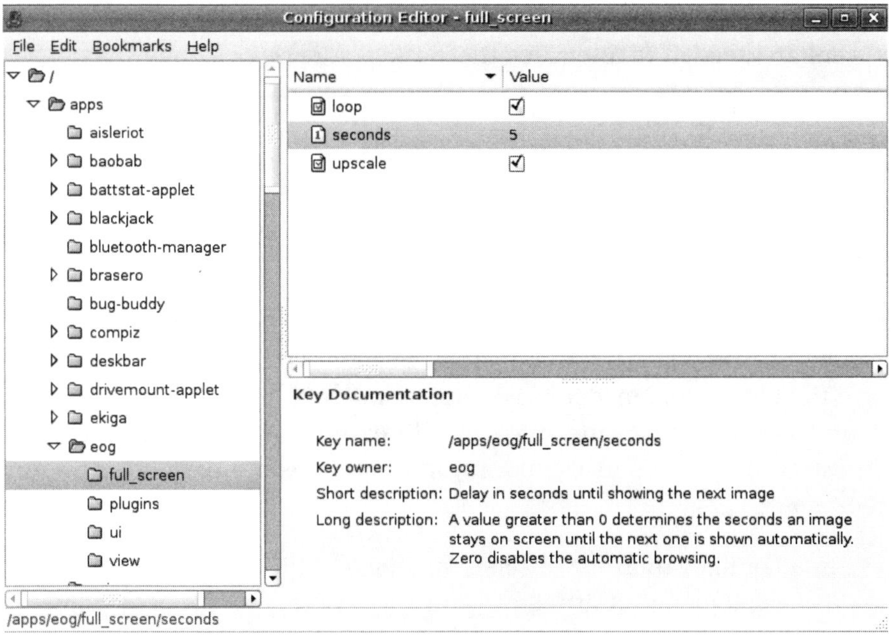

Figure 2.11: GCONF-EDITOR

a check in its box by clicking it. Incidentally, the tweak described here comes from Tip 27, on page 72, which explains how to activate the overburn mode of some CD-R/RW drives to squeeze more data onto discs.

Changes made in gconf-editor take effect immediately, often even if the application concerned is still open. In the majority of cases, there's no need to reboot or even log out and back in again (if there is, the tip in question will tell you).

If you make a mistake or if you find a setting you've changed isn't to your tastes, you can go back to the key in question, right-click it, and select Unset Key. This will return it to the original value.

Once you've finished using gconf-editor, just close it as usual.

2.6 Editing Configuration Files

Some of the tips in this book require that you edit configuration files by hand using a text editor. Under Ubuntu, system configuration files are usually located in the /etc folder. This is a root-owned folder, so root powers are needed to alter files there.

In every tip requiring it, I'll tell you the exact line within the config file you'll need to change, so there's no need to fret over details. However, some general points about configuration files are worth noting.

First, bear in mind that configuration files are plain-text format. They're never saved as anything more complicated, such as a rich-text file. Watch out for this if you have to create a new configuration file from scratch and save it for the first time. Second, configuration files often have the file extension .conf and usually not .cfg, as you might be used to under Windows. Some have no file extension at all, such as the /etc/fstab file that controls mounting of the basic storage devices on the system.

Within a configuration file, a hash symbol (#) at the beginning of a line has a specific meaning. It tells Ubuntu to ignore that particular line.[12] Thus, comments within the file inserted by its creator to aid understanding by everybody else are preceded by a hash symbol. Additionally, many configuration files come with examples of settings that aren't active by default and are therefore preceded by a hash. To enable that particular setting, all that's needed is to remove the hash.

Because the hash symbol is used to add comments to configuration files, you will often read instructions online where people advise you "comment out" a particular line. They simply mean add a hash to the front of the line so it will no longer be interpreted by Ubuntu.

A small amount of configuration files are in XML format, which are a little like HTML files—all the settings you can change are enclosed in tags (words surrounded by angle brackets). However, it's unlikely you will ever need to hand-edit an XML configuration file. For example, the GNOME desktop and associated applications used under Ubuntu use XML configuration files, but the gconf-editor program is provided to tweak these settings.

---

12. A hash at the beginning of a line in a file tells Ubuntu to ignore that line, with one exception. Script files, which contain chains of commands and are used throughout Ubuntu, start with a *shebang*—the characters #!. This tells Ubuntu that the file is a script. Usually following the shebang is the path to the shell that should run the script (for example, #!/bin/bash). But this is the only example of where a hash symbol is used for anything other than a comment.

2.7 Making and Keeping Backups

As mentioned, several of the tips in this book ask you to edit vital configuration files. If you follow the steps precisely, this shouldn't present any issues, but making backups before is always good idea.[13]

This doesn't mean just creating a backup of the configuration file itself. If you tweak a particular line within a configuration file, it's a good idea to make a copy-and-pasted copy of the original line too. As mentioned in the previous section, any line in a typical configuration file that's preceded by a hash symbol (#) is ignored. Therefore, you can simply copy and paste the line to a new line beneath and then precede it with a hash.

Let's look at an example. In Tip 78, on page 126, I discuss removing the login delay that occurs when you type a bad password. Take a quick look now. It involves editing the /etc/pam.d/common-auth file, so before carrying out the tip, you should create a backup of the file. This can be done using the Nautilus file browser, but it has to be running in superuser mode because the file in question is in a root-owned folder. Therefore, we need to start Nautilus with root powers—hit Alt+F2, and type gksu nautilus. Type your password when prompted. Then browse to /etc/pam.d, and locate the common-auth file. Right-click it, select Copy (as shown in Figure 2.12, on the next page), then right-click a blank space in the Nautilus window, and finally select Paste. This will automatically create a new file called common-auth (copy). Alternatively, you can select the file and click Edit → Duplicate.

If you want, you can back up the file at the command prompt instead, using the cp command. Just specify a new filename for the copied file, as follows:

```
$ sudo cp /etc/pam.d/common-auth /etc/pam.d/common-auth-backup
```

The tip goes on to tell you to open the file in the Gedit text editor and change the line auth requisite pam_unix.so nullok_secure so that it reads auth requisite pam_unix.so nullok_secure nodelay. Before doing this, you should highlight the line and copy and paste it to a new line just below. Add a hash (#) in front of it. Then make your change to the original line.

---

13. Of course, backing up *all* valuable files on a regular basis is a good idea. I explain how to back up data in Tip 286, on page 322.

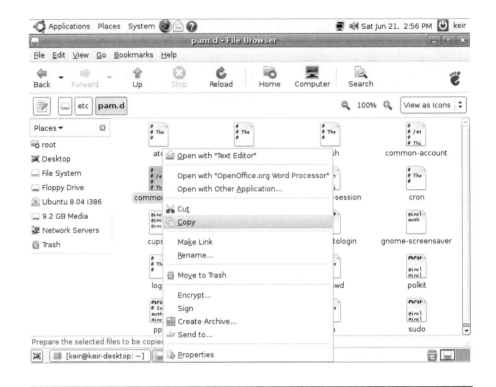

Figure 2.12: BACKING UP CONFIGURATION FILES

The benefit of creating a cut-and-pasted copy of the original line is, in many situations, you have a concrete example of the syntax of how the line should look. This can be particularly useful if you radically change the line.

So if you follow Tip 78, on page 126, you'll end up with two lines that look like this:

```
auth requisite pam_unix.so nullok_secure nodelay
#auth requisite pam_unix.so nullok_secure
```

After this, you can save the file and reboot, as the tip says, to test the settings. In the highly unlikely event of anything going wrong or the system not working as it should, you can once again use Nautilus to restore the original file (delete the old one and then rename the copy so it has the original filename; ensure you perform these two actions immediately after each other as quickly as possible in case the system calls on the file and finds it isn't there). Alternatively, you can open the file again in Gedit and restore the original line.

Once you're sure the tip has worked, you can either delete the backup file or just leave it there in case it's needed in the future.

2.8 Rescue Me! What to Do If It All Goes Wrong

Throughout this book I've tried very hard to ensure the tips not only work but were also tested on as many computers as possible (I have several computers in my test lab and also ran the tips on virtualized setups). Additionally, the book has been extensively technically reviewed by some people with very large brains and bags of Ubuntu experience. However, the fact is that all computers are different, and some tips may have an adverse effect on your particular setup. Not only that but human error—not just on my part but also yours, dear reader—means that occasionally things don't work as they should. Very occasionally, things might go really badly wrong. You might be left with a system that's unbootable.

The solution is to undo the changes you did. To do this, you'll need some method of accessing your broken installation's file system, and you can do this by using your original Ubuntu install CD in live distro mode. This is done by selecting the Try Ubuntu without any change to your computer option on the CD boot menu. When the desktop appears, remember that you're browsing the pseudo file system created in RAM by the Ubuntu live distro mode. To fix your system, you must mount your Ubuntu hard disk partition so that it's accessible.

To do this, click the entry on the Places menu relating to your Ubuntu partition. It will be identified on the Places menu by its size—for example, if it is 160GB in size, then it will be identified as 160 GB Media. After this, an icon will appear on the desktop, from where you can access the contents of the Ubuntu partition using Nautilus file browser.

Sometimes it's useful to make your Ubuntu partition into the root of the file system, as if you had just booted into it. It's not a good idea to do so while the live distro desktop is running, so you should switch to *single-user mode* (effectively a command prompt and nothing else) before attempting it.

Here are the steps required:

1. Once the desktop has appeared in live distro mode, hit $\boxed{\text{Ctrl}}$+$\boxed{\text{Alt}}$+ $\boxed{\text{F2}}$ to switch to a virtual console. Then type sudo telinit 1.

2. A text-mode menu will eventually appear. Select the option that reads root - drop to root shell prompt.

3. At the prompt, type the following (note that you automatically run as the root user in single-user mode, so there's no need to precede commands with sudo; remember that you shouldn't type the hash before each of the following commands, just like you shouldn't type the dollar when typing commands normally):

```
# mkdir ubuntu-partition
# mount /dev/sda5 ubuntu-partition
# chroot ubuntu-partition
# bash
```

As before, if Ubuntu is the only operating system on the disk, replace /dev/sda5 with /dev/sda1.

You should now find that you are browsing your Ubuntu partition, as if you had booted into it, and can carry out any repair commands.

Making a Clean Start

Sometimes the easiest thing if you've tweaked your system into oblivion is just to start over. It's not usually possible to reinstall Ubuntu "on top of itself" as you might have done with Windows, but if you choose to reinstall Ubuntu, it will offer to shrink your existing installation and install a new one alongside. You can then delve into the partition to get your data. Ensure you use the same username in the new installation because this will avoid complications with file ownership between the two partitions.

Alternatively, you might choose to keep your existing installation but create a new user account for yourself. This can be done by using the Users & Groups tool on the System → Administration menu. Click the Unlock button when it starts, and then the Add User button. Type the new details in the Username and User Password/Confirmation fields under the Set password by hand heading of the dialog box that appears (the rest can be left empty), and then click the User Privileges tab. Ensure the boxes alongside Administer the System and Manage Printers are checked.

After this, you can log in as the new user and import your data from your old /home folder. You will have to change the file/folder ownerships, however, to be able to both read and write the files. To do this, open an administrator Nautilus window (open a terminal, and type gksu nautilus), and then right-click the file/folder, click Properties, and then click the Permissions tab. Then select your new username from the Owner

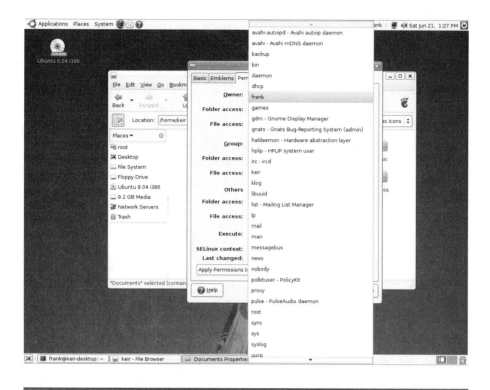

Figure 2.13: CHANGING FILE/FOLDER OWNERSHIPS

drop-down list, as shown in Figure 2.13 (note that, in the list, you will see several "non login accounts" used by the system; you can ignore them). Don't forget to close the administrator Nautilus window when you've finished.

2.9 Miscellaneous Things You Ought to Know

Here's a selection of topics that it might benefit you to know when trying some of these tips but that I have been unable to mention yet.

Understanding Disk Partitioning

When you installed Ubuntu, you probably repartitioned your disk. The hard disk partition containing Windows was shrunk, and two new partitions were created alongside it for Ubuntu: *root* and *swap*. The root partition is simply Ubuntu's main partition where all the data is stored.

The swap partition is the same as the swap file (which is sometimes known as the *paging file*) under Windows, except it is housed within its own partition.[14]

What's important to many tips in *Ubuntu Kung Fu* is how Ubuntu refers to the partitions. Every item of your PC's hardware under Ubuntu is represented as a virtual file in the /dev folder. If you installed Ubuntu in the standard way, opting for default installation choices and dual-booting with Windows, the Windows partition is referred to on a technical level as /dev/sda1, while Ubuntu's root partition is usually referred to as /dev/sda5 (assuming you're using Ubuntu 8.04 Hardy Heron or later).[15]

However, your computer *might* refer to the Windows partition as /dev/hda1 and Ubuntu's root partition as /dev/hda5. The only difference is that the *s* is swapped for an *h*. This difference in nomenclature is simply down to what hardware drivers are used for the motherboard chipset; there's absolutely no other significance in the case of a standard desktop or notebook computer.

To find out which side of the fence your PC sits on, open a terminal window, and type ls /dev/hda1. If you see the following error message:

```
ls: cannot access /dev/hda1: No such file or directory
```

then your computer uses the /dev/sda references. For an example, see Figure 2.14, on the facing page. If you see a file listed and no error message, then your computer uses the /dev/hda references. If that's the case, you will have to do some substituting when reading the tips—every time you read /dev/sda, regardless of the number that follows, you will have to type /dev/hda.

For example, Tip 223, on page 249, explains how to fix file system errors. At one point, you're told to type sudo fsck.ext3 -f /dev/sda5 into a terminal window. If your computer is one of those that refers to the hard disk partitions as /dev/hda, you would have to type sudo fsck.ext3 -f /dev/hda5 (incidentally, don't try this command without reading the tip first!).

---

14. Actually, the swap partition is not the same as Windows' swap file. The swap partition is also used to hold the RAM contents when the hibernation power-saving mode is used. This is why the swap partition will always be the same size as your RAM or larger.

15. The installer of Ubuntu 8.04 (and later versions) first shrinks the Windows primary partition and then creates an extended partition for Ubuntu's root and swap partitions. This explains why the root and swap partitions are numbered sda5 and sda6, respectively, rather than simply sda2 and sda3, as is the case with earlier releases of Ubuntu, where the root and swap partitions were created as additional primary partitions.

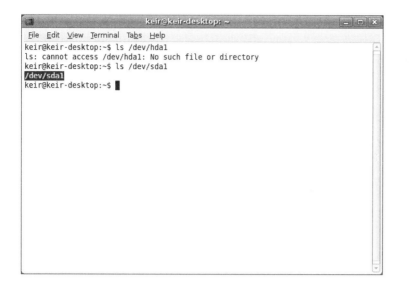

Figure 2.14: Checking to see how the hard disk is referred to

If you installed Ubuntu on a computer that had no operating system, Ubuntu's root partition will be the first on the disk, so it will be identified as /dev/sda1 (or, of course, /dev/hda1).

The boot loader software used under Ubuntu, known as GRUB, counts hard disk partitions not from 1 upward, but from 0. So, it would refer to /dev/sda5 as the *fourth* partition. On a dual-boot system with both Windows and Ubuntu installed on the hard disk, in the language used in the GRUB configuration file (hd0,4) refers to the Ubuntu root partition on most systems with Windows installed alongside. The Windows partition will be referred to as (hd0,0). If Windows isn't installed, then Ubuntu's root partition will be referred to as (hd0,0). It doesn't matter to GRUB whether Linux refers to your hard disk as sda or hda.

Watching Out for Wubi

From Ubuntu 8.04 onward, it's possible to install Ubuntu within the existing Windows file system if you intend dual-boot, thus avoiding repartitioning the disk. Effectively, the Ubuntu partitions (root and swap) are created as large files within the Windows file system.

However, aside from possibly being a little slower in operation, there is not much difference between a Wubi and standard Windows installation. The user chooses between Windows and Ubuntu at bootup, using the standard Windows boot menu, after which the Ubuntu boot menu appears as usual and everything that follows is the same as a standard Ubuntu session.

The main difference for readers of this book is that the tips in this book that talk about manipulating partitions won't apply. Additionally, accessing the Windows partition is handled differently; to view your Windows files, it's necessary to browse to the /host directory.

Getting Help If You Need It

Help is never far away when you're using Ubuntu. I mentioned the man command earlier in this chapter. Other built-in documentation worth reading is that contained in /usr/share/doc/. There you'll find a folder for virtually each piece of software installed on the system, and if you're lucky, inside will be a README file that will run through what the software does and how it can be used. This file can be read using the less command or opened in Gedit.[16] The README is usually more informal and not as strictly technical as man pages. There are usually several other files in the folder relating to copyright and authorship, but the one other file worth reading—if present—is README.Debian, which contains specific information about how the program is configured to run on your system.

As always, the Internet can be a gold mine of information. Your first port of call should be the *Ubuntu Kung Fu* community forum—http://www.ubuntukungfu.org/forum, where you can talk to other readers and, if I'm around, the author of this book. Other than this, the primary source of help for all Ubuntu users is undoubtedly http://ubuntuforums.org, which is the official meeting place for the Ubuntu community. Another forum worth visiting is http://www.linuxquestions.org, which, while catering to all renditions of Linux, has a very strong Ubuntu section.

Command-Line Text Editors

There was a time when discussing command-line text editors was the equivalent of walking into a lion's den wearing a shirt made of bacon. This was because of the intense rivalry between advocates of the emacs and vi text editors.

---

16. Some README files are gzipped, so have the .gz file extension, but these can still be read using less—decompression of the file is handled automatically.

But I'm not going to recommend either. If it's ever the case that you can't use Gedit to edit a configuration file, I advise you use nano. Although it runs at the command line, nano is not a million miles away from old-fashioned word processors you might have used. The cursor keys navigate around the text, and you can hit `Backspace` or `Delete` to remove text. To insert a new line, just go to the end of an existing one, and hit `Enter`.

To save the file, hit `Ctrl`+`o` (not `Ctrl`+`s`). Check that the filename is correct, and then hit Enter. To quit the program, hit `Ctrl`+`x`. If you've made any changes since you last saved, you'll be prompted with the Save modified buffer option. This is just another way of asking whether you want to save the file. Hit `y` to do so or `n` if you want to abandon your changes.

## Chapter 3

The Tips

The following pages—in fact, pretty much the rest of the book—contains the 300+ hints, hacks, techniques, tips, and tricks that make up the meat of *Ubuntu Kung Fu*. They're arranged randomly, although if one tip builds on another, then it will be listed immediately afterward.

Some seemingly disparate tips make reference to others too, and if you're reading the PDF or HTML version of this book, then you can click the relevant link to jump to that particular tip. If you're reading the dead-tree version, you have no choice but to wet your thumb and start turning pages (pending a truly amazing technical breakthrough from Pragmatic Programmers' secret lab, of course).

Few of these tips are absolutely specific to Ubuntu. Most will, with some minor adaptation, work on *any* version of Linux. Tips that describe command-line tricks will probably work without any changes on any version of Linux (or even versions of Unix, such as Mac OS X). However, my sole focus while writing the book was to attempt to ensure the tips worked perfectly under Ubuntu.

You should bear in mind the following before you start working your way through the tips:

- Working through more than 300 tips presents certain challenges, so alongside each tip heading is a checkbox. This is designed to let you to keep track of tips that interest you if you're reading the book away from your computer. Alternatively, you can put a check alongside tips you've already completed.

- If ever I need you to type something, it will be listed within the tip. For example, in Tip 2, on the facing page, I tell you to type the following:

```
$ history|less
```

You should type history|less, not $ history|less. The inclusion of the dollar prompt is simply a convention of computer books. In some of the tips, the prompt will change to #, grub>, or even C:\ when I describe some tips that need to be carried out using Windows. The same is true in each case—don't type the prompt character(s).

- In some tips, what I ask you to type is too long to fit on the book's page. In this case, an arrow symbol is used to indicate a line break. This doesn't mean you should hit Enter at that point. Just keep typing what appears on the following line, without even inserting a space.

- The tips were written using Ubuntu 8.04.1 LTS (Hardy Heron) as a base. Most tips are version-agnostic and will work on all versions of Ubuntu. However, a little common sense might be required if you're using a future release of Ubuntu.

1 Set Any Picture as Wallpaper with a Single Click

The easiest way of setting your own picture as a desktop wallpaper is to click and drag the image to the desktop using the middle mouse button (if the image is already on the desktop, then click and drag it a few inches to the left/right). On most modern mice, the middle mouse button is the scroll wheel, which also doubles as a third mouse button. On the menu that appears when you release the button, click Set as Background.

If that sounds a little too unorthodox for you (it can be hard to use the middle mouse button), you can also use Synaptic to install the nautilus-wallpaper package, which adds a simple Set as Wallpaper option to the menu that appears when you right-click an image file. After installation, you'll need to log out and then in again before the option becomes visible.

For more wallpaper-related enhancements to Ubuntu, see Tip 139, on page 171; Tip 144, on page 178; Tip 199, on page 227; Tip 237, on page 270; and Tip 290, on page 328.

2 See (and Reuse) the Most Recently Typed Commands

The command line includes a powerful history feature that can make life much easier. To see the recently typed commands, type history. This simply dumps to the screen a hidden file in your /home directory called .bash_history where up to 1,000 commands are recorded. Because this list will scroll off the screen when listed, it's a good idea to pipe the output into a text reader, such as less:

```
$ history|less
```

To reuse one of your commands, at the command prompt type an exclamation mark (!; known as a *bang* in bash-speak) and then the number alongside the entry in the history list. For example, on my system, I noted when viewing the history list that the command cp /etc/fstab ~/Desktop was command 591. To use it again, I typed !591 at the command prompt. If you ever need to simply repeat a command you've just used, type two exclamation marks—!!.

To actively rifle through your command history, hit Ctrl+r and then start typing the command in which you're interested. The prompt will "autocomplete" as you type. To use the command, hit Enter. To edit it before using it, hit Esc, and then make your changes.

Hitting the up and down cursor keys will also let you move through the most recently typed commands. Just hit Enter when you find the one you want to reuse.

For more command-line productivity tricks, see in particular Tip 46, on page 98; Tip 56, on page 108; Tip 105, on page 146; Tip 192, on page 222; Tip 259, on page 290; and Tip 193, on page 222, amongst others.

3   Add Cool New Visualizations to Totem/RhythmBox

Both Totem and RhythmBox include a funky animation that appears during music playback. Animations such as this are known as *visualizations*, but out of the box Ubuntu includes only one, rather than the hundreds found on the likes of Mac OS or Windows media players. However, you can add more to Ubuntu, for use in both Totem and RhythmBox, by using Synaptic to search for and install the libvisual-0.4-plugins package.

Once the package has been installed, to change the visualization in Totem that appears when a music track is playing, click Edit → Preferences, select the Display tab in the dialog box that appears, and make your choice from the Type of visualization drop-down list. Your choice will take effect immediately, so drag the Preferences dialog box out of the way to preview it.

In RhythmBox, click View → Visualization to start the animation, and then select from the drop-down list beneath the visualization.

4   Switch Monitor Resolutions with a Single Mouse Click

If you have an external monitor or projector you occasionally attach to a notebook computer, you might be used to switching resolutions on a regular basis. Unlike with Windows, this isn't just a right-click procedure—you must navigate the System → Preferences menu.

A good solution is to use Synaptic to search for and install resapplet. For some reason, although it's officially a GNOME applet, resapplet doesn't appear on the standard applet list. Instead, it must be configured to start at login. To do this, click System → Preferences → Sessions, ensure the Startup Programs tab is selected, and click the Add button. In the Name and Command fields of the dialog box that appears, type resapplet. Leave the Comment field blank. Then close the dialog box, and log out and back in again.

The new icon will then appear beside NetworkMonitor in the notification area. Clicking it will reveal a list of possible resolutions from which you can choose. Incidentally, it should be possible to instantly step up and down resolutions by pressing Ctrl+Alt and tapping the +/- keys on the numeric keypad. Unfortunately, this doesn't work on Ubuntu systems because of the way the graphical subsystem is configured. It may work on other Linux systems, however.

5 Closely Monitor the Power Consumption of a Laptop

Run gnome-power-statistics, and you'll see a graph of the exact power usage of your computer over the time since it booted up (provided your computer's hardware supports it). Try boosting the brightness of your screen or loading programs, and see how much of a drain they can be!

For laptop power-saving tricks, see Tip 106, on page 147, and Tip 128, on page 162.

6 Stop the Cursor from Blinking

I have nothing against a blinking cursor myself, but some find it distracting. To stop Ubuntu's cursor from blinking, open gconf-editor, navigate to /desktop/gnome/interface, and remove the check from cursor_blink. Then log out and back in again. Note that Evolution appears to ignore this setting, but most other applications will now have a still cursor.

Alternatively, by changing the value in cursor_blink_time, you can simply make it blink more slowly. A value of 5000 equates to five seconds—each unit is 1ms. Be aware that a setting such as 5000 means the cursor will be visible for five seconds at a time and then invisible for the same length of time.

☐ **7** # Scroll Without the Mouse in Firefox and Evolution Mail Windows

Both Firefox and Evolution have a hidden *caret browsing* feature. This is where a cursor appears in a web page or received email, just like in a word processing document. Just like in a word processor, its position can be controlled using the cursor keys. When the cursor reaches the bottom or top of the screen, the page (or email) scrolls.

Caret browsing was designed as an accessibility feature for those who find reading difficult, but it's proved popular for every kind of user. This is because it allows people to navigate web pages or emails without taking their hands off the keyboard (there's no need to reach for the mouse scroll wheel, for example) and also keep track of where they were last reading should they walk away from their computer. In addition to navigation, text can be highlighted in the usual way by holding down Shift and using the cursor keys. It can then be copied in the usual way by pressing Ctrl+c.

To activate caret browsing in either application, just hit F7 while the program is running. The cursor will appear at the top of the web page or email preview window, although it can be repositioned by clicking the mouse anywhere.

For more Evolution and general email hacks, see Tip 42, on page 90; Tip 156, on page 189; Tip 158, on page 190; Tip 172, on page 200; Tip 246, on page 277; and Tip 260, on page 291.

☐ **8** # Optimize Startup for Faster Boot Times

Few operating systems seem to boot quickly enough, and unfortunately Ubuntu is amongst them. However, you can do four things to reduce delays and generally speed up startup:

• Reduce or eliminate the boot menu countdown.

- Make boot runtime scripts start in parallel.
- Build a read-ahead profile personalized to your PC.
- Reduce the number of GNOME startup programs.

Some of these edits tweak essential system files, so check what you type against what you read on the page. Then check again before finally saving any files.

Reducing the Boot Menu Delay

If you dual-boot Ubuntu and Windows on your computer, the boot menu appears for ten seconds, during which you can select either Windows or Ubuntu. If you have only Ubuntu installed, a prompt appears for three seconds telling you that you can hit a key to see the boot menu.

This delay can feasibly be reduced to one second, provided you have quick enough reactions—hitting a key during that second will cause the countdown timer to stop so you can make your choice at leisure.

Alternatively, you can configure the system so the boot menu never appears. This will deny access to the other boot menu options, but if Ubuntu is the only operating system on your computer, then this could be a good arrangement.

Start by opening the boot menu configuration file in Gedit:

```
$ gksu gedit /boot/grub/menu.lst
```

Then search for the line that reads timeout 10, and change the 10 to read either 1 for a one-second countdown or 0 to disable the boot menu completely. An example from my test PC is shown in Figure 3.1, on the following page.

Save the file, and then reboot to test the settings.

Run Boot-Time Scripts in Parallel

Whenever Ubuntu boots, it runs several scripts that start necessary background services. By default, these are set to run one by one, but if you have a processor with more than one core, such as Intel's CoreDuo series or AMD's Athlon X2, you can configure Ubuntu to run the scripts in parallel. This way, all the cores are utilized, and you can save quite a bit of time at each boot.

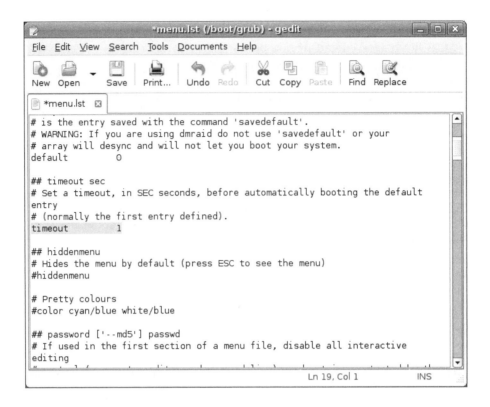

```
# is the entry saved with the command 'savedefault'.
# WARNING: If you are using dmraid do not use 'savedefault' or your
# array will desync and will not let you boot your system.
default        0

## timeout sec
# Set a timeout, in SEC seconds, before automatically booting the default
entry
# (normally the first entry defined).
timeout        1

## hiddenmenu
# Hides the menu by default (press ESC to see the menu)
#hiddenmenu

# Pretty colours
#color cyan/blue white/blue

## password ['--md5'] passwd
# If used in the first section of a menu file, disable all interactive
editing
```

Figure 3.1: CHANGING THE BOOT MENU COUNTDOWN

To make the change, type the following to open the necessary configuration file in Gedit:

```
$ gksu gedit /etc/init.d/rc
```

Look for the line that reads CONCURRENCY=none, and change it so it reads CONCURRENCY=shell. Then save the file and reboot your computer.

Using this method I managed to shave a massive twenty seconds off my desktop PC's usual startup time of just less than a minute.

Build a Readahead Profile Personalized to Your Computer

Ubuntu includes a software called readahead that, according to the official blurb, "allows the user to specify a set of files to be read into the page cache to accelerate first time loading of programs." In other words, it allows Ubuntu to cache frequently accessed files to avoid searching

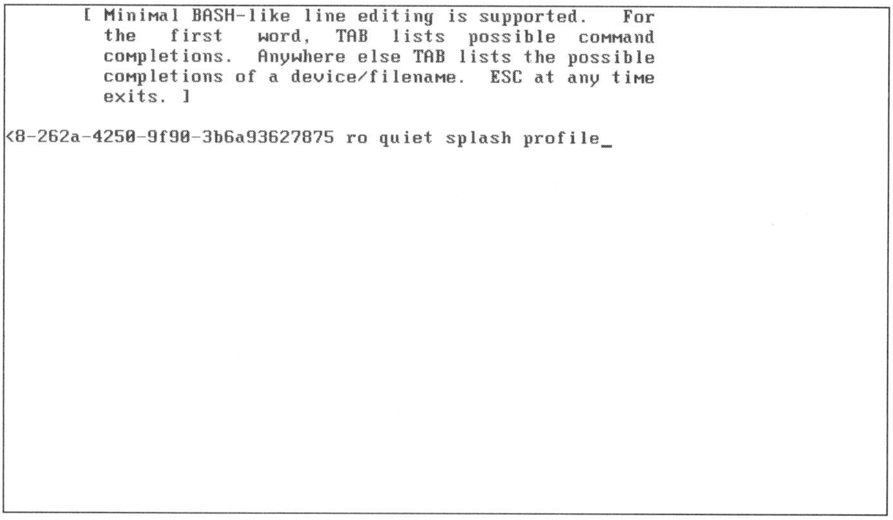

```
   [ Minimal BASH-like line editing is supported.   For
   the   first   word,   TAB   lists   possible   command
   completions.   Anywhere else TAB lists the possible
   completions of a device/filename.   ESC at any time
   exits. ]

<8-262a-4250-9f90-3b6a93627875 ro quiet splash profile_
```

Figure 3.2: RESETTING UBUNTU'S READAHEAD PROFILE

around for them at startup. A default readahead profile is included with Ubuntu, but you can create your own, tailored to your system.

Reboot Ubuntu, and at the boot menu, ensure the usual Ubuntu entry is highlighted. Then hit e. This will let you temporarily edit the boot menu entry. Use the cursor keys to move the highlight down to the second line, which begins with the word kernel, and hit e again. Use the right arrow key to move to the end of the line, and after the words quiet and splash, add the word profile. For an example taken from my test PC, see Figure 3.2. Then hit Enter and then b to boot your computer. Note that the first boot will be slow because the readahead cache will have to be rebuilt. In subsequent boots, however, you should see speed improvements.

I experienced a couple of seconds of improvement by building a new readahead profile. This isn't a dramatic increase, but it was certainly worth doing.

Trimming the GNOME Startup Programs

Once you've logged into the GNOME desktop, you'll face yet another delay as all the GNOME background software starts. You can save a few seconds by trimming this list using the GNOME Sessions program

(System → Preferences → Sessions). Ensure the Startup Programs tab is selected, and then look through the list for items you might want to prune. For example, if you're never going to use Evolution's alarm function, then you can disable Evolution Alarm Notifier by removing the check alongside it. One word of warning: Volume Manager isn't related to audio. Instead, it enables the automatic detection of external storage devices that are attached to your computer. As such, it should always be enabled. Nor should you disable NetworkManager—this is necessary to get Ubuntu online if you're using wifi. (If you absolutely have to disable it, follow the instructions in Tip 43, on page 91, which explains how to configure Ubuntu's network component using the older Network Settings tool.)

For another optimization hack, see Tip 293, on page 330; if you're using Wubi to run Ubuntu, Tip 19, on page 65.

9 Graph the System Bootup Performance

If you've followed Tip 8, on page 54, which described how to optimize Ubuntu's bootup, you might also be interested in Bootchart. As its name suggests, this creates charts displaying exactly what starts during bootup and the time it takes. Once installed by Synaptic (search for the bootchart package), it runs as a background service, and no configuration is necessary. After each boot, you'll find the chart it has generated in the /var/log/bootchart/ directory—to view it, just precede its filename at the command line with eog, or browse to it using Nautilus and double-click it.

The chart shows the total time taken to boot along the vertical axis and, beneath this, shows the time taken by each of the startup services to complete. For an example taken from my test computer, see Figure 3.3, on the facing page.

Remember that programs such as Bootchart that log bootup speeds can themselves impact performance. When you've finished with it, be sure to use Synaptic to remove the package.

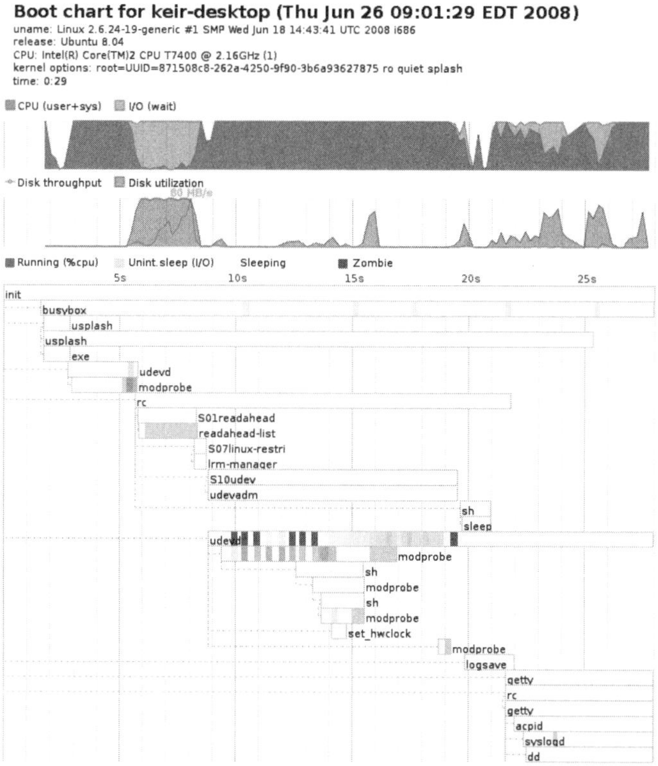

Boot chart for keir-desktop (Thu Jun 26 09:01:29 EDT 2008)
uname: Linux 2.6.24-19-generic #1 SMP Wed Jun 18 14:43:41 UTC 2008 i686
release: Ubuntu 8.04
CPU: Intel(R) Core(TM)2 CPU T7400 @ 2.16GHz (1)
kernel options: root=UUID=871508c8-262a-4250-9f90-3b6a93627875 ro quiet splash
time: 0:29

■ CPU (user+sys)　■ I/O (wait)

─Disk throughput　■ Disk utilization
80 MB/s

■ Running (%cpu)　Unint.sleep (I/O)　Sleeping　■ Zombie
5s　　　10s　　　15s　　　20s　　　25s

init
busybox
usplash
usplash
exe
udevd
modprobe
rc
S01readahead
readahead-list
S07linux-restri
lrm-manager
S10udev
udevadm
sh
sleep
udevd
modprobe
sh
modprobe
sh
modprobe
set_hwclock
modprobe
logsave
getty
rc
getty
acpid
syslogd
dd

Figure 3.3: A CHART PRODUCED BY BOOTCHART (SEE TIP 9)

10　Change Gedit's Printing Font

Gedit shouldn't really be used for printing stuff. That kind of thing is better handled by OpenOffice.org. But if you occasionally run off a quick block of text or look at hard copy of some code, you'll have noticed that Gedit always prints in Monospace font, even if you've set the screen font to something else in Edit → Preferences. To change the printing font, fire up gconf-editor, and navigate to /apps/gedit-2/preferences/print/fonts.

Change the print_font_body_pango entry to read whatever you want—use Gedit's own font selector dialog box to get the font name you should enter (Edit → Preferences, click Fonts and Colors, and click the Editor Font drop-down list). For example, to print using a sans-serif font[1] at 9 points, you could type Bitstream Vera Sans 9. For a serif font, you could type Times 9. To get a preview of how the new font will look, click File → Print Preview within Gedit.

For another rough-and-ready printing tip, see Tip 61, on page 112.

11 Shrink or Enlarge Images at the Command Line

GIMP can do just about anything to an image, but it can be time-consuming to fire it up just to resize an image. For ultra-quick manipulation, consider Imagemagick, a command-line image manipulation program. It doesn't come installed by default, and you'll need to install it via Synaptic (search for and install imagemagick). Once installed, the convert command should be used with the addition of the -resize command option. For example, the following will shrink filename.bmp to half its original size:

```
$ convert -resize 50% filename.bmp filename_small.bmp
```

The following command will enlarge filename.bmp to twice its original size (although there will be an obvious degradation in quality):

```
$ convert -resize 200% filename.bmp filename_larger.bmp
```

For further command-line image manipulation fun, see Tip 154, on page 188; Tip 214, on page 239; and Tip 268, on page 297.

---

1. You will, of course, know that a *serif font* is one with "bits hanging off the edges" of the lines that make up the letters, while *sans-serif* fonts don't have these bits. A good rule of thumb is that serif fonts are normally used for the text in newspapers, while sans-serif fonts tend to be used for headings. This book follows the same principle.

12 View All a Digital Photo's Technical Information

☐

Most pictures taken by digital cameras are saved in EXIF JPEG format. This means that they record technical details about the shot along with the actual image data. The information includes the exposure time, the aperture used, whether the flash was active, and so on.

In Ubuntu you can view this information by right-clicking any image, clicking Properties, and then looking at the Image tab. To view even more information, double-click the image so it opens in Eye of GNOME (the default Ubuntu image viewer), and then click File → Properties. Then click the Metadata tab, and click the Details fold-down chevron. Remember that even dialog boxes within Ubuntu can be enlarged by clicking and dragging the corners—this can really help view all the available information.

To view the information at the command line, use Synaptic to install the exif package. Then, to view the EXIF information, simply type exif photo.jpg, replacing photo.jpg with the name of the file.

13 Have Ubuntu Speak to You

☐

Ubuntu includes a built-in speech synthesizer called espeak. It's there to work in partnership with the Orca screen reader, which provides support for those who are partially sighted,[2] but it can also be called from the command line, as follows:

```
$ espeak "Ubuntu Kung Fu"
```

As you'll be able to tell, it's not the most sophisticated speech synthesizer in the world (it has a feel of Speak & Spell about it), but it can be fun to play around with.

---

2. To enable the Orca screen reader program, click System → Preferences → Assistive Technologies, and select Enable assistive technologies. Then log out and back in. Then click System → Preferences → Preferred Applications. Click the Accessibility tab, and put a check alongside Run at start under the Visual heading. Then log out and back in once more.

By simply typing espeak and then hitting ⌷Enter⌷, whatever you type after this will be spoken. To quit, type ⌷Ctrl⌷+⌷d⌷.

To switch voices, use the -v command option, but first you will need to find out the available voices, which can be done by typing espeak --voices=en. For example, to have the phrase "How about a nice game of chess?" spoken in a Jamaican voice, you could type this:

```
$ espeak -s 140 -v en-westindies "How about a nice game of chess?"
```

In this example I also added the -s command option, by which you can specify the speech speed in words per minute. The default value of 170 tends to be a little fast, especially when it comes to longer sentences.

14 Instantly Search for Files in Nautilus

What this tip describes is very obvious, yet almost nobody knows it's possible. To quickly search through a list of files in a Nautilus window, simply ensure the window is topmost, and start typing the search term. A small search text field will appear near the bottom right of the window, and files/folders will be matched as you type.

For another tip about finding the files you want using Nautilus, see Tip 72, on page 118. For general file-searching tips, see Tip 77, on page 123.

15 Take Photos or Record Videos with Your Webcam

Use Synaptic to search for and install cheese, and you'll be able to turn your computer into a virtual photo booth and/or camcorder! Once you've installed it, you'll find the program on the Applications → Graphics menu. Using it is simple and self-explanatory, especially if you've ever used Mac OS X's PhotoBooth software, which it is clearly modeled upon. Once you've taken a snap, right-click it, and select Save As to write it to the hard disk. See Tip 63, on page 113, for instructions on how to get your webcam working if you see nothing when using Cheese (or if you see a test pattern image).

To learn how to record the contents of your screen to a movie file, see Tip 312, on page 355.

16 Add RAR File Compression Support to Ubuntu

Although ZIP is the main compression file format used on most desktop computers, some people prefer to use the RAR format. To install support for extracting files from a RAR archive, use Synaptic to search for and install unrar. After this, File Roller—Ubuntu's default archive manager—will be able to extract files from RAR archives. You can also use the command from the prompt by simply typing unrar e filename.rar, replacing filename.rar with what you downloaded. Note that unrar doesn't require a dash before the e command option.

To be able to create RAR files, you'll need to install the rar package using Synaptic. But beware that this is a shareware program—after installation, you must register at http://www.rarlab.com within 40 days. To create an archive at the prompt once the package is installed, use the rar command, first specifying the a command option, then specifying the name of the new archive, and finally specifying the file or folders. For example, to create a rar archive of filename.doc, type rar a filename.rar filename.doc. To create an archive of your Desktop directory, type rar a desktop.rar ~/Desktop/. Once the rar package is installed, you will also be able to create a RAR archive in the usual manner for Ubuntu, by right-clicking a file, selecting Creating Archive, and selecting .rar in the drop-down list of compression types.

17 Add a Swap File or Expand Existing Swap Space

It's a myth to say that Ubuntu (or any Linux) needs a swap partition. This is certainly the preferred way of working and is most efficient, but

Linux can also use a single swap file located in the root partition, just like Windows or Mac OS X. There are times when this is advantageous, such as if you're able to create only one partition for Ubuntu (for example, Apple's Boot Camp software allows the creation of only a single non-Mac partition when dual-booting).

To create a swap file, you need to first create a dummy file of sufficient size, then format it as a swap file, and finally ensure that Ubuntu uses it at bootup. The following steps do just that (be extremely careful entering these commands; check what you type against what's on the page, and then check again before saving the files):

1. Open a terminal window, and create an empty file in the root of the file system using the dd command, as follows (this creates a 1GB file—you should ideally adjust the count= figure to at least match the size of your memory, bearing in mind that there are 1,024MB in 1GB):

   ```
   $ sudo dd if=/dev/zero of=/swapfile bs=1M count=1024
   ```

2. Now we need to format it as a swap file:

   ```
   $ sudo mkswap /swapfile
   ```

3. The final step is to make Ubuntu mount it at boot, which is done by editing /etc/fstab:

   ```
   $ gksu gedit /etc/fstab
   ```

   Then make a new line at the bottom of the file, and add the following:

   ```
   /swapfile none swap sw 0 0
   ```

   You can align the entries on the line under the column headings in fstab, like the other entries in the file, but it doesn't matter so long as there is at least one space between each entry on the line. Once done, save the file, and reboot your computer.

Once the computer has rebooted, you can test to see whether the swapfile is being utilized by typing cat /proc/meminfo|grep Swap.

These steps can also be used to add more swap space to a system that has an existing swap partition. You might want to do this if you're editing extremely high-resolution photographs, for example, or working with large video files.

18 Get Rid of the Virtual Console Legal Boilerplate

☐

Whenever you log in to a virtual console, you'll see a few paragraphs of legal boilerplate, reminding you that Ubuntu is free software and is supplied without warranty. Once you've read this, you're unlikely to forget it, so to stop it appearing each time you log in, type the following into a terminal window, which will delete the contents of the "message of the day" (motd) file, which is responsible for the message:[3]

```
$ sudo rm /etc/motd
$ sudo touch /etc/motd
```

Of course, rather than deleting the file, you might just choose to replace the text within it with something else. It's a simple text file. To load it into Gedit, type gksu gedit /etc/motd, and change its contents to whatever you want.

For further virtual console-related productivity tips, see Tip 46, on page 98; Tip 179, on page 210; Tip 193, on page 222; Tip 198, on page 226; Tip 207, on page 232; and Tip 233, on page 267.

19 Make Wubi Installations of Ubuntu Run Faster

☐

Try defragmenting your hard disk from within Windows after installing Ubuntu using Wubi. With a Wubi installation, the Ubuntu file system is stored in one large file (C:\ubuntu\disks\root.disk), as is the swap partition (C:\ubuntu\disks\swap.disk), and if these are spotted around the Windows partition as fragmented files, then performance might suffer. Of course, defragmenting the disk *before* installing Ubuntu using Wubi is an even better idea.

See also Tip 186, on page 216.

---

3. Actually, the two commands first delete /etc/motd and then re-create an empty file with the same name using the touch command.

☐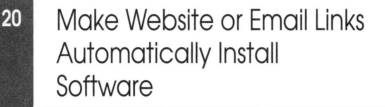

20 Make Website or Email Links Automatically Install Software

Sometimes if you're trying to help somebody fix a problem, you'll have to tell them how to install software. Yet for some Ubuntu newbies, even this can be confusing. The solution is to create a "software install" hyperlink within a web page (such as a forum posting), new email window, or Pidgin message window. To do this, simply click the "create link" button on the web page or within the email (the precise name of this will vary depending on the software/website used), and then type apt:packagename in the URL field, replacing packagename with the precise name of the package as listed in Synaptic.

For example, let's say you want to tell somebody how to install the thunar package, as referenced in Tip 92, on page 136. If you're creating an email with the instructions, ensure the new mail uses HTML (ensure HTML is checked on the Format menu), and then click Insert → Link. In the URL field, delete what's there, and type apt:thunar. Don't worry about the Description field—leave it with the default contents that will probably mirror what's in the URL field. You can see an example in Figure 3.4, on the next page. Then click Close. Note that there's a slight bug in Evolution that means, for some reason, the hyperlink won't actually appear as a link until you type some more into the new mail window or click the Send button.

Perhaps it goes without saying that should you ever receive such a link in an email, or see one on a website, you should be very wary (especially if there are also additional instructions telling you to add a new software repository). It would be easy to disguise a malicious link as something seemingly benign, although you will always be prompted to confirm the choice of software before installation.

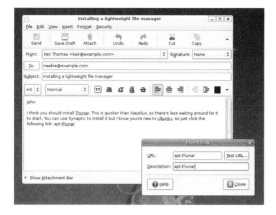

Figure 3.4: ADDING A "SOFTWARE INSTALL" LINK TO AN EMAIL (SEE TIP 20)

21 Make Fonts Look Superb

Most fonts contain within them "hints" laid down by their designer about how they should look onscreen. However, Ubuntu ignores them and uses a system called *autohinting*, which improvises the hints based on the shape of the letters.[4] It works well, and Ubuntu's fonts look far from ugly, but you might also want to try *bytecode hinting*. This uses the hinting built into the fonts and is said to work particularly well with Microsoft fonts (you can learn how to install them in Tip 170, on page 197).

To activate bytecode hinting, open a terminal window, and type the following:

```
$ sudo dpkg-reconfigure fontconfig-config
```

Using the cursor keys, select Native from the menu, and then hit Enter. On the next screen you will be asked whether you want to activate subpixel rendering. This is good for TFT screens, so make the choice (or

---

4. *Autohinting*, as described in Tip 21, is used to avoid patenting issues with bytecode hinting technology in some countries. This isn't an issue for you, as an end user, but it's why organizations like Ubuntu prefer to distribute Ubuntu with autohinting activated.

just select Automatic). Next you'll be asked whether you want to activate bitmap fonts, which are non-TrueType fonts good for use at small point sizes. There's no harm in using them, so select yes.

The program will quit when it's finished. Once that's happened, type the following to write the changes to the system and update files:

```
$ sudo dpkg-reconfigure fontconfig
$ sudo dpkg-reconfigure defoma
```

Click System → Quit → Logout, and then log back in again. The difference should be noticeable immediately. Specifically, letters will appear more rounded, and the antialiasing will appear better.

Bytecode hinting isn't to everybody's taste. If you don't like it, just repeat the steps, and enable autohinting again.

For more font-related tips, see Tip 101, on page 144; the aforementioned Tip 170, on page 197; Tip 280, on page 313; and Tip 283, on page 319.

22 Download Updates Faster

Every now and again the Ubuntu update servers become a little congested, particularly when there's a new release of Ubuntu. If you find this happening, switch to an alternative server, preferably located near where your computer is located—there are many servers around the world, all mirroring the same repositories. Click System → Administration → Software Sources. Click the Download From drop-down list, and then select Other. In the list of servers, choose any you want. You'll need to reload the package lists from the server when prompted.

Don't worry about the possible security implications of signing up to a server you've never heard of. All Ubuntu software packages are digitally signed, so fakery is technically impossible (caveat: never say never, but I'd be extremely surprised if any faked packages got onto a repository server).

23 | Slow Down a Touchpad's Scrolling

If you have a notebook computer, you might be used to *edge scroll* on the touchpad when running Windows. This is where the right edge of the notebook's touchpad is used as a virtual scrollbar—by running a finger up and down, the currently active window scrolls up and down correspondingly.

You might already have realized that you can activate the edge scroll functionality in Ubuntu using the Touchpad tab of System → Preferences → Mouse. The problem I had was that the scrolling was just too fast. A light touch on the pad caused the web page or file listing to fly up or down the screen. The solution was to add a line to the xorg.conf configuration file, as follows:

1. Open the Xorg configuration file into Gedit:

   ```
   $ gksu gedit /etc/X11/xorg.conf
   ```

2. Look for the two lines that read as follows:

   ```
   Section "InputDevice"
     Driver   "synaptics"
   ```

   Then, beneath all the lines that begin Option, add a new line as follows:

   ```
   Option "VertScrollDelta" "50"
   ```

   You can align the words with the other entries in the list if you want, although this doesn't matter. For an example taken from my test notebook, see Figure 3.5, on the following page.

3. Save the file, close any open programs, and then hit Ctrl+Alt+Backspace to restart the X server. Log in again as usual, and the changes should be instantly visible.

If the scrolling is now too slow, try changing the value of "VertScrollData" to 25 or perhaps even less—the lower the value, the more sensitive the edge scroll becomes.

To make Firefox scroll fewer lines as you drag and scroll, start Firefox, and type about:config into the URL bar. Agree to carry on despite the

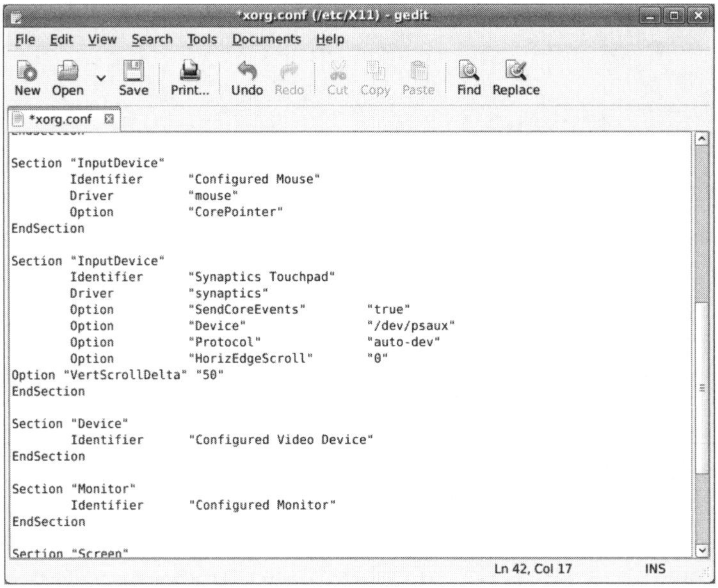

Figure 3.5: SLOWING DOWN A TOUCHPAD'S EDGE SCROLL (SEE TIP 23)

warning about voiding a possibly warranty. Then, in the search bar, type mousewheel.withnokey.sysnumlines. In the list of results, double-click the entry so that it reads false and turns bold. Now try the new scroll speed by opening a new tab and browsing to a website.

To speed up the scroll slightly, type mousewheel.withnokey.numlines, and change the value to anything greater than 1. For the ultimate in scrolling, click Edit → Preferences in Firefox, click the Advanced icon, and put a check in Use smooth scrolling.

24 Ensure Your Windows Partition Is Always Available Under Ubuntu

Do you find that sometimes your Windows partition isn't available in Ubuntu? You will know because you'll see the error message "Cannot mount volume." This probably happens because Windows crashed or hung during shutdown. If Windows is not cleanly shut down, then Ubuntu will refuse to mount the partition. If, even after Windows is cleanly shut down, the Windows partition refuses to appear, then run a chkdsk on the partition from within Windows. See also Tip 38, on page 87, which describes how to repair the Windows partition from within Ubuntu.

25	Improve the GNOME Terminal Look and Feel

☐

Both the color scheme and font of GNOME Terminal can be tweaked. This can be a good way of improving legibility and also the amount of space GNOME Terminal hogs onscreen, because a smaller font size makes the window smaller too.

To change the font, click Edit → Current Profile, and remove the check from Use the system fixed width font. Then click the Font drop-down list, and select either a different font or perhaps just a smaller point size (I find 8 point is best). Not all fonts are suitable for use in GNOME Terminal—generally speaking, it works best with Courier or Mono-style nonproportional fonts, although a handful of proportional fonts suffice too. For the ultimate in small but still legible fonts, try selecting Bitstream Vera Sans Mono 8 point. Also consider installing the ttf-inconsolata package—this provides a high-quality monospace font for use at small point sizes. Once it's installed, close any open GNOME Terminal windows, and then follow the previous instructions to change the font, selecting the Inconsolata entry in the list.

To change the color scheme, click Edit → Current Profile, and select the Colors tab. Then remove the check from Use colors from system theme, and select a replacement from the Built-in schemes drop-down list. For a retro feel, try the Green on Black scheme. The Palette drop-down list refers to how items in things like file listings are colored. Generally speaking, there's no need to change this. Consider combining changing the color scheme with Tip 236, on page 269, which explains how to make the GNOME Terminal window translucent.

If you want to really save screen space, click Edit → Current Profile, and remove the check from Show menubar by default in new terminals. This will then hide the menus in any new terminal windows you open. To get it back temporarily, right-click the terminal window, and select Show Menubar from the menu.

☐

26 Ensure Ubuntu Always Knows the Time

Several of my computers sometimes mysteriously lose minutes when switched off so that the time they display slowly becomes more and more behind. Luckily, I have Ubuntu installed. This can periodically synchronize with the main Ubuntu time server and thus never let the computers get out of step with the rest of the world.

To set this up, use Synaptic to install the ntp package. Once the package is installed, restart your computer. Configuration is automatic.

If, after rebooting, you find that the time display is still wrong, it's likely that you have Ubuntu set up for the wrong time zone. To fix this, right-click the time/date display at the top right of the Ubuntu desktop, and select Adjust date and time. Then click the Unlock button in the window that appears. Then click the Time Zone button, and click the nearest city to you on the map that appears. Once done, click Close. The changes will take effect immediately.

☐

27 Get More Data onto CD-R Discs

Overburn is the process of cramming a little extra data onto CD-Rs, in excess of the manufacturer's recommendations. Typically an average 700MB CD-R will take 734MB. Sometimes it works, sometimes it doesn't, and discs created this way aren't guaranteed to work on all computers (there have been some suggestions that overburning can even damage CD-R/RW drives). To enable overburn for Nautilus' CD/DVD Creator (Places → CD/DVD Creator), entirely at your own risk, open gconf-editor, and head over to /apps/nautilus-cd-burner. Then put a check alongside overburn on the right.

For another CD/DVD burning tip, see Tip 157, on page 189.

| 28 | Share Files Across the Network (Without Tearing Your Hair Out) |

If you opt to share folders across a network under Ubuntu, you'll find they're protected with your username and password, which you might not want to share with others. The Shared Folders dialog box allows you to set up guest access, but at the time of writing, this had a serious bug that rendered it unusable.[5]

The following describes a method of securely, painlessly, and easily sharing files with colleagues or other computers in your house across the network, regardless of whether they run Ubuntu, Windows, or Mac OS X. It involves creating a dummy guest account solely for the purpose of hosting the shared files and folders.

Note that these instructions were written using Ubuntu 8.04.1:

1. Use Synaptic to install the samba and libpam-smbpass packages. These are the background programs that are needed for file sharing and user authentication.

2. Create a guest account. You will use this for hosting the shared folder(s), and the other computers will use its login details to access the shared folder. To create the account, click System → Administration → Users and Groups. Click Unlock and then the Add User button. Give the new user the username guest, and give it a simple password in the User Password field that you'll be able to share with others. Leave the other text fields as they are. Click the User Privileges tab, and check Share Files with the Local Network.

3. Log out of your account and into your new guest account. Create the folder(s) you want to be used for sharing (it doesn't matter where—you might as well create it on the desktop; nor does it matter what name you give it). Then right-click it, and select Sharing

---

5. The bug with guest access on shared folders (on an Ubuntu 8.04.1 installation) is that files added to the folder by other users are owned by user "nobody," and the Ubuntu user whose shared folder it is has only read access. To change the ownership and permissions, you will need to use admin powers at the command prompt each time a file is placed there.

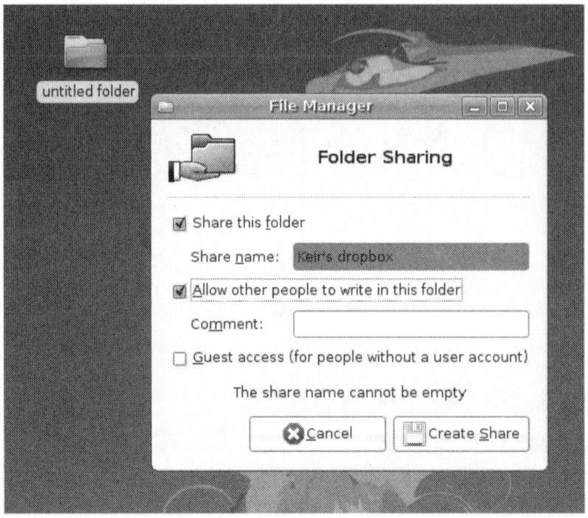

Figure 3.6: THE SHARING DIALOG BOX MIGHT REPORT AN ERROR, BUT THIS IS A BUG (SEE TIP 28).

Options. Click Share This Folder, and type a share name in the relevant text box (you might see error messages while doing this, but don't worry, as shown in Figure 3.6; it appears the dialog box is a little buggy). Check Allow Other People to Write in This Folder, but *don't* check Guest access! Then click Create Share. You'll be prompted to add permissions automatically, so click to do so. Right-click any other folders you want to share, and repeat this step; then log out and log back into your main user account. Note that there is no need to leave the account logged in—its shared folders are available to everybody even if the account is logged out.

4. Now you have to create a permanent launcher in your regular account for the new shared folder so you can access it in the future. Right-click the desktop, and select Create Launcher. In the Name field of the dialog box that appears, enter a memorable label, like Shared Folder. In the command field, type nautilus smb://localhost. Leave the Comment field empty, and then click OK. Double-click the new launcher, and you should see the shared folder(s). Double-click the shared folder, and in the dialog box that appears, enter guest in the Username field and the password you created in the relevant text field. Then check Remember Forever. You should now have access to your shared folder. A useful tip is to hit Ctrl+d to

create a Nautilus bookmark. In the future, you can simply select this bookmark, on the Bookmarks menu, to access the shared folder.

5. Other computers should now see your shared folder appear in My Network Places, just like any other Windows computer with shared files. They should use the username guest and the password you created earlier. Don't click the "guest access" option—specify guest as the username.

There should never be any need to directly log in to the dummy guest account in the future, unless you specifically want to create new shared folders.

For another method of painlessly sharing files with others, see Tip 226, on page 255.

29   Save Ink When Printing

□

Ink-jet fluid is one of the most expensive liquids in the world, and replacing cartridges on a regular basis can be depressingly wallet-draining. One quick hint is to print pages using draft mode and also to reduce the scaling of the print so that either more fits onto the page you're printing or less ink is used if you're printing something like a photo.

In the Print dialog box that appears when you click File → Print, ensure your printer is selected in the list, and select the Advanced tab. Change the Print Quality drop-down list to read Draft, Economy, or whatever you want (the range of options will vary depending on the make and model of printer).

To reduce the scaling, click the Page Setup tab, and alter the setting in the Scale box. I found that a setting less than 60% was a step too far (at least for my eyesight) and that about 75% was a comfortable compromise. If you're printing from within Firefox, you'll also need to click the Options tab and uncheck Ignore Scaling and Shrink to Fit Page Width.

To learn how to print more than one picture per page, see Tip 151, on page 186.

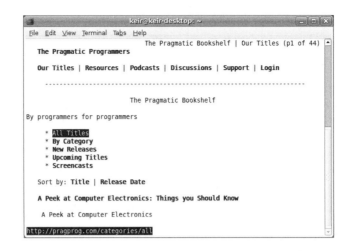

Figure 3.7: LINKS (SEE TIP 30)

☐ ## 30 Browse the Web from the Command Line

Call it a form of insurance, but I like to have a command-line web browser installed in case anything goes wrong with either Firefox or the entire GUI system. I can then look up help and solutions from a virtual console or just check the news while I'm waiting for things to get better.

Command-line browsers are pretty primitive. There are no images, for example, or even color. The page design always gets mangled. In other words, they're not for use all the time, unless you're a masochist. Or a command-line fanatic.

There are two competing text-mode browsers—links and lynx. links is perhaps the better of the two (see Figure 3.7) because it understands frames and thus gets the layout of pages slightly more correct, but both are only a download away via Synaptic.[6]

---

6. While installing links, you might see something called links2, which seems to promise image support. It does! Sadly, this won't work on Ubuntu because the necessary frame buffer graphics mode isn't activated for reasons of overall system stability.

Once either program has started, hit g to enter a URL (with lynx, you'll also need to type http:// if the address doesn't start with www). Once the page has loaded, use Page Up and Page Down to scroll the page. Use the up/down cursor keys to cycle through each link onscreen until you find the one you want, and then hit Enter to follow it. To go back a page, hit the left cursor key. To download a file that's linked to, highlight the link, and hit d. You can search for words using a forward slash (/), in the same way as with man pages (see Tip 167, on page 195). Hitting Esc in links will cause a rudimentary menu to appear—use the cursor keys to navigate, and hit Enter to select a menu option. Once you're done, hit q to quit the program.

If links is used in a terminal window, you'll be able to click each link using your mouse. If gpm is installed (see Tip 233, on page 267), you'll have rudimentary mouse control over the browser and can click links in a virtual console window.

31 Create an "Ubuntu Install" USB Stick

If you don't fancy carrying the delicate Ubuntu installation CD around with you, you can copy its contents to a USB key stick and use that to install Ubuntu onto computers (provided those computers can boot from USB, and most modern computers will be able to).

This is also a handy way of creating a portable USB installation of Ubuntu on a small USB key (in other words, 1/2GB) for use on other computers (if you have a larger USB memory stick, see Tip 305, on page 345). The only problem is that the system software cannot be updated, and you'll always be running as the root user, because that's how the live distro mode of the install CD operates.

This tip is relevant only for users of Ubuntu 8.04 (Hardy Heron) or older. Ubuntu 8.10 (Intrepid Ibex) has built-in tools to install to create an installer USB key stick.

To make the process easier, a member of the Ubuntu community called Probono has created the fantastic Liveusb software that will entirely automate the creation of a USB install stick. To install it, first add his software repository—click System → Administration → Software

Sources, select the Third-Party Software in the window that appears, and then click the Add button. Then type the following into the APT line text field:

```
deb http://ppa.launchpad.net/probono/ubuntu hardy main
```

Click OK, then click the Close button in the parent dialog box, and then click to reload the list of packages when prompted. Then use Synaptic to search for and install liveusb. You'll be told the package isn't authenticated, but this is fine.

Insert the USB stick, insert your Ubuntu install CD, and then start the program by clicking System → Administration → Install Live USB. In the Options section, you can select to install Flash Player on the USB stick and also whether you want to make the USB stick "persistent," which is to say, any files you save after booting from it will stick around, rather than being wiped each boot.

Note that a bug in the Ubuntu 8.04 Hardy Heron installation CD means that it is impossible to activate persistent mode on the USB key stick. This has been fixed in the Ubuntu 8.04.1 install CD.

32 Add a Menu Entry for Ubuntu's Compression Tool

File Roller is Ubuntu's behind-the-scenes compression (zip) program. In truth, there's no need for you to come into direct contact with it because it will automatically step in to decompress archives when you double-click them and compress files when you select Create Archive from the right-click menu. However, if you want to run it separately (perhaps if you want to create empty archives with the intention of filling them later or if you just can't get over how WinZip does things), you can add an Applications → Accessories menu item for it. Click System → Preferences → Main Menu, and select Applications → Accessories in the list on the left. Then put a check alongside Archive Manager on the right. Then close the program window.

From now on, you can find File Roller on the Applications → Accessories menu.

For other file compression tips, see Tip 16, on page 63, and Tip 174, on page 205.

33 Quickly Run Applications Without Opening a Terminal Window

☐

If you want to run a GUI application that doesn't have a menu entry (for example, gconf-editor), there's no need to fuss with a terminal window. Just hit Alt + F2 . Then type the name of the program. If it needs to run with root privileges, just type gksu beforehand. If the program is command line, check the Run In Terminal box. This will then open a terminal window and run the command, but be aware that the terminal window will then close as soon as the command has finished, so you won't be able to inspect the output.

34 Instantly Search Google for Any Word or Phrase

☐

Have you ever been reading a document and wanted to look up something in Google? In Firefox you can just highlight the word or phrase, right-click it, and select Search Google. However, what if you're reading, say, a PDF file? Or a man page in a terminal window?

A very simple but effective solution is Googlizer, which you can install using Synaptic. Once installed, it's added to the Applications → Internet menu, so you'll have to manually drag and drop it to a blank spot on the panel for quicker access.

How it works is simple. Highlight any text, in any application, and then click Googlizer's icon to instantly search Google. If a Firefox window is open, a new tab will be added showing the search results. Otherwise, Firefox will be started, and the search results will be shown. Try it. It's one of those simple things that might just change the way you work forever.

Googlizer can be personalized so that it searches the version of Google localized to your country or even a non-Google search engine. To do this, you'll need to discover the search URL for the engine you want to use. To do so, just perform a search using either the localized version of Google (for example, http://www.google.co.uk, if you live in the UK) or

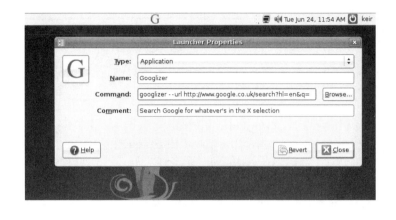

Figure 3.8: ALTERING GOOGLIZER'S DEFAULT SEARCH (SEE TIP 34)

a different search engine. Then look at the URL for the part where your search term appears, and highlight/copy all that comes before it.

For example, if I search for *Ubuntu Kung Fu* using http://www.google.co. uk, I get the following URL for the search results page:

```
http://www.google.co.uk/search?hl=en&q=Ubuntu+Kung+Fu&btnG=Google+ ↩
Search&meta=
```

...so I chop the end off, from the Ubuntu+Kung+Fu part onward, and I'm left with the following, which I copy into the clipboard (highlight the text, and hit Ctrl+c):

```
http://www.google.co.uk/search?hl=en&q=
```

Once you have the information, right-click the Googlizer panel icon, and select Properties. In the Command line, add --url after googlizer, and then paste your Google URL. For example, I ended up with the following, as shown in Figure 3.8 (note that I resized the dialog box for the purposes of the figure):

```
googlizer --url http://www.google.co.uk/search?hl=en&q=
```

You can also change the icon if you want by clicking the icon preview at the top left of the dialog box.

When finished, click the Close button, and then test the new localized search.

Here are some URLs that will make Googlizer use other search engines —just add these addresses after the --url part of the Command line, as described earlier:

Yahoo.com: `http://search.yahoo.com/search?p=`
Ask.com: `http://www.ask.com/web?q=`
Microsoft Live: `http://search.live.com/results.aspx?q=`

35 Ensure You're Informed About the Newest Releases of Ubuntu

If you have Ubuntu 8.04.01 LTS (Hardy Heron) installed, by default Ubuntu will tell you only when the next long-term support (LTS) release of Ubuntu is available. However, newer versions of Ubuntu are released every six months. To make Ubuntu inform you whenever *any* new release is made available, open Software Sources (System → Administration), click the Updates tab, and select Normal Releases from the Release Upgrade drop-down list.

36 Create a File Delete Command That Uses the Trash

As mentioned several times in this book, the rm command doesn't have a trash facility. Once files are deleted, they're gone forever. However, you can create your own trash command, which, when used at the prompt, will move files and/or folders to Ubuntu's standard trash folder. The files can then be recovered, if desired, or permanently deleted in the usual way by emptying the trash folder.

To add the new command, you'll have to create an *alias*. Aliases are discussed more in Tip 259, on page 290, but for now it's enough to know that you'll need to edit the .bashrc file in your /home folder and add a line to the bottom, as follows:

1. Open a terminal window, and type gedit ~/.bashrc.
2. At the bottom of the file, add the following new line:
   ```
   alias trash="mv -t ~/.local/share/Trash/files --backup=t"
   ```

Save the file, close Gedit, and open a new terminal window to test your new command. To delete filename.doc, for example, you would type trash filename.doc. The new command will work on folders too, and multiple files/folders can be specified one after the other (for example, trash filename1.doc filename2.doc).

Another method to achieve the same goal, but without the need to create a command alias, is to use Synaptic to install the gvfs-bin package. Then use the gvfs-trash command in the same way as the trash command created earlier, by specifying files and/or directories (for example, gvfs-trash filename1.doc filename2.doc).

☐ | 37 | Configure Ubuntu's Firewall

You might not realize it, but Ubuntu has a very powerful firewall built in. However, it isn't activated out of the box. Some firewall configuration tools are provided but aren't easy to use and definitely aren't recommended for those less versed in networking fundamentals.

The firewall isn't activated because Ubuntu has no *outward-facing services*—there's no programs that allow incoming connections from the Internet, apart from those under the user's control, like Firefox and Evolution, where any incoming connections are requested. The analogy is that Ubuntu is a house without windows or doors, so enacting further defenses against intruders isn't necessary.

But a firewall provides more than simple protection against incoming connections. It can protect you against unauthorized outgoing connections too, such as those enacted by spyware[7] and also switch off some network diagnostic tools that hackers have been known to exploit.

To easily configure Ubuntu's firewall, you can use Firestarter. This is a simple GUI program that lets you control both incoming and outgoing connections. It works on the principles of *policies* and *rules*. Policies are sets of rules that define what outside agents can and can't access your computer (and, conversely, what your computer itself can and can't access across the network/Internet).

---

7. Ubuntu, and all versions of Linux, has yet to see any spyware. It's pretty unlikely too, considering open source software and the generally higher level of awareness of Ubuntu users. But never say never....

Installing Firestarter

Firestarter can be installed via Synaptic (search for and install the firestarter package) and subsequently found on the Applications → Internet menu. When it first starts, you'll need to complete a setup wizard. The default choices are usually correct, although, if you use a wifi connection, be sure to select the right type of connection you want Firestarter to protect from the Detected device(s) drop-down list. You can find out the device that provides your network connection by right-clicking the NetworkManager icon, selecting Connection Information, and looking at the end of the line that's headed Interface. When the wizard finishes, opt to save the settings.

Configuring Incoming Connections

Once installed, Firestarter enacts a default policy of turning away unsolicited incoming connections (incoming connections that are requested, such as when Firefox requests a web page, are still allowed). Although extremely safe when it comes to security, turning away unsolicited connections isn't always desirable. For example, the file-sharing software BitTorrent relies on other people connecting to your computer unsolicited in order to download file fragments. Additionally, services like network file sharing rely on others being able to connect to your computer whenever they want to grab or drop off files.

Therefore, it's sometimes necessary to allow some incoming connections, which is done by creating an inbound rule, as follows:

1. Start Firestarter, and click the Policy tab. Ensure Inbound traffic policy is selected in the Editing drop-down list. Then right-click in the lower part of the window, underneath the Allow service heading. In the menu that appears, click Add Rule.

2. In the dialog box that appears, select the type of incoming connection you want to allow from the Name drop-down list. If you want to allow network file sharing, select Samba (SMB). Once you've made your selection, the Port text field will be automatically filled in. There should be no need to change this. For an example taken from my test PC, see Figure 3.9, on the next page.

3. Under the When the source is heading, you can select Anyone to allow literally any Internet-connected computer to connect to your computer (advisable in the case of BitTorrent) or IP, host or network to restrict it to a particular computer or range of computers. To

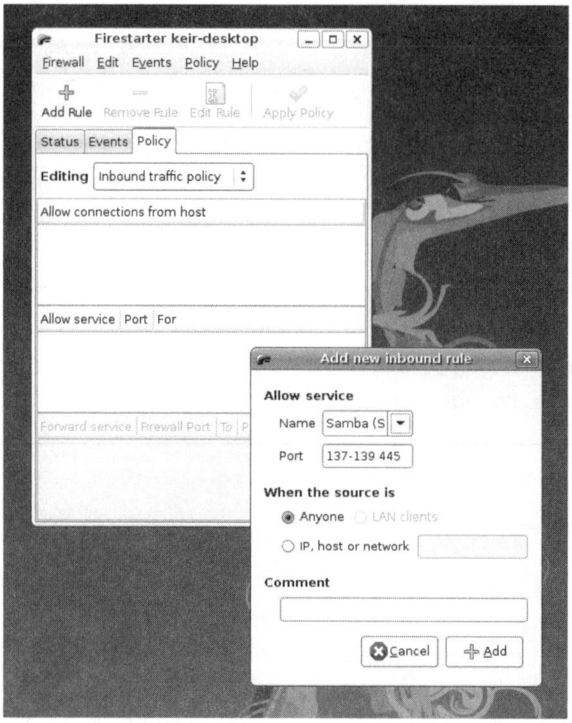

Figure 3.9: CONFIGURING AN INBOUND RULE IN FIRESTARTER

allow only those computers in your private network to connect, for example, you might type 192.168.1.1-255. This would add a layer of security if you simply want to enable network file sharing, for example.

4. Click the Add button, and then click the Apply Policy button on the main toolbar. The change will take effect immediately, and there's no need to reboot. Once configuration is complete, you can close the Firestarter program (remember that Firestarter is simply a configuration program for the firewall, not the firewall itself; it doesn't need to be running for the firewall to function).

Configuring Outgoing Connections

By default, Firestarter allows all outgoing connections. For example, should Firefox or Evolution attempt to connect to a website or mail server, it won't stop them. This is known as a *permissive policy*. To block all outgoing network connections from software, apart from that which you sanction, Firestarter needs to be switched to *restrictive policy*. The following steps describe how to enact a restrictive outgoing policy and then create rules so that software is allowed to make outgoing connections (this is also known as creating a *whitelist* because only software you list is allowed through):

1. Start Firestarter, and ensure the Policy tab is selected. Then select Outbound traffic policy from the Editing drop-down list. Then select Restrictive by default, whitelist traffic.

2. Right-click underneath the Allow service heading at the bottom of the program, and select Add rule from the menu that appears.

3. In the Name drop-down list, select the type of connection you'd like to pass through unhindered. For example, to allow Firefox (and also Ubuntu's software management subsystem) to work properly, you'll need to select HTTP, because HTTP is how web traffic is referred to technically. You will almost certainly want to allow this. Once that's done, the Port text field will be filled in automatically. There should be no need to change this unless you know what you're doing.

4. If you need to manually create a rule (which is to say, those offered don't fit your requirements), type the port into the Port text field, and then type the name of the new rule straight into the Name field (the Name field works as both a drop-down list and a text field). You can give the new rule any name you want.

5. Regardless of whether you create your own rule or use one that's already defined, don't change anything under the When the source is heading. In this case, the settings are for use only when Firestarter is protecting a shared Internet connection. Just click the Add button to create the rule.

6. Click the Apply Policy button on the toolbar. The changes will take effect immediately, and there's no need to reboot.

If you opt for a restrictive outgoing policy, at the very least you should create rules to allow HTTP, HTTPS, POP3, and SMTP. The first two will allow Firefox to fetch web pages unhindered, while the latter two are necessary for getting and sending email (if you use IMAP instead of POP3, then, obviously, you should select that instead).

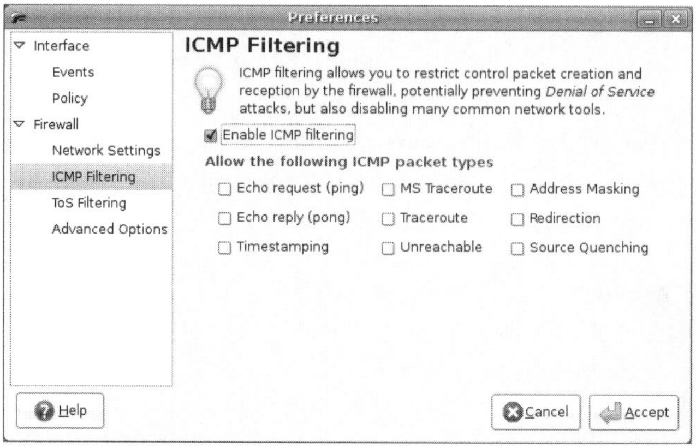

Figure 3.10: TURNING OFF DIAGNOSTIC TOOLS RESPONSES IN FIRESTARTER (SEE TIP 37)

A restrictive policy can be a pain to maintain because some websites ask Firefox to fetch data using non-HTTP or HTTPS ports. In particular, this can be the case if certain types of plug-ins are used. In that case, you need to create a rule for each port that gets used, and that involves some technical knowledge of what port is being requested. Additionally, if you install new software that requires Internet access, the port it uses will need to be added.

Turning Off Network Diagnostic Tools

Firestarter has another trick up its sleeve. It can stop network diagnostic responses being sent from your computer. Network diagnostic tools can be useful in problem-solving situations, but there have been a number of occasions when they have been exploited by hackers. To turn off the ports, click Edit → Preferences within Firestarter, select ICMP Filtering on the left of the dialog box that appears, and put a check in the Enable ICMP filtering box (*don't* then put a check in any of the boxes beneath—that will *reenable* the ports!). For an example from my test PC, see Figure 3.10. Then click Accept. You can quit Firestarter after this.

38 Repair Windows from Within Ubuntu

☐

If Windows is refusing to boot, for whatever reason, you can try repairing the file system from within Ubuntu. Use Synaptic to search for the ntfsprogs package. Once it's installed, unmount your Windows partition (if it's mounted), and type sudo ntfsfix /dev/sda1 to check and fix the partition (assuming your Windows partition is /dev/sda1—likely if you installed Ubuntu in a dual-boot configuration on a computer already running Windows).

This tip is also useful if you see the "Cannot mount volume" error when attempting to access your Windows partition from within Ubuntu.

To learn how to repair the Ubuntu file system, see Tip 223, on page 249.

39 Empty the Trash Even If Told You Can't

☐

When emptying the trash, you might see an error saying that the files can't be deleted. This is probably because files have ended up in there either that are owned by root or that have adverse file permissions. The solution is to empty the trash using administrator powers. To do so, open a terminal window, and type the following two commands, replacing username with your username:

```
$ sudo rm -rf ~/.local/share/Trash/{files,info}/
```

For additional trash talk, see Tip 173, on page 204, and Tip 228, on page 260.

☐ **40** | # Log On Automatically After Bootup

If you want to stop seeing the username/password prompt when you start Ubuntu, click System → Administration → Login Window. Then click the Security tab, and put a check in Enable Automatic Login. From the User drop-down list, select your username. Then click Close. Bear in mind that this is obviously insecure because it gives virtually anybody access to your desktop and files.

There is a slight downside if you're using a computer with a wifi network card: a dialog box will appear each time you log on, asking you to enter your password to unlock your keyring. This is needed by NetworkManager so it can grab your wifi network key from the protected keyring password file. Previously, logging in manually was enough to unlock the keyring.

Short of massively overhauling Ubuntu's authentication and security system, there are a handful of possible solutions—using Wicd to replace NetworkManager or using Ubuntu's older network configuration tool. See Tip 41, and Tip 43, on page 91, respectively.

☐ **41** | # Use an Alternative Wifi Connection Manager

Wicd (http://wicd.sourceforge.net/) is an excellent swap-in replacement for NetworkManager. NetworkManager is the system software that sits in the notification area and handles network connections. Wicd does the same job but uses a piece of software that's almost entirely independent of existing Ubuntu infrastructure and packs in a few extra features too, such as the ability to configure static IP/DNS addresses and use non-ISP-specific DNS servers such as that offered by OpenDNS (http://www.opendns.org).

Here's how to install and configure Wicd:

1. You'll need to add a new software repository. To do so, click System → Administration → Software Sources, click the Third-Party Software

tab, then click the Add button, and enter deb http://apt.wicd.net hardy extras. Click Close and then the Reload button to refresh the list of software.

2. Use Synaptic to search for and install wicd. Once you have it installed, you'll need to reboot, and then you'll find Wicd on the Applications → Internet menu. Note that the wicd package will remove the NetworkManager packages during installation. You might see a brief error message that the "NetworkManager applet could not find some required resources." You can ignore this. Once Wicd has been installed, reboot the system, although if you want to set up a notification area icon for Wicd, follow the instructions in the next step first.

3. To add a notification area icon, similar to that of NetworkManager, a few manual steps are necessary. Click System → Preferences → Sessions, and click Add. Type wicd into the Name field and /opt/wicd/tray.py into the Command text area. Leave the Comment text field clear. Then close the dialog box and reboot.

4. When you start Wicd (it can be found on the Applications → Internet menu), it will automatically scan for nearby wifi networks. If no networks are shown, click the Refresh toolbar button.

5. Before you can connect, which is done by clicking the Connect link, "unfold" the configuration options by clicking the little chevron alongside the wifi base station's entry on the list. Then unfold Advanced Settings, and put a check in Use Encryption. Select the type of wifi protection the base station uses from the list, and and type the key or password in the text box provided. Of course, if the network has no protection (usually described as an *open network*), then you can skip this step. Then click the blue Connect link. Once you've connected to the network, you can quit the Wicd configuration program.

To revert to using NetworkManager, should you want, use Synaptic to install the network-manager package and uninstall the wicd package. Then stop Wicd's notification area applet starting at GNOME startup— click System → Preferences → Sessions, select the entry you created for Wicd, and click the Remove button. The reboot the computer.

For more network configuration magic, see Tip 43, on page 91; Tip 60, on page 111; Tip 70, on page 117; and Tip 119, on page 157.

☐

| 42 | Make Evolution More Like Outlook (Just a Little Bit) |

Nobody can reasonably suggest that Microsoft "got it right" with Outlook, the email component provided as part of its office suite. However, if you're been using it for some time and have switched to Evolution, you might be annoyed by the slight differences. The good news is that Evolution can be made slightly more Outlook-like with just a little tweaking.

- Forward email inline: Whenever you forward an email, Evolution will attach it as a file that the recipient must then open. This can cause confusion. To make Evolution forward email as text within the new message (known as *forwarding inline*), click Edit → Preferences, click Composer Preferences on the left side of the dialog box, and click the Forward Style drop-down list. Then select Quoted.

- Change the plain text font: If you send or receive emails that aren't HTML (that is, plain text), Evolution will use a monospace font to display the text. This can look ugly. To switch to the standard sans proportional font, click Edit → Preferences, select Mail Preferences on the left side, and then remove the check alongside Use the Same Fonts as Other Applications. In the Fixed Width Font drop-down list, select Sans from the list beneath the Family heading and 10 pt from the size list.

- Always create HTML email: The fact is that, although the world once sent plain text messages, nowadays we prefer color. That means HTML email. To make HTML format the default for new mail, click Edit → Preferences, click Composer Preferences on the left side of the dialog box, and put a check alongside Format Messages in HTML. It's worth bearing in mind that some Ubuntu mailing lists, such as those hosted at http://www.ubuntuforums.org, will reject HTML email postings—plain text must be used.

- Vertical message preview window: Most versions of Outlook default to a three-pane vertical view for the program window, with the mailboxes at the far left, the list of messages in the middle, and the contents of each mail on the right. To switch to this view in Ubuntu, click View → Preview → Vertical View. For an example, see Figure 3.11, on the facing page.

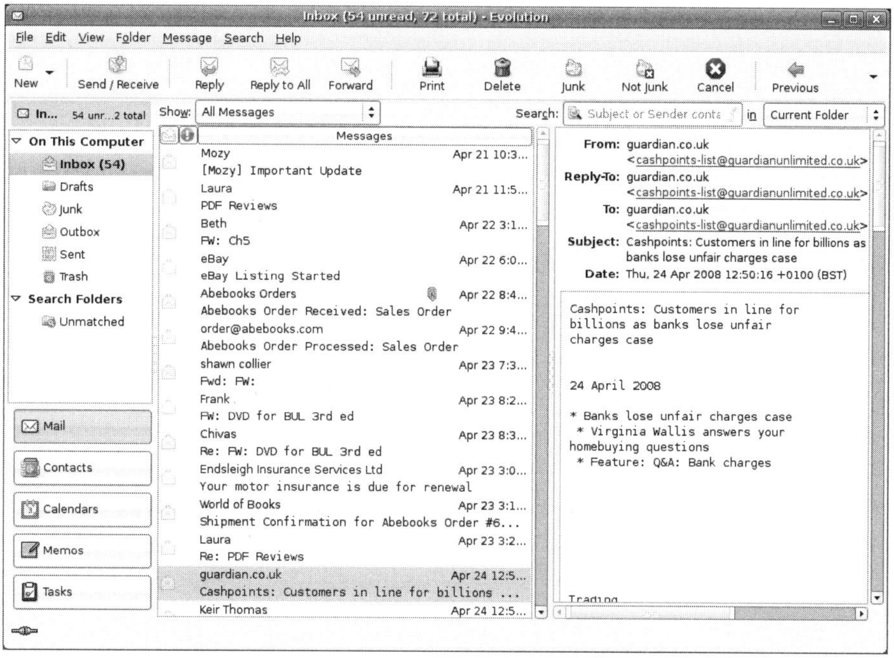

Figure 3.11: MAKING EVOLUTION MORE LIKE OUTLOOK WITH A THREE-COLUMN PROGRAM VIEW (SEE TIP 42)

For more Evolution tips and tricks, see Tip 7, on page 54; Tip 156, on page 189; Tip 158, on page 190; Tip 172, on page 200; Tip 246, on page 277; and Tip 260, on page 291.

43 Give Ubuntu a Static IP Address

Network configuration in Ubuntu is handled by the NetworkManager tool, and it does a superb job. However, it's primarily geared toward wireless networking and always assumes a DHCP server is in use.[8] You

---

8. A DHCP server automatically assigns network addresses to other computers. Every broadband modem and the majority of workplaces or other institutions use DHCP servers because they simply make joining a network as fuss-free as possible. In the case of Ethernet (cabled) connections, you can just plug in and go. In the case of wifi, once the base station password has been entered, you're ready to go.

might choose to use a static IP address, which is to say one that you set yourself. A handful of workplaces insist their workstation computers use static IP addresses.

If this is the case, then you might consider using Ubuntu's older but still very functional Network Settings configuration tool. It comes with some caveats, however. It's compatible with wireless networking but doesn't have the ability to *roam* (detect other networks automatically), so if you move into an area with a different wireless network, you'll need to manually reconfigure. Because of this, Network Settings is better suited for situations where you'll only ever connect to one wireless network. Network Settings also deactivates the NetworkManager icon that shows the strength of your wifi connection. If you want to configure a static IP address for a wifi card, consider using Wicd instead, which features its own notification icon that shows signal strength and allows the configuring of a manual IP address—see Tip 41, on page 88

Using Network Settings is easy. To do so, follow these steps:

1. Click the NetworkManager icon, and select Manual Configuration, or select Network from the System → Administration menu. Click the Unlock button, and enter your password when prompted.
2. Double-click the entry that reads either Wireless Connection or Wired Connection, depending on whether you want to configure a wifi or Ethernet connection.
3. In the dialog box that appears, uncheck Enable Roaming Mode. If you're configuring a wifi card, enter your base station details and password into the Network Name and Network password boxes. Select the type of wifi protection in use from the Password type drop-down list. If you click the drop-down arrow in the Network Name text box, you might see that the base station has automatically been detected, although I found this wasn't always reliable.
4. In the Configuration drop-down list, select Static IP address. Then fill in the IP address, Subnet mask, and Gateway address boxes. Click OK when done.
5. Still in the Network Settings dialog box, click the DNS tab, and then click the Add button. Then type the first of the DNS addresses. Once done, hit [Enter], and repeat the step for the second (or perhaps even third) addresses. After this, close Network Settings, and then reboot your computer for the changes to take effect.

Should at any time you want to return to using roaming mode/Net-workManager, just repeat the previous steps, but put a check in the Enable Roaming Mode box. Then configure your network by clicking the NetworkManager icon as usual.

For more network configuration tricks, see Tip 41, on page 88; Tip 60, on page 111; Tip 70, on page 117; and Tip 119, on page 157.

44	Format a USB Memory Stick (or Camera Memory Card)

□

Sometimes if a USB memory stick or memory card stops working cor-rectly, the best plan is to reformat it. To do this under Ubuntu, fol-low the next steps, first backing up any data on the stick, if possible, because the steps will completely wipe the USB stick. Note that the instructions are extremely thorough—first the partition on the memory stick is deleted; then a new one is created and subsequently format-ted. This should return virtually any USB stick to life, provided it isn't suffering from a hardware failure:

1. With the memory stick/card inserted so its icon appears on the desktop, look for what it's called (its *label*) and make a note.

2. Now you must find how Ubuntu refers to it on a technical level so you can use the information later when formatting. Open a terminal window, and type mount. Look through the list of results for the label you noted, and then make a note of the beginning of the line, which will begin /dev. For example, on my test system, the beginning of the line reads as follows:
   ```
   /dev/sdb1 on /media/KINGSTON type vfat (rw.nosuid,nodev ...
   ```
   So, I made a note of /dev/sdb1. For an example from my test PC with the relevant line highlighted, see Figure 3.12, on the following page. What you discover may be different from my test PC because this identifier depends on how many hard disks and other remov-able storage devices that you have attached to your computer.

3. Right-click the desktop icon for the memory stick, and select Un-mount Volume.

4. Back in the terminal window, type the following:
   ```
   $ sudo cfdisk /dev/sdb
   ```

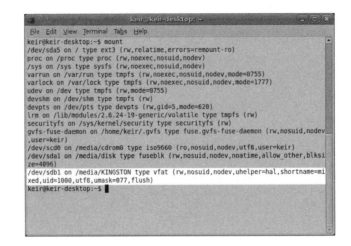

Figure 3.12: FINDING OUT HOW A USB STICK IS REFERRED TO ON A TECHNICAL LEVEL (SEE TIP 44)

You should replace /dev/sdb with what you discovered earlier—note that you will need to drop the number from the end. You should now see a listing showing the partition on the USB stick, as shown in Figure 3.13, on the next page. If you see an error message instead, hit any key to quit cfdisk, and try the following:

```
$ sudo cfdisk -z /dev/sdb
```

5. If you didn't see an error message, hit d to delete the partition. Then, regardless of whether you saw an error message or not, hit n to create a new partition, and hit Enter twice to accept the default suggestions of partition type and size. Then hit t, hit Enter, and type 0C (that's zero, then C) to set the new partition type. Finally, hit W (that's Shift plus w), type yes, and once the partition table has finished being written to disk, type q to quit cfdisk (do not worry about the error messaging saying that no primary partitions are marked bootable—this is irrelevant in this case).

6. If, at this stage, the USB stick's icon suddenly reappears on the desktop, right-click it, and once again select Unmount volume (close the file-browsing window first, if one has appeared). Then type the following into the terminal window to format the new partition:

```
$ sudo mkfs.vfat -F 32 -n USBSTICK -I /dev/sdb1
```

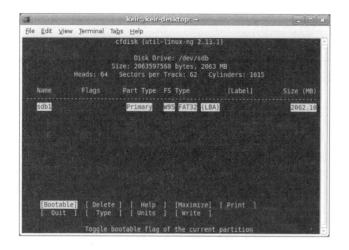

Figure 3.13: REPARTITIONING THE USB MEMORY STICK USING CFDISK (SEE TIP 44)

You should replace USBSTICK with the label you want to apply to the device and /dev/sdb1 with the hardware identification you discovered earlier. Once the format has completed, the USB memory stick should automatically mount on the desktop. If not, remove it, and then reinsert it.

To learn how to do cool things with USB memory sticks, see Tip 31, on page 77; Tip 113, on page 151; Tip 145, on page 178; Tip 229, on page 261; Tip 305, on page 345; and Tip 309, on page 352.

45 Protect Ubuntu So It Can't Be Booted Without a Password

You can lock the boot menu so that selected boot options won't work unless the menu is unlocked by hitting $\boxed{p}$ and typing a password. Additionally, unless the menu is unlocked, it won't be possible to edit the boot menu entries, so an intruder can't edit a boot menu entry to get around the protection.

To be honest, a password-protected boot menu doesn't offer any serious security because it's easily overcome by booting from the Ubuntu installation CD, which will provide unrestricted access to the hard disk contents.[9] However, the technique might be useful to protect your data from nosy family members or work colleagues who are casually nosy but not technically adept.

Start by opening a terminal window and typing the following:

```
$ grub-md5-crypt
```

You'll then be prompted for a password. This will be the boot menu password, so type it carefully. Then type it again when prompted to confirm it. As with any password, it can include letters, numbers, symbols, or spaces.

Once the password has been entered, a *password hash* is outputted at the prompt—a stream of seemingly random letters, numbers, and/or symbols. This is the password in encrypted form. It's encrypted so that it can be added to the boot menu configuration file in a way that people won't be able to decode it by looking at the file.

To add it, open the boot menu file using Gedit:

```
$ gksu gedit /boot/grub/menu.lst
```

...and, at the top, add a new line that reads password --md5; then, immediately following, copy and paste in the password hash you created. Here's how the line looked on my test machine:

```
password --md5 $1$Qeb3b$X0.1bPvj47A3GEywBcR6m
```

After this, look for the line in the boot menu file that refers to your Ubuntu installation. It'll probably be something like the following and will be immediately after a line that reads ## ## End Default Options ## (note that I've truncated the third line of the entry for reproduction here):

```
title      Ubuntu 8.04.1, kernel 2.6.24-19-generic
root       (hd0,4)
kernel     /boot/vmlinuz-2.6.24-19-generic root=UUID= ...
initrd     /boot/initrd.img-2.6.24-19-generic
quiet
```

---

9. Better protection for a PC with a password-protected boot menu, as described in Tip 45, on the preceding page, can be had by simply removing the floppy and CD/DVD drive hardware from the PC, thus limiting the opportunities to use a boot media that will give root access. You should also disable booting from removable storage in the PC's BIOS and add a BIOS password. Even after all this, I can still think of a few ways of getting around the protection, but it's perhaps as good as it can get, short of locking away the PC or mounting 24-hour surveillance on it.

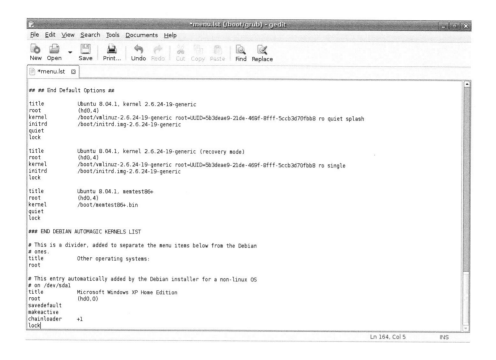

Figure 3.14: Adding password-protection to the boot menu file
(see Tip 45)

Add a new line at the end of the entry, and type the word lock.

Here's how the entry looked after I'd finished editing it (again, with the
third line truncated):

```
title          Ubuntu 8.04.1, kernel 2.6.24-19-generic
root           (hd0,4)
kernel         /boot/vmlinuz-2.6.24-19-generic root=UUID= ...
initrd         /boot/initrd.img-2.6.24-19-generic
quiet
lock
```

Add lock to all the other boot menu entries too, assuming you want to
stop somebody booting them without typing the password—if you want
to stop Ubuntu only being booted, then no further work is needed. If
lock isn't added to an entry in the boot menu file, then any user will be
able to select that entry and boot into it.

For an example of how the boot menu file looked on my computer once
I'd added lock to each entry, see Figure 3.14.

Once done, save the file, and quit Gedit. After this, test your password protection by rebooting. Once the computer restarts, you'll see that the boot menu appears as usual, and you'll be able to move the selection highlight up and down using the cursor keys. But you won't be able to select any to boot into—if you try, you'll see the error message Error 32: Must be authenticated. You'll then be prompted to hit a key and return to the boot menu. Hitting e to try to edit an entry won't work either.

To authenticate, hit p when the boot menu appears. Then type the password you chose earlier (the actual password, not the encrypted hash!). After this, you'll be able to select any entry on the boot menu and subsequently boot the computer.

To remove the password protection, simply repeat the previous steps, removing the lock entries from each entry in the menu.lst file. You should also remove the earlier password... line.

To do another interesting thing to the boot menu, see Tip 139, on page 171.

| 46 | Dump the Text on a Virtual Console to a File |

If you're trying to fix a problem, you might want to capture the output of a command for reproduction on a website forum, along with the command you typed to get the results. If you're working in a terminal window, you can cut and paste, but what if you're working at a virtual console? If you simply want to capture the result of a command, just redirect the output:

```
$ ls > output.txt 2>&1
```

This will send both the output and error output (if any) of the ls command to output.txt. If you want to capture the command you typed and any other command-line detritus (including output), use the screendump command. The following will send everything currently on the current screen (command-line prompts included) to a text file called output.txt:

```
$ sudo screendump > output.txt
```

The command has to be issued as root because of permission issues, but the resulting file will be owned by you.

For further virtual console tricks and tips, see Tip 18, on page 65; Tip 179, on page 210; Tip 193, on page 222; Tip 198, on page 226; Tip 207, on page 232; and Tip 233, on page 267.

47 Eliminate the Time Period During Which sudo/gksu Powers Hang Around

By default, sudo/gksu will "remember" your password for a short while after you use them so that if you use sudo/gksu again, you won't be prompted. This can make using sudo/gksu less annoying but can also create security concerns—if you temporarily leave your computer unattended, for example, anybody who uses it will have sudo powers for that short period.

If you type sudo -K after each use of sudo, the password will be required again the next time sudo/gksu is used. To do away with the grace period forever, you need to edit the /etc/sudoers file, and to do that, you need to issue the following command at the terminal: sudo visudo. This opens the vim text editor, which is rather less than intuitive, but it's not hard to use. Use the cursor keys to move down to the end of the line that reads Defaults env_reset, and hit [a]. Then type timestamp_timeout=0 so that the complete line now reads as follows:

```
Defaults    env_reset,timestamp_timeout=0
```

Then hit [Esc], type :wq, and hit [Enter]. This will save the file and quit vim.

The change will take effect immediately. If, for any reason, you want to make sudo/gksu *never* forget your password so that you won't be prompted after you initially use sudo/gksu (until you log out of that particular command-line session), change the line to read this:

```
Defaults    env_reset,timestamp_timeout=-1
```

This is obviously very insecure, however. Note that if you make a mistake while editing the /etc/sudoers file, hit [Esc], type :q!, and hit [Enter].

This will quit the text editor without making any changes. Then try again.

To reverse the changes so sudo and gksu act like they should, simply repeat the previous steps, and remove timestamp_timeout=0 or timestamp_timeout=-1.

For more sudo and password-related tweaks, see Tip 271, on page 301; Tip 200, on page 228; and Tip 78, on page 126.

☐ ## 48 Access Ubuntu Files from Windows

If you dual-boot, Ubuntu is kind enough to provide access to your Windows partition (Places → xGB Media, where x is the size of your Windows partition). However, Windows isn't nice enough to return the favor, and you can't access Ubuntu files from within Windows—well, not without an ext2/3 file system driver for Windows.

A couple of such drivers are available, and perhaps the best is the Ext2 Installable File System for Windows. This is freeware (not open source, alas) and lets you both read and write files within your Ubuntu partition while Windows is up and running. It comes in the form of a standard Windows executable and can be downloaded from http://www.fs-driver.org/download.html. During installation, you'll be prompted to assign a drive letter to Ubuntu's ext3 partition (any will do so long as it's not in use—I like to use Z:; you can see an example in Figure 3.15, on the facing page), after which you can simply access the Ubuntu files using My Computer.

If you must have open source software, consider Explore2fs (http://www.chrysocome.net/explore2fs), although it doesn't integrate with Windows' system tools and simply shows the Ubuntu files in its own program window. It also doesn't install automatically and instead is simply an executable plus .dll files that must be copied to a folder of your choice and run from there. [10]

---

10. When using Explore2fs (as described in Tip 48), if you run into problems using the program under Vista, right-click the program's .exe file, and select Run as Administrator each time you want to use it.

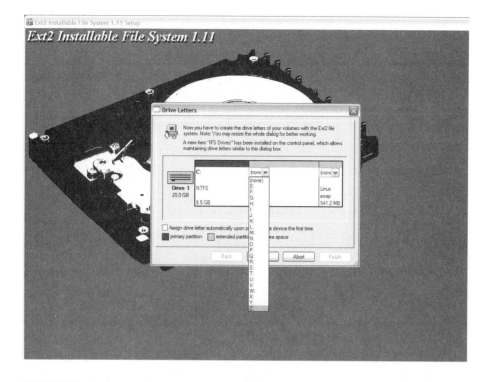

Figure 3.15: INSTALLING EXT2 INSTALLABLE FILE SYSTEM FOR WINDOWS (SEE TIP 48)

Note that writing files to the Ubuntu file system from within Windows gave me slight palpitations. I would do it only if I had no other choice. Otherwise, I'd treat it as a read-only volume.

To learn how to fix the Windows file system from within Ubuntu, see Tip 38, on page 87.

49 Kill a Crashed GUI

This is an oldie but worth mentioning in case you don't know. To kill the GUI, for whatever reason, such as a crash, hit `Ctrl`+`Alt`+`Backspace`. There's no warning dialog boxes when you do this—any open applications will be terminated and data lost. You'll be returned to the GNOME login screen, where you can log in afresh.

If you're working on a virtual console and want to kill the GUI for any reason, typing the following will kill GNOME Display Manager (gdm), which "owns" the desktop processes:

```
$ sudo killall gdm
```

To get the GUI back after this, start gdm again:

```
$ sudo gdm
```

To go on a virtual killing spree within Ubuntu, see Tip 133, on page 166.

50 Make Ubuntu Safe for Children to Use

Ubuntu can be as kid-safe as any other operating system with a little work. Essentially, two things can be done. First, you can create a new restricted user account for the child (or children) that stops them from doing anything that might break the system or from attempting to bypass any protective measures you enact. Second, you can install a web-filtering system so that nothing that isn't entirely child-safe gets through when they're using Firefox.[11]

Creating a Restricted User Account

The first thing you should do is create a restricted user account for the child. This will give them their own login on the machine so they won't have to share your administrator account. To create the account, click System → Administration → Users & Groups. Once the program starts, click the Unlock button. Then click the Add User button. Fill in the Username, Real name, and password fields. In the Profile drop-down list, select Unprivileged. This stops the new user from administrating the system, thereby potentially getting around your lockdown measures by, say, installing or removing software. When done, click OK.

---

11. Note that no type of filtering software is perfect. There's an old saying: "Where there's a will, there's a way." The instructions in Tip 50 are primarily for younger children who have no interest in bypassing web filters. The only way to be 100% sure of stopping children of any age from seeing objectionable material is to prevent them from using the computer in the first place.

Installing Web-Filtering Software

Dansguardian is filtering software that filters by content. This means that anything requested by your web browser that includes objectionable words is blocked. This includes both outgoing and incoming requests, so if the child sends a request to Google that includes objectionable words, no results will be returned.

To install Dansguardian, follow these steps:

1. Use Synaptic to search for the dansguardian package. Whilst there, also install tinyproxy, which is a system component Dansguardian needs.

2. Once the two are installed, you'll need to tweak a couple of configuration files. Open the tinyproxy configuration file in Gedit, as follows:

   ```
   $ gksu gedit /etc/tinyproxy/tinyproxy.conf
   ```

   ...then look for the lines that read as follows:

   ```
   # Port to listen on.
   #
   Port 8888
   ```

   Change Port 8888 so that it reads Port 3128. When done, save and close the file.

3. Back at the terminal, type the following to open the Dansguardian configuration file in Gedit:

   ```
   $ gksu gedit /etc/dansguardian/dansguardian.conf
   ```

   Look for the third line down that reads UNCONFIGURED - Please remove this line after configuration, and type a hash symbol (#) at the beginning so it reads #UNCONFIGURED - Please remove this line after configuration. Then save the file.

4. After this, type the following to start Dansguardian (and also tinyproxy, a system service it relies upon):

   ```
   $ sudo /etc/init.d/tinyproxy restart
   $ sudo /etc/init.d/dansguardian restart
   ```

   You might see a warning message when Dansguardian restarts about an out-of-date virus database. You can ignore this. The anti-virus component of Dansguardian updates itself automatically.

5. The user account now needs to be set up to let Dansguardian filter the incoming pages. To do this, you'll need to change the

web proxy settings so that any application that attempts to access the Web (such as Firefox or any other browser you might install) will be routed through the Dansguardian software. To do this, log into the new account you made for the child, and click System → Preferences → Network Proxy.

6. Select the Manual proxy configuration radio button, and check Use the same proxy for all protocols. Then, in the HTTP proxy text field, type localhost. Leave the Port field as it is, and click the Close button.

The changes take effect straightaway, so, still in the child's user account, try using Firefox to browse to a website containing objectionable material (for example, http://www.playboy.com; for an example of what you should see, refer to Figure 3.16, on the next page). You should see a page informing you that it has been blocked. I strongly advise you to thoroughly test Dansguardian's filtering before allowing your children unrestricted access to the computer.

I'd also advise you visit http://dansguardian.org to learn more about how it works. There are two key things worth knowing. First, if you find that Dansguardian blocks a site that you know to be fine, you can add it to the "exception" list (/etc/dansguardian/exceptionsitelist). Open the file in Gedit (gksu gedit /etc/dansguardian/exceptionsitelist), and add the address to the bottom, without the http:// or www components. For example, to add http://www.ubuntukungfu.org, you would add ubuntukungfu.org to the bottom of the file on a new line. Once done, save the file, close Gedit, and then restart the Dansguardian background service:

```
$ sudo /etc/init.d/dansguardian restart
```

On the other hand, if there's a site that Dansguardian "lets through" that perhaps it shouldn't, then you can add it in the same way to the file /etc/dansguardian/bannedurllist. You might choose to add various search engines to this list if you want to stop children from being able to seek out objectionable material. For example, to stop Google from being used, you could add google.com to the list. Bear in mind that you'll also need to add the Google domain for the country you live in if you live outside the United States (for example, you would need to add google.co.uk if you lived in the United Kingdom). Once you've added the site to the list, don't forget to restart Dansguardian, as mentioned earlier.

To remove Dansguardian, first repeat the previous step that describes how to configure a network proxy, and click the radio button along-

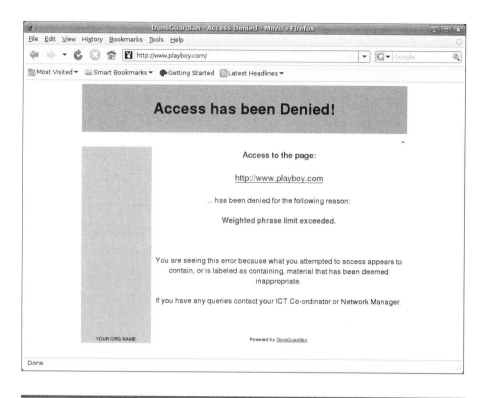

Figure 3.16: DANSGUARDIAN BLOCKING AN OBJECTIONABLE WEBSITE (SEE TIP 50)

side Direct Internet Connection. Then use Synaptic to uninstall the dansguardian and tinyproxy packages.

When child-proofing Ubuntu, you might also be interested in Tip 294, on page 331, which describes how to use the Ubuntu Tweak program to "lock down" Ubuntu to disable certain features of the desktop.

51 Run Two (or More) Desktops at the Same Time

Ubuntu offers the handy User Switcher applet at the top right of the desktop to switch between the desktop of two or more users. This is cleverer than it might first seem. When it's used to switch to a second user, a new X server is started for them in addition to the existing one. You're supposed to use the applet to switch between the two users, but you can switch between X servers by holding down $\boxed{\text{Ctrl}}$+$\boxed{\text{Alt}}$ and hitting $\boxed{\text{F7}}$ and $\boxed{\text{F9}}$.

Should you need to, you can manually start your own additional X servers for users. Assuming you've created a new account, switch to a virtual console (this won't work from a terminal window!), and then log in as the new user. Then type the following:

```
$ startx -- :1
```

A desktop GUI will then start for the new user. To switch back to the already-logged-in user's desktop, hit $\boxed{\text{Ctrl}}$+$\boxed{\text{Alt}}$+$\boxed{\text{F7}}$. To switch to the new user's desktop, hit $\boxed{\text{Ctrl}}$+$\boxed{\text{Alt}}$+$\boxed{\text{F9}}$.

The previous step can be repeated to create yet more concurrent desktops for other users: for example, to concurrently run a desktop for a third user, just switch to the next virtual console, log in as that user, and type startx -- :2. That user's desktop will then appear, and you can switch to other desktops as described earlier and back to the third user's desktop by hitting $\boxed{\text{Ctrl}}$+$\boxed{\text{Alt}}$+$\boxed{\text{F10}}$.

Once you've finished your work on the second desktop, just log out of the second desktop in the usual way, and then type exit to quit the virtual console that started the additional X session.

52 Go Completely Full-Screen in Virtually Any Application

Some apps have a "full-screen" mode causing the title bar, GNOME menus, and GNOME panel to temporarily disappear. This can be useful for maximizing screen real estate or just working without background distractions. If the option is available, it will show up on the View menu.

However, even if an app is capable of full-screen mode, it isn't always shown as an option, and defining a global keyboard shortcut key will force even reluctant apps to go full-screen. To do so, open Keyboard Shortcuts (System → Preferences), and look in the list for the entry that reads Toggle Fullscreen Mode. Then click in the Shortcut column of the entry, and type your preferred keyboard combination (I recommend

Ctrl+Alt+f). Then close the Keyboard Shortcut program window, and test the new shortcut in your favorite application. It works with nearly every application. The only ones I found that didn't work were those that rely on dialog box interfaces, such as Ekiga.

53 Make Calculator Round Up (or Down) to Two Digits

If you use Ubuntu's Calculator application to work out nothing but trivial financial transactions in dollars and cents (or euros/cents, pounds/pennies, and so on), then you can force it to always round its results to two decimal places, depending on which side of half a cent/penny the result is. Start gconf-editor, and navigate to /apps/gcalctool. Then double-click the accuracy entry on the right, and change it to 2. Note that, after this, Calculator will still let you enter numbers with more than two decimal places, but it will always round up the answer to just two decimal places.

54 Follow the Moon's Phases

If you're into astronomy or have a romantic streak, you might be interested in Lunar Clock, which adds a moon phase indicator to the panel. To install it, use Synaptic to search for and install glunarclock. Once it's installed, right-click a blank spot on the panel where you want the applet to appear, select Add to panel, and then select Lunar Clock from the list.

Before using it, you must tell it where you are on the earth so it's accurate. To do this, right-click its icon, click Preferences, and then the Location tab. You'll need your latitude and longitude figures—these can be obtained by typing the name of your town/city into http://www.geonames.org.

55 Import Internet Explorer Settings into Firefox

During setup, Ubuntu offers to let you import your Internet Explorer favorites, but what about after this? Boot into Windows, and within Internet Explorer, click File → Import and Export (if using IE 7 or later, you might first need to click a blank spot near the tab bar and put a check alongside Menu Bar).

The Import/Export Wizard will start, and it should be obvious which options to choose. You should end up with a file called bookmark.htm. Now boot into Ubuntu, start Firefox, browse into your Windows partition, and click and drag the file on top of the open Firefox window. This will open the file in Firefox, and your favorites will be listed at the bottom. Right-click each link you want to import into your Firefox bookmarks, and select Bookmark this Link.

56 Drag and Drop Files onto the Terminal Window

If you are using a terminal command on a file and cannot bear to type the entire path to the file, just drag and drop it onto the terminal window using the mouse. The filename and path will then be auto-completed for you.

For more cool terminal tricks and tips, see Tip 25, on page 71; Tip 236, on page 269; and Tip 247, on page 278.

57 Use Older Digital Cameras with Ubuntu

Do you have a vintage camera that won't work under Ubuntu because it's not a removable storage device (which is to say, its contents don't

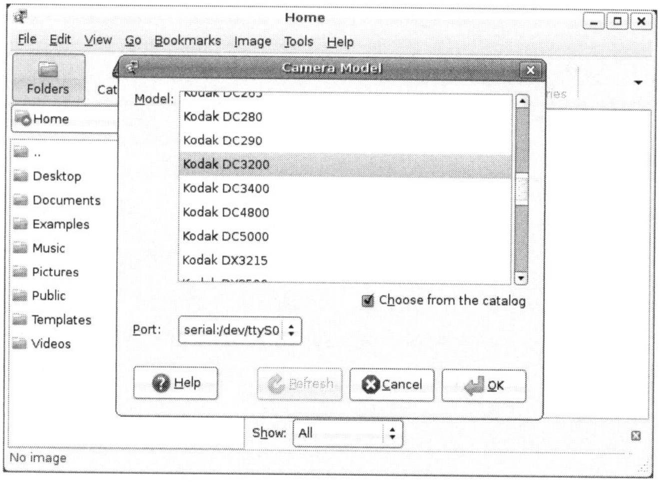

Figure 3.17: CONFIGURING GTHUMB (SEE TIP 57)

appear in a file-browsing window when you attach the camera)? If the camera connects via a serial, USB, or parallel port, it's very likely you'll be able to use the gThumb software to access it. This can be found and installed via Synaptic (search for the gthumb package) and, once installed, will appear on the Applications → Graphics menu.

To set up your camera, attach it to your computer, and switch it to data transfer mode (if applicable). Then click File → Import Photos in gThumb. Then click the icon above the words No Camera Detected. All being well, your camera should be automatically detected, and you can click OK. If not, you can click Choose from the Catalog and select the model from the list, as shown in Figure 3.17. The Port drop-down list should then be filled in automatically, but you should inspect it to make sure. Clicking OK will then cause gThumb to probe the camera and import thumbnails, which you can then download. To make gThumb start automatically when you connect a USB camera, click System → Preferences → Removable Drives and Media. Then, in the Command text box under the Digital Camera heading, replace f-spot-import with gthumb --import-photos.

Note that this will cause gThumb to start whenever you insert any kind of digital photograph storage device, such as a memory card reader.

58 Use the Ultra-quick xterm to Bash Out Commands

GNOME's terminal program is very powerful but can take a few seconds to appear, and I tend to be impatient. So, often I use xterm instead, which is the ultra-simple terminal program supplied on all Linux computers that have the X graphical system installed. Hit `Alt`+`F2`, and then simply type xterm. Alternatively, you can create a desktop launcher—right-click the desktop, select Create Launcher, and type xterm into both the Name and Command fields. Leave the Comment field blank. Click the icon button if you want to assign a more descriptive icon. If you want a scrollbar to appear in the xterm window (far too fancy for my tastes!), change the command in the launcher to read xterm -sb -rightbar.

59 Install All the Program Compilation Tools You'll Need

Sometimes there's no other option than to compile software from source code. Typically this is the case if you want the very latest version of a software package that has yet to make it into Ubuntu's repositories or if you want to support an esoteric piece of hardware with a kernel module.[12]

Usually you'll need to install the compilation toolchain piece by piece, but a quick shortcut is to install build-essential using Synaptic. This installs make, gcc, and a handful of other packages essential for the familiar configure, make, make install sequence.

---

12. If you are building software against the kernel, there should be no need to download the kernel source. The kernel headers are installed by default under Ubuntu (the package concerned is linux-headers-x, where x is the hardware architecture). If you do need to download the kernel source code for whatever reason, install the linux-source package.

```
                    *hosts (/etc) - gedit
File  Edit  View  Search  Tools  Documents  Help

 New   Open    Save   Print...    Undo  Redo    Cut  Copy  Paste    Find  Replace

  *hosts

127.0.0.1          localhost
127.0.1.1          keir-desktop

# The following lines are desirable for IPv6 capable hosts
#::1       ip6-localhost ip6-loopback
#fe00::0 ip6-localnet
#ff00::0 ip6-mcastprefix
#ff02::1 ip6-allnodes
#ff02::2 ip6-allrouters
#ff02::3 ip6-allhosts




                                           Ln 9, Col 24              INS
```

Figure 3.18: EDITING THE /ETC/HOSTS FILE TO DISABLE IPv6 (SEE TIP 60)

60 Avoid Network Slowdowns and Incompatibilities

Do you know what IPv6 is? If you don't, then it's unlikely you need it, even though it's activated by default under Ubuntu. IPv6 is the new network addressing scheme that's designed to replace IPv4, which is used across the Internet right now. One day we'll probably all use it, but at the moment you'll struggle to find it used outside academic institutions and some corporate environments. The trouble is that having IPv6 enabled can cause program incompatibilities and even network slowdowns, especially with certain types of router and/or ISPs. To disable it, follow these steps:

1. Open a terminal window, and then type gksu gedit /etc/modprobe.d/ aliases. In the Gedit window, look for the line that reads alias net-pf-10 ipv6, and change ipv6 to off so it reads alias net-pf-10 off. Then save the file.

2. Open the /etc/hosts file in Gedit (gksu gedit /etc/hosts), and after the line that reads # The following lines are desirable for IPv6 capable hosts,

put a hash at the beginning of each line following that contains ip6 (so the first line reads #::1 ip6-localhost ip6-loopback;, the second reads #fe00::0 ip6-localnet, and so on). For how the file looked after editing on my test PC, see Figure 3.18, on the previous page. Once done, save the file, and quit Gedit.

3. Start Firefox, and in the address bar, type about:config. You can ignore the warning that appears about changing settings. In the Filter text field, type ipv6. Then double-click network.dns.disableIPv6 so that it now appears in bold (and you might notice that, at the end of the line, false changes to true). Then close Firefox, and reboot your computer.

☐ ## 61 | Print at the Command Line

You can quickly send text or configuration files to the printer using the lp command. For example, to print the /etc/fstab configuration file, you would type lp /etc/fstab. The formatting of the printed page is rough (no margins, and Courier font used), but it's OK for quick hard-copy viewing. If you want, you can set a top page margins using the -o page-top= command option. The following will print the same file with a 1-inch (72 point) margin at the top:

```
$ lp -o page-top=72 /etc/fstab
```

Note that for the lp command to work, you'll need to first make your printer the system default (even if it's the only one attached). To do so, click System → Preferences → Default Printer. Select your printer, and then click Set Default. Then click Close.

☐ ## 62 | Find the Ubuntu Version and Code Name

If you're sitting in front of somebody else's Ubuntu computer and want to quickly identify which version of Ubuntu it's running (not always easy to do from the look and feel if it's heavily customized), do the following: open a terminal window, and type cat /etc/lsb-release. You can also click Help → About Ubuntu, although bear in mind this won't show the "point release" (for example, on my 8.04.1 installation, Help → About Ubuntu mentioned only the 8.04 release).

This trick can also be used to ensure that you've upgraded to a newer version when one is released.

See Tip 129, on page 163, to learn how to find out the GNOME desktop version number.

 ## 63 Get Your Webcam Working in Ubuntu

Open a terminal window, and type gstreamer-properties. Click the Video tab, and click the Test button under the Default Input heading. A video window should appear showing what the webcam sees. If you receive an error, try selecting the Video for Linux (v4l) option from the Plugin drop-down list. If you still receive an error, the webcam is probably incompatible with Ubuntu. Note that once the selection is made in the Plugin drop-down list so that the webcam works, all applications that use webcams (such as Ekiga or Cheese, as described in Tip 15, on page 62) will be able to utilize it.

64 Downgrade to Firefox 2

Ubuntu 8.04 (Hardy Heron) uses Firefox 3, which brings in a handful of new and pioneering features. To be frank, some of these irritated me a little bit (the URL history completion and slow startup times in particular), so I downgraded to the older and more established Firefox 2. To do this, I searched for firefox-2 in Synaptic. Once installed, I could run it by typing firefox-2 at the command line or by creating a desktop launcher.

To switch the entire system over to Firefox 2 so that all new links are opened in it (links clicked in Evolution emails and so on), click System → Preferences → Preferred Applications. Click the Internet tab, and then, under the Web Browser heading, select Custom from the drop-down list. In the Command field, type firefox-2 %s. Close the dialog box, and then log out and back in again.

Note that Firefox 2 uses the older Plugin Finder service, which might not work well or offer the same degree of choice as the newer Plugin Finder 2 service included with Ubuntu 8.04 and used by Firefox 3. If you need to install a plug-in, it might be better to use Firefox 3 to install it—Firefox 2 will subsequently pick up on the plug-in and use it. To run Firefox 3, just type firefox at the prompt, first ensuring any currently open Firefox window is closed.

65 Install All the Multimedia Playback Codecs You'll Ever Need

Ubuntu will install the codecs you need for a multimedia file whenever you try to play it. The problem is that you have to be online for this to work. What if you've just installed Ubuntu and are about to hop on a plane, with the intention of watching movies during the journey? To install all the usual codecs before leaving the house, click Applications → Add/Remove, and then in the Show drop-down list select All Available Applications. Ensure All is selected in the list on the left, and then use the Search box to search for gstreamer. In the list of results, put a check alongside the following—once done, click the Apply Changes button:[13]

```
GStreamer extra plugins
GStreamer ffmpeg video plugin
Ubuntu restricted extras
GStreamer plugins for mms, wavpack, quicktime, musepack
GStreamer plugins for aac, xvid, mpeg2, faad
GStreamer fluendo MPEG2 demuxing plugin
```

Once the software is installed (it may take some time, and you might have to agree to one or two license agreements that will pop up), click the Close button in the dialog box that appears.

To enable DVD movie playback, you'll need to complete one extra step. Ensure Synpatic is closed (and no other software installation applica-

---

13. While following the instructions in Tip 65, pay attention to the dialog box warnings about the potential issues surrounding the installation of certain codec software; you'll find a broader discussion of the issues raised at https://help.ubuntu.com/community/RestrictedFormats.

tion is currently running, such as Update Manager), and then open a terminal window. Type the following:

```
$ sudo /usr/share/doc/libdvdread3/install-css.sh
```

Note that you will need to install the Xine version of the Totem movie player if you want fuss-free DVD movie playback. See Tip 66.

See also Tip 231, on page 263, which describes how to install alternative media players under Ubuntu.

66 Get Better DVD Movie Playback

If you followed Tip 65, on the preceding page, to enable DVD movie playback, you might have noticed that Totem doesn't provide access to individual chapters from the Go menu. In fact, in my tests, clicking entries on the Go menu while a DVD movie was playing did nothing.

To get around this, you can install the Xine version of Totem instead. This uses the Xine multimedia back end, which is used in the KDE desktop but is otherwise nearly completely identical. It fully supports DVD menus and chapter navigation using the Go menu.

Simply open Synaptic, and then search for and install totem-xine. Once it's installed, you'll need to tweak a setting so that totem-xine automatically starts when a DVD movie is inserted. Open a terminal window, and type the following:

```
$ sudo update-alternatives --config totem
```

Then type 2 to select the second option from the list presented. After this, *all* movies will play back in the Xine version of Totem. Unfortunately, with Ubuntu 8.04 at least, there appears to be no way of making just DVDs play back in the Xine version of Totem (changes to the system configuration using gconf-editor that should do the trick don't work). However, the Xine version of Totem is functionally identical to Xine, so there should be no difference in usability.

If you ever get confused about which version of Totem you're using (Ubuntu's own or Xine), click Help → About, and look at the line that begins Movie Player using.... The native Ubuntu version will read Movie Player using GStreamer, while the Xine version will read Movie Player using xine-lib....

See also Tip 231, on page 263, to learn what alternative media player applications are available, most of which can also play DVD movie disks.

67 | Run the Terminal with a Single Keypress

I don't know about you, but I spend about 50% of my time at the command prompt, so being able to open the terminal program quickly is a real help. To assign a keyboard shortcut, click System → Preferences → Keyboard Shortcuts, and look in the list for Run a Terminal, which will be under the Desktop heading. Click the word Disabled alongside it, and then hit Ctrl + Alt + t.

Any shortcut key combination can be used, aside from those involving the Windows keys (those to the left and right of the spacebar and usually with a Microsoft Windows logo on them, although these can be forced to work with a little system configuration—see Tip 195, on page 224). Even key combinations that are already in use by other programs can be used—any key combination set in the Keyboard Shortcuts program window will take precedence. For example, Ctrl + t could be used to cause the terminal program to start, although it will override the shortcut used by Firefox to create a new tab.

68 | See the APT Cow

The apt-get command has an interesting if bizarre Easter egg. Open a terminal window, and type apt-get moo to see it.

Not to be outdone, the aptitude software installation command has a similar Easter egg. Type aptitude -v moo to see it. Then try adding some more v characters to see what happens—aptitude -v moo, aptitude -vv moo, aptitude -vvv moo, and so on.

Programmer humor, eh? Can't beat it. Can't understand it.

If you like cows, see Tip 245, on page 277.

69   See What Firefox Plug-ins Are Installed

Start Firefox, and in the address line, type about:plugins. The headings show the type of content the plug-in is designed to pick up, and after that the Ubuntu plug-in that handles the content is listed.

To see what add-ons are installed, click Edit → Preferences, and in the dialog box that appears, click the Manage Add-ons button.

70   Kill the Network Connection Instantly

Think your computer is in the process of being hacked? Or have you just clicked Send on that nasty email to the boss and instantly regretted it? Whatever the case, simply right-click the NetworkManager icon (top right of the desktop in the notification area), and uncheck Enable Networking. Bang. Network gone. NetworkManager will even display a little exclamation mark to tell you. To get your network back, repeat, but check the entry in the menu. Next time count to ten before you click Send.

71   Post Blog Entries from your Ubuntu Desktop

I'm not a particular fan of blogs, believing that it is better to be an idiot in silence than to write a blog and prove it to the world. However, I realize I am in the minority, as do the GNOME developers (probably), who provide an excellent piece of software to create quick blog entries straight from your Ubuntu desktop.

Use Synaptic to search for and install gnome-blog. Once installed, right-click a blank spot on the panel, and select Add to panel. Then select Blog Entry Poster from the list.

The program is designed to work with blogs hosted at Blogger.com, Advogato, or LiveJournal. Alternatively, you can configure the software to work with MovableType, Pyblosxon, or WordPress installations on your own website.

When it runs for the first time, the program will ask you to set up your blog details. You'll need to set the blog type in the Blog Type drop-down list and then set your username and password (if you're attempting to access blog software you've manually installed on a website, you'll also need to provide the URL). Then click the Lookup Blogs button both to confirm the details are correct and to retrieve the list of blogs that you can use the applet to contribute to. Once the lookup has completed, select its entry from the Blog Name drop-down list. Note that you can contribute to only one blog using the applet.

To make a new posting, just click the applet's button on the panel. Type the title, as prompted, and then the body of the posting into the window. Then click the Post Entry button. Pictures can be dragged and dropped onto the posting window for inclusion too.

72 Intelligently Select Only the Files You Want

Imagine the following: you're working on a project and have been saving the files in your Documents folder, which is where all your files tend to end up, regardless of project. This particular project involves pictures (of varying file types), word processing documents, and spreadsheets.... You spend a few minutes considering how chaotic it all is, and then your boss asks you to send all the files to him. However, there are hundreds, and you can't sort by file extension or alphanumerically, because they're all different.

Assuming all the files contained the project name, you could use Nautilus's Select Pattern function, which is found on the Edit menu. For example, assuming the project is called Falken and this word appears somewhere within project files' filenames, you could type the following into the Select Pattern dialog box:

```
*falken*.*
```

This uses *wildcards*, in the form of asterisks, to indicate characters within the filename that could equate to anything. So, the files could start with any text, could end with anything, and could have any file extension, but if it contains the word falken somewhere within it, it will be selected, as if you'd just clicked it. Assuming several files match the pattern, they will all be selected, and you can then click and drag them to the email you're about to send to your boss. Note that the pattern selection tool is case sensitive.

For more Nautilus tips, see Tip 85, on page 132; Tip 104, on page 146; Tip 144, on page 178; Tip 261, on page 292; Tip 272, on page 302; Tip 295, on page 333; Tip 165, on page 194; and Tip 132, on page 165.

73 Temporarily Disable a User Account

If you've followed Tip 50, on page 102, which describes how to make Ubuntu suitable for children, you might also want to occasionally deactivate your child's account—as punishment for misdeeds, perhaps, or just to force them to do something other than browse the Internet all day!

The following command will effectively deactivate a user's password, making it so they can no longer log in. All settings and files belonging to the user will remain intact:

```
$ sudo passwd -l username
```

Replace username with the user's username.

To reenable the account after the errant youngster has paid a penance, type the following:

```
$ sudo passwd -u username
```

☐

| 74 | Take Complete Control of Desktop Effects and Animations |

As you probably know, Ubuntu includes several desktop effects and animations. For example, windows visually shrink to the panel when minimized.[14] You might also have realized that you can activate more of these effects by clicking System → Preferences → Appearance, selecting the Visual Effects tab, and clicking the Extra radio button. This will add "wobbly windows" to the visual mix, amongst other things.

To take more control over the desktop effects, consider installing one of two packages. The first is Simple Compiz Config Setting Manager, which can be installed via Synaptic by searching for the simple-ccsm package. Once installed, you'll find the software on the System → Preferences menu. At its simplest, the program lets you select between more profiles (collections of effects) compared to Ubuntu's default tool. To select a different profile, just select from the drop-down list at the top of the program window. Alternatively, you can personalize the setup by tweaking the Animations, Effects, Desktop, Accessibility, and Edges tabs. Animations lets you change the minimize/maximize effects. Effects lets you change the animation that appears when you Alt+Tab through applications. Desktop lets you control the animation that appears when you switch virtual desktops. Accessibility controls screen magnification, while Edges lets you define the hotspots at the sides of the screen; these are needed by some effects.

For ultimate control over desktop effects, use Synaptic to search for and install the compizconfig-settings-manager package (note that if you installed Simple Compiz Config Settings Manager, this will already be installed). Once installed, this can be found on the System → Preferences menu and is referred to as Advanced Desktop Effects Settings (although the program refers to CompizConfig Settings Manager, which is how it's referred to in the wider Ubuntu community). This lets you

---

14. If you don't see any visual effects, then it's possible your computer isn't capable of supporting the effects. Alternatively, you might not have the correct graphics drivers installed—click System → Administration → Hardware Drivers, and if necessary, put a check alongside the entry in the list representing your graphics card.

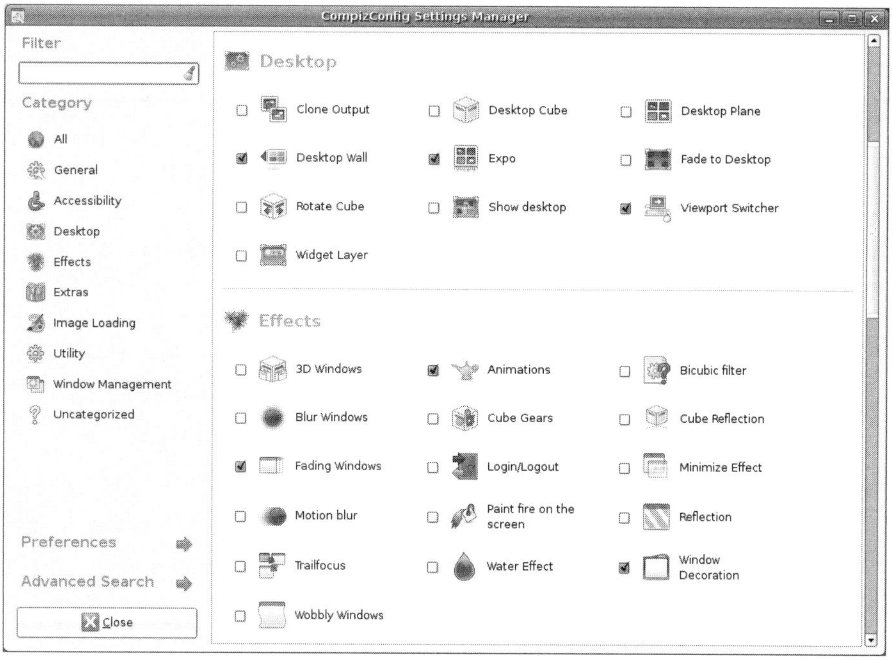

Figure 3.19: COMPIZCONFIG SETTINGS MANAGER (SEE TIP 74)

manually activate and deactivate all the plug-ins that provide the desktop effects functionality, as shown in Figure 3.19, as well as tweak their settings by double-clicking their entries in the list. Some effects require a key combination to activate them, and this can also be found (or changed) by double-clicking the entry of the effect within the list.

Ubuntu's desktop effects can be hard to understand at times, and a good place to start your desktop effects adventure is at the Ubuntuforums.org forum dedicated to the purpose:

http://ubuntuforums.org/forumdisplay.php?f=330.

For more tricks to add zing to your Ubuntu desktop, see Tip 21, on page 67; Tip 79, on page 127; Tip 147, on page 183; Tip 199, on page 227; Tip 220, on page 246; Tip 274, on page 304; and Tip 289, on page 328.

75 Do Some Desktop Publishing

It's possible to do just about anything on Ubuntu, and desktop publishing presents no challenges. Simply use Synaptic to search for and install the scribus package. Scribus is professional-level DTP software designed to compete with the likes of Adobe InDesign and QuarkXPress. As such, it features CMYK color, color separations, press-ready output, and much more. Indeed, several major publishing houses use it for compositing. Once installed, Scribus can be found on the Applications → Office menu.

Need to create sophisticated diagrams and used to the power of programs like Adobe Illustrator or CorelDraw? No problem. Just use Synaptic to search for and install the inkscape package. Inkscape is a professional-level vector drawing package that can be used for just about any task and is used to create much of the GNOME desktop artwork. It features node editing, complex path operations, the ability to trace bitmaps, and lots more. Files are outputted in the industry-standard SVG file format. Once installed, Inkscape can be found on the Applications → Graphics menu.

If you'd like to try creating your own TrueType fonts or modify existing ones, you might be interested in the Fontforge (use Synaptic to search for and install fontforge). Once it's installed, it can be found on the Applications → Graphics menu.

If you're interested in desktop publishing on Ubuntu, see also Tip 101, on page 144, to learn how to install 465 excellent fonts. A handful more fonts are available in Synaptic, and generally speaking their package names start with ttf-.

76 Control Volume Levels at the Command Prompt

Ever been working away at the command prompt and wanted to mute the sound (or ever been working away at the prompt and wanted to crank up the sound when your favorite track comes on)? Simply type alsamixer. Hey, presto—primitive but useful text-mode faders. Use the left and right cursor keys to move between faders. Use the up and down keys to change the values. Hit [Esc] to quit.

To play MP3s from the prompt, even if there's no GUI up and running, see Tip 292, on page 329.

| 77 | Search the Ubuntu File System |

A little known fact is that the average human spends a high proportion of time looking for things that have been lost. Ubuntu helps avoid this, at least in computing terms, by including a number of powerful file search functions for both command-line and GUI users.

Command-Line Searching

There are essentially two methods used to search for files at the command line: locate and find. The difference is that locate relies upon a database of files and locations, while find literally searches the file system each time you use it.

locate is partnered to a back-end program—updatedb—that is run periodically and automatically by the system to update the database of files. This highlights a weakness of the system—locate's results are only as good as the last time the database was updated. Therefore, it's often a good idea to manually update the database using the updatedb command (as root—sudo updatedb) before using locate. There are several different versions of the locate software, and the version provided with Ubuntu—called mlocate—is designed to update its database quickly by looking for and adding only new files. This means updatedb doesn't take long to run each time.

Using locate is easy. Just type locate and then the search word or search phrase. If the search phrase includes symbols or spaces, enclose it in quotation marks. For example, to search for any files or folders that include fstab in their names, you would type locate fstab. To search for the file accounts 2008.xls, you might type locate "accounts 2008". locate can use wildcards. To search for any MP3 files on the system, you could type locate *.mp3.

Using find is a little different. First you must specify the search location and then the search term. For example, to search for the file accounts 2008.xls in your /home directory, you could type find /home/username -name "accounts 2008". You should of course replace username with your

Figure 3.20: TRACKER (SEE TIP 77)

own details. To search the entire file system, specify the file system root instead: find / -name "accounts 2008".

Both locate and find use *regular expressions* (known as *regexes*) to specify search terms. It's beyond the scope of this book to go into this rather arcane field, but several very good beginner guides can be found by searching Google. Regexes permeate all of Linux, and spending some time learning how to use them can be very rewarding.

Searching at the Desktop

Ubuntu includes the Tracker tool for all desktop searching needs. Like recent developments in Mac OS X and Vista, this is designed to catalog all kinds of data, above and beyond just files. Recently visited websites are cataloged, for example, as are programs installed on the system. Tracker also indexes the *contents* of emails and also files (provided it understands the file format). Thus, a PDF file containing a certain phrase can be searched for, even if its filename is obscure and/or unrelated.

Thus, Tracker can actually be an alternative access point for day-to-day use of Ubuntu. Rather than using Nautilus to navigate to a file in the Documents directory, simply open a Tracker window and type its name (or part of its name). Then double-click to open it. Rather than clicking Applications → Office → OpenOffice.org Writer, just type writer, and then double-click the program that appears in the search results.

Tracker isn't enabled by default in Ubuntu 8.04 Hardy Heron because some believe it can slow the system down. It runs a background service that's always monitoring the file system and thereby using resources, and it also performs an indexing run each time you log in. That said, many report no problem using it, and there's little reason to give it a try. The same instructions that describe how to enable it can also be used to disable it.

Before activating it, it's a good idea to install the wv package using Synaptic. This allows Tracker to index the contents of Word documents (.doc files). Then, to activate the Tracker service, click System → Preferences → Search and Indexing, and click the checkboxes alongside Enable indexing and Enable watching. If you're using a notebook computer, you might also want to check the box alongside Disable all indexing when on battery.

Click the OK button. You'll be told the tracker daemon has to restart. This is fine. After this, a new magnifying glass icon will appear in the panel. Clicking this provides access to Tracker's search tool. However, you can't use it just yet! First you must let Tracker index your hard disk and files. This might take some time. You'll know when it's finished because the Tracker icon will change to an orange magnifying glass, rather than a clear one. In the future, the glass might change again, but this simply indicates that Tracker is "catching up"; you'll still be able to search.

To use Tracker, just click its panel icon, type the search term (or phrase, if you want to search for content within documents), and then click the Find button. The categories of search results will be listed on the left of the program window (actual files, folders, applications, documents, and so on), and the specific search results will be listed on the right. To open any file or folder, simply double-click it. For an example, see Figure 3.20, on the facing page.

Tracker can also be used from the command line, once Synaptic has been used to install the tracker-utils package. Once the package has been installed, just type tracker-search followed by your search term.

78 Remove the "Bad Password" Wait Period

Whenever you mistype a password, Ubuntu will pause for two seconds before letting you try again. This is for a good reason, because hackers often try "brute-force" techniques to guess the password. This involves using a computer program to try millions of passwords until the right one is found. The two-second delay when a bad password is supplied makes such an approach much more impractical.

However, if you—like me—sometimes seem to have one too many fingers and constantly mistype the password, you can reduce the delay to zero.[15] This will mean that, upon a bad password being entered, you'll immediately be prompted to try again.

Start by opening the /etc/pam.d/common-auth password in Gedit by typing the following into a terminal window:

```
$ gksu gedit /etc/pam.d/common-auth
```

Then look for the line that reads auth requisite pam_unix.so nullok_secure, and add nodelay to the end, so it now reads auth requisite pam_unix.so nullok_secure nodelay. Then save the file, and reboot the computer.

You should be able to test your change at the Ubuntu login prompt— deliberately try a bad password, and see what happens.

Note that this tip will reduce the bad password delay in *all* password entry situations, including requesting sudo/gksu powers, and so on.

To reverse this change, if you want, edit the file again, and remove the nodelay addition you made. Then save the file and reboot.

---

15. Perhaps it goes without saying that you should never use Tip 78 on a computer that's directly accessible on the Internet, such as a server or a workstation with a fixed nonprivate range IP address. Any computer connected to a server will see probings by hackers on a daily if not hourly basis, and a brute-force attack to guess a password is highly likely.

79 | Make Desktop Icons Really Big

Is your eyesight not what it was? Right-click any desktop icon, and click Stretch Icon. Then pull the handles at the corners of the icon. Most icons can go to a quarter of the screen size, but some look better than others. Those that look good are Scalable Vector Graphic (SVG) icons. The default Human icon set is SVG. To make icons small again, right-click them, and click Restore Icon's Original Size.

For more look-and-feel tweaks, see Tip 74, on page 120; Tip 21, on page 67; Tip 147, on page 183; Tip 199, on page 227; Tip 220, on page 246; Tip 274, on page 304; and Tip 289, on page 328.

80 | Run Ubuntu...Without the Linux Components!

It's unlikely you'll have some fundamental objection to the Linux kernel, but if you fancy scrapping it and perhaps moving closer to Linux's Unix ancestry, then give Nexenta a try. Nexenta is an entirely different operating system that ditches the Linux kernel in favor of Sun Microsystem's OpenSolaris operating system base. However, it is otherwise very similar.

OpenSolaris grew directly out of the original Unix, unlike Linux, which was effectively a re-creation of much of the Unix system. The Open-Solaris kernel is perhaps more geared toward server hardware, and its hardware drivers might be less comprehensive (particularly when it comes to wifi hardware or graphics drivers), but many people consider it a rising star of the open source world. It comes with a handful of system tools, such as dtrace (http://www.sun.com/bigadmin/content/dtrace/), that offer many advantages over anything currently offered within typical Linux systems.

For additional details and to download an ISO image so you can burn a bootable CD to install Nexenta on your computer, visit http://www.nexenta.org.

☐ ### 81 · Instantly Hide a File or Folder

Any file or folder whose name is preceded with a period (.) is hidden from view in Nautilus and also won't appear in the list of shell commands such as ls, unless the user specifically chooses to view hidden files (ls -a, or clicking View → Show Hidden Files in Nautilus). So to hide a file or folder, just rename it (select it and hit F2), and then put a period in front of the filename. Gone. If the file doesn't vanish, hit F5 to refresh the file listing. To return the file to view, just remove the period.

If you want to make a file disappear from Nautilus's view of files (including the desktop) but still appear in command-line listings, add a tilde symbol (~) to the end. For example, to hide partypicture.jpg, change its filename to partypicture.jpg~. To hide text file, change its name to text file~.

This might seem like a secure method of avoiding prying eyes from seeing your personal files, but it's not really. For genuine privacy and security, you should encrypt files. See Tip 145, on page 178, and Tip 250, on page 280, to learn how.

☐ ### 82 Scan for Viruses

Put simply, viruses just aren't an issue for Ubuntu. It's unknown the number of viruses out there that target Linux, but the number has been said to be less than fifty. Most of those affect server software, such as the Apache web browser. When it comes to the desktop, Linux is entirely virus-free.

Of course, there's no guarantee this state of nirvana will last forever, and anyhow, installing antivirus software on your computer is so easy that there's little excuse not to do so. Any viruses found are likely to be Windows viruses, which pose no danger to you, but at least you'll be able to keep your unfortunate Windows-using friends safe.

This tip describes how to install ClamTK,[16] which is a graphical front

---

16. Note for the technically curious: The program name ClamTK implies the use of the Tk libraries but in actual fact ClamTK uses the GTK2 libraries, like all GNOME applications. Its name is a legacy from a time some years ago when it *did* use the Tk libraries.

end for the ClamAV command-line virus scanner, available online from http://www.clamav.net. ClamAV is designed for heavy-weight server use and as such is an industrial-strength tool. However, there's no reason why you can't employ it on your desktop.

Installing and Configuring ClamTK

To install ClamTK and also ClamAV, use Synaptic to search for the clamtk package. ClamAV will be installed automatically as a dependency. Once the program is installed, it can be found on the Applications → System Tools menu, under the title Virus Scanner.

But before using ClamTK to scan for viruses, it's necessary to run it as root so that the virus database can be updated. Start by typing gksu clamtk into a terminal window. Once the program runs, click Help → Update Signatures. Once the update is finished (look under the Information heading of the program), close ClamTK, and then open it from the Applications menu, as described earlier. Note that future updating will be carried out automatically and periodically in the background as a scheduled task.

Scanning for Viruses

To scan the entire system, click the Options menu, and click Scan Hidden Files. Then, to start the scan, click File → Recursive Scan, and on the left of the file-browsing dialog box that appears, select File System. Then click OK. There are several important things to note about a full-system scan:

- A full-system scan is very CPU and disk-intensive. Because of this, for a minute or two it might even seem that ClamTK has crashed.
- The nature of the Ubuntu file system means that there are some files ClamTK won't scan, such as those in the /proc directory. These will be reported in the program window as "excluded," as shown in Figure 3.21, on the next page.
- With a full-system scan, it's likely that you will have at least one *false positive* result, meaning that ClamTK will identify a file as containing a virus when it actually doesn't. This is because of a limitation in ClamAV (it's primarily designed to be used on servers to scan emails) but also is a statistical likelihood because of the huge number of files on an average system. The way to check a result to see whether it's a false positive is to use Google to search for the name of the virus that's reportedly infecting the file, adding

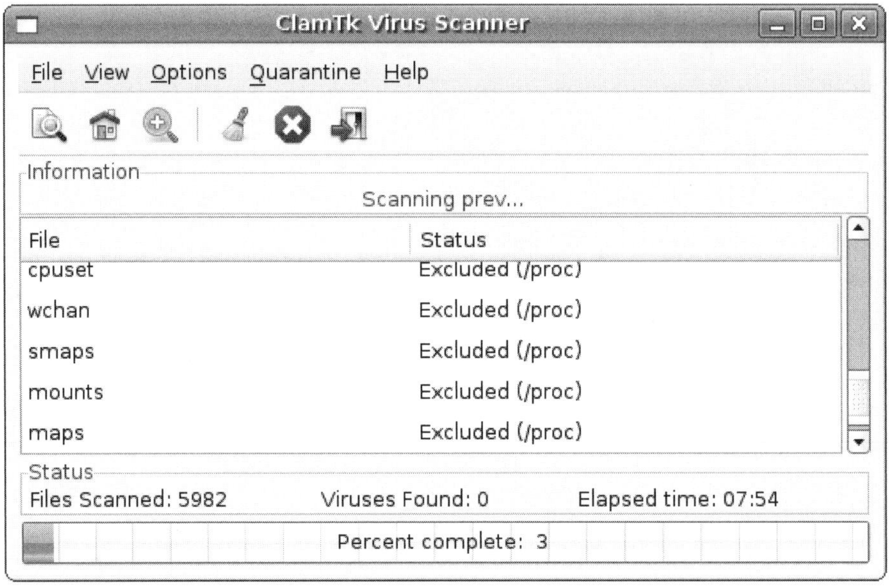

Figure 3.21: ClamTK performing a virus scan

clamav and the filename to the search phrase. This will show what others have found—it's likely that others will have experienced the same results as you.

Because system scans are problematic, you might want to keep them to a minimum and simply scan your /home directory on a periodic basis. After all, this is where you normally download files, so it's where viruses are most likely to be found. Simply repeat the previous steps, this time selecting your /home directory from the file-browsing dialog box.

If ClamTK finds a virus, it will list the suspect file in the program window, along with details of the virus it thinks is infecting the file. Note that ClamTK can't remove viruses from files. Instead, dealing with the suspect file is up to you. Assuming you've ruled out the possibility of a false positive, as described earlier, bear in mind that it's *extremely* likely that it will be a Windows virus and therefore of no danger to you.

ClamTK includes a "quarantine" function that can copy the file to a special directory, but you may as well use Nautilus to browse to the file and either delete it or, perhaps more sensibly, examine it in more detail.

Adding a Right-Click Scan-on-Demand Function

ClamTK comes into its own as an on-demand scanner, although it must be manually configured to do this. To add an option to the right-click menu within Nautilus that will cause ClamTK to scan that file or folder, follow these steps:

1. Open Gedit (Applications → Accessories → Text Editor), and save a new file called virus_scan to your /home directory.

2. Type the following into the Gedit window:

```
#!/bin/bash
# Scan the selected file in clamtk
clamtk "$@"
```

Then save the file and close Gedit.

3. You must now mark the new file as executable and copy it to the nautilus-scripts directory so that it integrates with Nautilus's right-click menu. To do this, type the following (both these commands should be typed into a terminal window; ensure you're in your /home directory before typing these commands):

```
$ chmod +x virus_scan
$ mv virus_scan .gnome2/nautilus-scripts/
```

After this, you can scan any file by right-clicking it and selecting Script → virus_scan.

---

83 Temporarily Log In as the Root User at the Command Line

If you have a lot of administrative tasks to do, you can temporarily switch to the root user at the command prompt, even if you haven't followed Tip 111, on page 149, to permanently enable the root user account login. You have a choice of methods—type either sudo su or sudo -i (the difference is that, with sudo -i, you'll also use the root user's environment settings so will be switched to the /root folder, for example).

You'll know you're root user because the prompt will change to a hash (#), rather than a dollar sign (treat this as a warning!). To return to being a normal user, just type exit, or hit Ctrl+d.

☐

84 Start the Screensaver from the Command Line

If you're hacking away at the terminal command line and need to leave your computer unattended, you might consider deliberately starting the screensaver. If a password has been set, you'll also benefit from password protection. To start the screensaver, just type the following:

```
$ gnome-screensaver-command -a
```

See Tip 259, on page 290, to learn how to turn this into a simple single-command alias to save typing.

☐

85 Get the Most Out of (or into) a Nautilus Window

By default, the Nautilus file-browsing windows tend to be a little relaxed when it comes to the spacing of icons. Actually, there's so much space between them that you could drive a bus through them. To tighten things up, click Edit → Preferences in a Nautilus window, ensure the View tab is selected in the dialog box that appears, and put a check in Use Compact Layout. Just like the days of Windows 95!

For more Nautilus tips, see Tip 72, on page 118; Tip 104, on page 146; Tip 144, on page 178; Tip 261, on page 292; Tip 272, on page 302; Tip 295, on page 333; Tip 165, on page 194; and Tip 132, on page 165.

☐

86 View Images at the Command Line

To quickly view a picture from the command line, just type eog filename. For example, eog holiday.jpg will open and display holiday.jpg. To view the picture full-screen, type eog -f filename. See Tip 208, on page 233, to learn how to start a slideshow of pictures in a particular directory.

See Tip 268, on page 297, to learn how to view pictures even if there's no GUI up and running.

 ## Administer the Printer from a Web Browser

Like most Linuxes (and also Macintosh OS X), Ubuntu relies upon the CUPS software for its printing subsystem. In addition to Ubuntu's configuration software on the System → Administration menu, CUPS can be configured using your web browser. Just type localhost:631 into the Firefox address bar to access the CUPS control panel. You can administer any printer setup on the system by clicking the Printers tab in the web page that appears and looking at the list of print jobs currently pending by clicking the Jobs tab. Remember that you might need to refresh the page to see when jobs join/leave the print queue.

To learn how to administer your entire system from a web browser (from any computer), see Tip 143, on page 175.

 ## Move a Window Without Clicking the Title Bar

To move any unmaximized window around, hold down Alt, and then click and drag anywhere in the window. The cursor will change to a grab hand. This can be especially useful for moving windows whose title bars have accidentally moved outside the desktop boundaries. It's also useful if you're running Ubuntu on a very small screen, where program windows are too big to fit and the OK/Cancel buttons are often hidden below the bottom of the screen.

☐

> ## 89 Connect to Shared Folders from the Command Line

If you work in an office environment or have more than one PC in your home, you might be used to connecting to shared folders across the network. Ubuntu's Places → Network view should show the computers that are local to you and let you connect.

If you're working at the command line and want to access shared folders, then it's a little trickier. Once a shared folder has been accessed by Nautilus, you'll find it mounted in the hidden .gvfs folder of your /home folder. But if the desktop isn't up and running or if the shared folder isn't mounted, then it won't be accessible.

In such a case, you might want to use smbclient, which effectively lets you "ftp" into a shared folder and use almost exactly the same commands to download/upload files as the command-line ftp program (see Tip 131, on page 164, for details of how the ftp command-line program works).

1. Start by using smbclient with the -L option to list the shared resources on the computer to which you want to connect. You can specify either the computer's network name or the IP address. You can find out the computer name on a Windows XP computer by right-clicking My Computer, selecting Properties, and then looking on the Computer Name tab for the Full computer name entry. You can also click the Change button to assign a new name if the existing one is too complex. To find out the IP address of a Windows computer, click Start → Run, and type cmd. In the DOS box that appears, type ipconfig, and in the output, look for the line that reads IP address.

2. Here's how to list what's available on a computer with the network name keir-windows:

```
$ smbclient -L keir-windows
```

You might be prompted for a password. It was enough in my tests just to hit ⎡Enter⎤ at this stage. Then look in the output for listings under the Sharename heading. Those that have disk in the Type heading equate to the shared folders available on the computer. You must specify a particular shared folder when you want to connect—you can't just connect to a computer and then switch to whichever folder you want to access.

3. Connecting to the shared folders is a little strange because the network name needs to be specified in an unusual way. Just like Windows, smbclient uses backslashes (\) for addresses (rather than forward slashes, as is typical with Linux/Unix), but these have a quite distinct meaning at the Linux command prompt, and this causes problems. Backslashes are used to tell the shell not to interpret the next character you type in the way it normally does. See the sidebar on page 22 for more information.

Perhaps ironically, we therefore have to use another backslash to tell the command line not to interpret the backslash in the way it normally does. Confused? Don't be. The simple fact is that, when using the smbclient command to connect to a shared folder, one slash should be replaced by two slashes. So, an address like \\keir-windows\sharedfolder\, normally used under Windows, becomes \\\\keir-windows\\sharedfolder\\. Here's how I'd connect to a folder called sharedfolder on the keir-windows computer:

```
$ smbclient \\\\keir-windows\\sharedfolder\\
```

4. If the share name has a space in it or a strange character (such as an exclamation mark), it too will need to be escaped with a backslash. So to connect to the shared folder accounts 2009! on the computer called keir-windows, we would type this:

```
$ smbclient \\\\keir-windows\\accounts\ 2009\!\\
```

Once connected, you can manipulate files on the shared computer using FTP commands. See Tip 131, on page 164, for a brief rundown of the ftp command-line program. As in ftp, type help for a list of commands.

90 Deactivate Caps Lock

☐

If you find yourself sometimes accidentally hitting the [Caps Lock] key, this tip will be a godsend. Just open a terminal, and type xmodmap -e "clear Lock" to disable it. On my system, the keyboard LED for the key still lit when it was hit, but there was no other effect within Ubuntu.

To make this tweak permanent, open your .profile file in Gedit (gedit ~/.profile), and add the command as a new line at the end of the file. Then save the file, and log out and back in to see the changes.

To reverse the changes, just edit the .profile file again, and delete the line you added. Then log out and back in again.

If you'd like to leave the ⎡Caps Lock⎤ key active and simply be told when it's been hit, see Tip 241, on page 274.

91 Format Floppies

Still use floppy disks? To format the disks under Ubuntu, hit ⎡Alt⎤+⎡F2⎤, and type gfloppy. Pretty much all the options are identical to what you might be used to under Windows' floppy formatting tool.

To learn how to format a USB memory stick or other memory card, see Tip 44, on page 93.

92 Switch to a Lightweight File Manager

Thunar is the default file manager used in the stripped-back Xfce4 desktop of Xubuntu. It starts quickly and has a low-memory footprint, yet it is very powerful and provides all the features you are likely to need. In fact, it beats Nautilus in many departments when it comes to features.[17] It can be used to replace Nautilus within the Ubuntu desktop for some operations, although bear in mind that Nautilus windows will still appear sometimes, such as when using Nautilus CD-R/DVD Creator.

---

17. One feature of Thunar I particularly appreciate is the ability to rubber-band-select many files in list view, something Nautilus doesn't allow. Thunar also includes the ability to define your own right-click functions, something that is possible in Nautilus but only if you add the Nautilus Actions component, as described in Tip 295, on page 333.

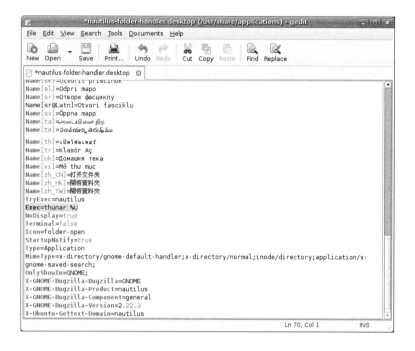

Figure 3.22: CONFIGURING THE SYSTEM TO USE AN ALTERNATIVE FILE MANAGER (SEE TIP 92)

Follow these steps to switch to Thunar:

1. Start Synaptic, and search for and install the thunar and thunar-archive-plugin packages. After installation, you can run Thunar by typing thunar in a terminal window.

2. To cause Thunar to open whenever you click an entry in the Places menu, you'll need to edit a configuration file: open a terminal window, and type the following:

```
$ gksu gedit /usr/share/applications/nautilus-folder-handler.desktop
```

Scroll to the bottom of the file, and look for the line that reads Exec=nautilus --no-desktop %U. Change it so it reads Exec=thunar %U. For an example taken from my text PC, see Figure 3.22.

Then save the file and test the changes by selecting Places → Home.

This tip works equally well for any alternative file manager. Others you might like to try are Konqueror (KDE's file manager), Dolphin (KDE4's file manager), and Rox-filer, a stripped-down file manager that is extremely lightweight. Just use Synaptic to search for and install konqeuror, doplhin, or rox-filer, respectively. When altering the earlier nautilus-folder-handler.desktop file to make Rox-filer the default, change the line to read Exec=rox-filer, without the %U; Dolphin and Konqueror still require the %U after the command. Note that Rox-filer's configuration is carried out by right-clicking a blank spot in its program window. It doesn't use a traditional menu system, like most application windows.

If you want a lightweight command-line file manager, install Midnight Commander (search for and install the mc package using Synaptic). Then type mc at the prompt to start the program. Once it's started, hit Alt+1, use the cursor keys to highlight Contents, and then hit Enter. This will display the help file explaining how to use the program. If you ever used Norton Commander back in the days of DOS, you'll find Midnight Commander very familiar, because it's modeled on that product.

To go back to using Nautilus after installing Thunar (or Konqueror/ Dolphin/Rox-Filer), just edit the nautilus-folder-handler.desktop file again, and change the line you edited to read Exec=nautilus --no-desktop %U. Then save the file, and log out and back in again.

93 Use Syntax Highlighting in Gedit

Programmers will be pleased to hear that Gedit includes syntax highlighting. However, it doesn't appear until the document is saved. It can be enhanced by clicking Edit → Preferences and checking Highlight Matching Bracket, which, as its name suggests, will highlight the opening and closing brackets of any command or phrase. If for any reason you want to deactivate syntax highlighting, open gconf-editor, navigate to /apps/gedit-2/preferences/syntax highlighting, and remove the check alongside enable on the right side.

For other Gedit tricks, see Tip 10, on page 59; Tip 134, on page 167; and Tip 155, on page 188.

94 Stop ZIP Files That Are Emailed to Colleagues from Getting Lost

☐

When you create a ZIP file from a file using the right-click Create Archive function, the .zip file extension will be appended to the end of the file. However, the old file extension will still be there. If you compressed document.doc, for example, you'd end up with document.doc.zip. The problem with this is that some Windows virus scanners interpret two file extensions as the sign of a virus and will strip them out of any emails you send. Therefore, if you plan to send the archive to Windows users, simply delete the first file extension, leaving only .zip.

95 Use an Alternative Email Client

☐

The default mail client provided with Ubuntu, Evolution, is something of a benign monster. It's packed with features and is aimed squarely at business users. It's quite clearly modeled on Microsoft Outlook. Personally, I can't help feeling it's overkill for more modest needs. The following are two alternatives, each of which can be installed using Synaptic and each of which is more than adequate.

Claws Mail

This is an email client with the emphasis on simplicity, although that doesn't mean it's light on features. It integrates well with the GNOME desktop used by Ubuntu and, in my opinion, has the look and feel that email clients used to have back in the 90s, before they started trying to organize our lives (although the look and feel can be changed via themes—see http://www.claws-mail.org for more information and downloads). Thus, there's no calendar or to-do list, and even composing HTML email is apparently one feature too many (although you can view HTML mail sent by others). You do get live spell checking and email filtering, however, amongst other up-to-date and indispensable features, and the program utilizes a plug-in structure, so many additional functions can be downloaded from the website (see http://www.claws-mail.org for downloads).

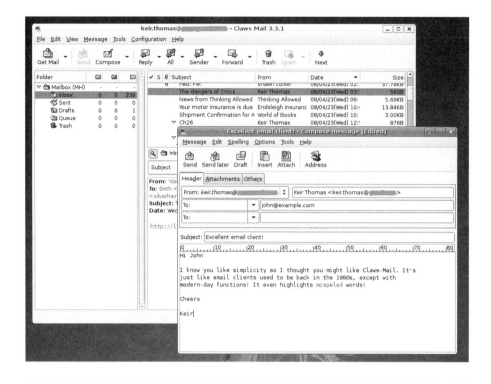

Figure 3.23: CLAWS MAIL (SEE TIP 95)

You can install Claws Mail by searching for and installing the claws-mail package. For an example of the program running on my test PC, see Figure 3.23. Once installed, Claws Mail can be found on the Applications → Internet menu. When first run, it walks through a setup wizard in which you must enter your mail server details.

Thunderbird

Few people realize that Firefox isn't Mozilla's only product. Thunderbird is its email client offering and is perhaps the second-most popular open source email client in use today. And that's not without reason—Thunderbird packs in the features you might expect of a modern email client, such as powerful search, filtering, and junk mail detection, but it keeps everything simple and usable. It also integrates a Usenet (news groups) reader program and comes already configured to work with Gmail accounts. As you might expect, it features the same HTML-rendering technology as Firefox, so HTML emails always look like they should.

Like Firefox, Thunderbird is extensible via add-ons, many of which can be downloaded from https://addons.mozilla.org/en-US/thunderbird and some of which actually improve Thunderbird's functionality extensively. To install add-ons, right-click the download link, save the add-on to the hard disk, and then click Tools → Add-ons. Then click the Install button, and navigate to the downloaded file.

Thunderbird can be installed using Synaptic. The best way of doing so is to search for and install the thunderbird-gnome-support package, which will install Thunderbird along with software that helps it integrate into the GNOME desktop used by Ubuntu. You might also want to add the relevant language settings package for your area so that spell checking will work correctly—use Synaptic to search for thunderbird-locale, and select the correct package from the list.

Once installed, the program can be found on the Applications → Internet menu. When it first starts, it will walk through a wizard during which you can configure it to work with your email servers.

96 Ensure People Hear You When Using a Microphone

Ensure the Microphone slider is not muted in the mixer window by double-clicking the volume control icon and clicking the speaker icon beneath the Microphone slider so it no longer has a cross against it. You might also have to activate the +20db microphone boost: click Edit → Preferences on the mixer window, and in the dialog box that appears, put a check in Mic Boost (+20dB). Click Close, and back in the mixer window, click the Switches tab, and put a check alongside Mic Boost (+20dB). Note that you might not see the +20dB boost option with your particular sound hardware.

97 Quickly Browse to a Location

Want to browse to a file system location but too lazy to grab the mouse and click the Places menu? Hit the forward slash (/), and then type the path into the dialog box that appears.

☐

98 Turn Off the Beep

Whenever you made a mistake or if Ubuntu simply wants to tell you something isn't possible, it will cause the computer to beep. This can become annoying and doesn't really serve much purpose. To turn it off, click System → Preferences → Sound, and then click the System Beep tab. Then remove the check from the Enable System Beep box. You might want to enable the check in Visual System Beep, because this will flash either the screen or the topmost program's title bar to indicate the same type of error.

☐

99 Add a Second Hard Disk

If you run out of space on your main hard disk, you might choose to add a second hard disk.[18] When adding a new disk, two things need to be done. First the disk must be partitioned. Then it must be formatted. If you want to make it accessible under Windows as well as Ubuntu, the FAT32 format must be used. Before you can do either task, you need to identify how Ubuntu refers to the new hard disk on a technical level.

The following steps will do all of this:

1. Boot into Ubuntu with the hard disk attached to your computer. Open a terminal window, and type sudo fdisk -l.

   Here are the results I saw on my test system:

   ```
   Disk /dev/sda: 81.9 GB, 81964302336 bytes
   255 heads, 63 sectors/track, 9964 cylinders
   Units = cylinders of 16065 * 512 = 8225280 bytes
   Disk identifier: 0x1c381c37

      Device Boot  Start    End    Blocks   Id  System
   /dev/sda1    *       1    4742  38090083+   7  HPFS/NTFS
   ```

---

18. The instructions in Tip 99 assume you've installed a new hard disk. If you connect an old hard disk that already contains an operating system, you should find the disk is detected automatically on the Places menu within Ubuntu. Rather than repartitioning and reformatting, you may as well just wipe the files from the hard disk using Nautilus and then use the existing partition. Ensure that you select the right disk and don't accidentally wipe the files from your Windows partition!

```
/dev/sda2          4743      9964     41945715    5  Extended
/dev/sda5          4743      9744     40178533+  83  Linux
/dev/sda6          9745      9964      1767118+  82  Linux swap/Solaris
```

```
Disk /dev/sdb: 120.0 GB, 120034123776 bytes
255 heads, 63 sectors/track, 14593 cylinders
Units = cylinders of 16065 * 512 = 8225280 bytes
Disk identifier: 0xb94838a4
```

```
Disk /dev/sdb doesn't contain a valid partition table
```

There are two hard disks listed in the results: look for the headings Disk /dev/sda and Disk /dev/sdb. Beneath each heading is technical information about the disk, and beneath that the partitions on that disk are listed.

It should be obvious that, on my test computer, /dev/sdb is the new hard disk because it has no partitions (it "doesn't contain a valid partition table"), while /dev/sda has the standard partition layout of a dual-boot Ubuntu system.

2. Type the following to start the cfdisk partitioning program:

```
$ sudo cfdisk -z /dev/sdb
```

You should replace /dev/sdb with what you discovered earlier. Then press ⃞n to create a new partition, and hit ⃞Enter twice to create a primary partition and accept the size suggestion. This will create a partition that fills the entire disk.

3. Hit ⃞t, and then hit ⃞Enter to scroll the list. Then type 0C (note that's *zero* and then *C*). Hit ⃞Enter. Then press ⃞W (note that's ⃞Shift+⃞w). Type yes to confirm your choice. Once the program has finished writing the new partition table, press ⃞q to quit the program.

4. Now you must format the new partition. In order to do this, type the following:

```
$ sudo mkfs.vfat -F 32 /dev/sdb1
```

You should replace the /dev/sdb component of the previous line with what you discovered earlier, although ensure you end it with a 1 (in other words, if you found the new disk was identified as, say, /dev/sdc, then you would type sudo mkfs.vfat -F 32 /dev/sdc1).

After this, the hard disk is ready for use. To have it appear on Ubuntu's Places menu, restart the computer (it will be identified by its size—for example, if it is a 160GB hard disk, it will appear on the Places menu as 160 GB Media). The new disk should be automatically detected and made available within My Computer when you boot into Windows.

100 Update Ubuntu in the Background

One of the best things about Ubuntu is the frequency of updates. It's nice to know your system has the latest security-patched software. Yet this can also be annoying, because Update Manager seems to be constantly pestering you to confirm new downloads. To bypass this and automatically download and install updates in the background, open Software Sources (System → Administration), click the Updates tab, and select Install Security Updates without Confirmation under the Automatic Updates heading.

101 Install 465 Open Source Fonts

All credit to Brian Kent (http://www.aenigmafonts.com) who's not only an excellent font designer but is also committed to the ideals of open source software and has made 465 of his font creations available to Ubuntu users. To install the fonts, you'll need to add a new software repository: click System → Administration → Software Sources, then click the Third-Party Software tab, and finally click the Add button. Then type the following into the dialog box that appears:

```
deb http://ppa.launchpad.net/corenominal/ubuntu hardy main
```

Click the Add Sources button, then the Close button. When prompted, agree to reload the package lists. Then use Synaptic to search for and install the ttf-aenigma package. Once installed, the fonts will be available for use straightaway in all applications.

To learn how to get other fonts for your system, see Tip 75, on page 122; Tip 170, on page 197; Tip 280, on page 313; and Tip 283, on page 319.

102 Be Careful Not to Badly Name Files/Folders in Your Windows Partition

☐

This is less of a tip and more of a warning. As you might know, Windows doesn't let you use the following characters when naming files or folders: \/:*?@<>|.

Unfortunately, Ubuntu isn't quite as fussy and allows some of those characters in filenames. It also doesn't realize you shouldn't use them when accessing a Windows partition. If you create new files or folders on your Windows partition from within Ubuntu containing these characters, they will be rendered inaccessible when you boot into Windows. In fact, Windows will become so confused that it won't even let you rename the file or folder (even at the DOS prompt). The only solution is to boot back into Ubuntu and rename it there.

103 Make Your Windows Partition Read-Only

☐

Ubuntu can both read and write files to your Windows partition, and the software behind this (ntfs-3g) is said to be very reliable. However, it still gives me sweaty palms—the possibility of data loss is too high. So, I decided to make the NTFS partition read-only whenever it's mounted. To do this, start gconf-editor, and navigate to /system/storage/default_ options/ntfs-3g. In the right of the window, double-click the mount_options entry, and in the dialog box that appears, click the Add button. In the Add New List Entry dialog box, type ro into the New List Value text box, and then click OK. Click OK to close the parent dialog box. The changes take effect immediately, although you will have to unmount if it's already mounted and then remount. Note that this will make read-only *any* hard disk you attach to your computer that contains an NTFS file system.

To reverse these changes, simply open gconf-editor again and remove the entry from the mount_options key by selecting the ro entry under the Values heading and clicking the Remove button. You will have to unmount and then remount your Windows partition for the changes to take effect.

104	Stop Nautilus from Neatly Arranging Icons

Nautilus sorts all file and folder icons into a grid pattern. If you want something more chaotic, whereby icons stay exactly where you drop them, click View → Arrange items → Manually. Each folder can have its own setting in this regard. To make Nautilus default to manual arrangement with new folders it creates, start gconf-editor, navigate to /apps/nautilus/icon_view, and put a check alongside default_use_manual_layout. To stop desktop icons from being arranged to a grid, just right-click a blank spot on the desktop, and uncheck Keep Aligned.

For other Nautilus hints and hacks, see Tip 72, on page 118; Tip 85, on page 132; Tip 165, on page 194; Tip 144, on page 178; Tip 261, on page 292; Tip 272, on page 302; and Tip 295, on page 333.

105	Run GUI Programs from a Terminal Window Without Tying Up Input

Running GUI programs such as gconf-editor from a terminal window tie it up, so no other commands can be entered until it is quit. To avoid this, add an ampersand (&) to the end of the line. This makes the program run as a bash background task (known technically as a *job*), although it will still work fine. For example, to run gconf-editor so it is possible to subsequently use the terminal for further commands, type gedit &.

To see a list of programs you've started in this way, type jobs at the prompt. Remember that the new program will still quit when the terminal window is exited. To get around this, see Tip 300, on page 340.

106 Set the CPU Speed from the Desktop

☐

With some types of CPU, it's possible to manually alter the clock speed while the system is running. This can be useful with a notebook computer, for example, where you might choose to throttle down the CPU speed when on battery power to save juice or to minimize heat generation when the computer is resting on your lap.

The CPU Frequency Scaling Monitor applet takes care of this function, but before it can be used, some additional configuration is necessary.

Open a terminal window, and type the following:

```
$ sudo dpkg-reconfigure gnome-applets
```

You'll see a warning about how enabling the cpufreq-selector program could be a security risk if it is given root powers. This is true, but, as always, usability must be balanced against security. The chances of a hacker exploiting this are very slim. Hit Enter; then, on the next screen, use the cursor keys to highlight Yes, and hit Enter again.

After this, right-click a blank spot on the top panel, click Add to panel, and then select CPU Frequency Scaling Applet from the list. A new applet will be added, showing the current speed of the CPU. By clicking it, you'll be able to set either the speed you want the CPU to run at or the power-saving mode it should use (these modes vary in name and nature from chip to chip, but what they offer should be obvious from their names).

If your CPU has more than one core, such as Intel's CoreDuo series, each core must be configured separately. For example, a dual-core chip will need two CPU Frequency Scaling Monitor applets. Just right-click the panel as explained to add another. To alter which particular core each applet controls, right-click an applet, select Preferences, and choose the CPU core under the Monitored CPU heading.

Note that each core can run at a different speed compared to the other core and be switched to a different power-saving mode.

To see the benefits or otherwise of scaling the CPU speed, see Tip 5, on page 53, which explains how to graph your computer's power consumption. You might also be interested in Tip 240, on page 273, which explains how to monitor CPU load.

107 Switch to Kubuntu, Xubuntu, or Edubuntu Without Installing from Scratch

To switch to Kubuntu, Xubuntu, or Edubuntu, use Synaptic to search for and install kubuntu-desktop, xubuntu-desktop, or edubuntu-desktop, respectively (if you want the KDE4 release of Kubuntu, look for kubuntu-kde4-desktop). These are *metapackages*[19] on which the whole of the Kubuntu, Xubuntu, and Edubuntu packages rely. Kubuntu, Xubuntu, or Edubuntu will be installed alongside the standard GNOME desktop (in the case of Edubuntu, the additional educational software will be installed along with the Edubuntu kids' GUI theme; this will be applied automatically upon installation, and you can manually switch back to the Human theme if you want).

To use Kubuntu or Xubuntu instead of GNOME, log out, and click the Options button at the bottom left of the login screen. Then click Select Session, and select KDE or XFCE from the menu. To return to the GNOME desktop, repeat this step, and select GNOME instead.

108 SSH into Ubuntu from Windows

As discussed in Tip 190, on page 218, SSH is possibly the ultimate remote administration tool. Alas, it's completely unsupported by Windows (although it comes as standard on Mac OS X). However, you can

---

19. Metapackages are effectively empty packages that have dependencies on a lot of other packages. A metapackage is the standard way of installing larger applications such as OpenOffice.org that come in lots of bits and pieces.

install PuTTY (http://www.chiark.greenend.org.uk/~sgtatham/putty/) to get instant SSH/SFTP support on Windows.

109   Recover a Damaged Desktop   ☐

If you've been tweaking your system to the point of breaking and find that the GNOME desktop no longer appears when you attempt to log in, click the Options button on the login screen, and click Select Session. Next select Failsafe GNOME, and click Change Session. Then log in as usual. From here you should be able to repair your desktop or possibly even use the Users and Groups program to create a new account to use in the future (nothing like a fresh start, eh?).

110   Recover a Damaged Desktop #2   ☐

If you've having trouble logging into your GNOME desktop, first see Tip 109. If that doesn't work, you can try deleting your GNOME desktop configuration files and starting again. This is possible because, if GNOME doesn't find configuration files where they should be, it will automatically create some afresh. Deleting these files is very radical because it will delete all your desktop settings, plus those for GNOME applications (although your Evolution mail and account settings will remain because they're stored in the .evolution folder). However, if you have no other choice...

Log out of the desktop, and then switch to a new virtual console (Ctrl+ Alt+F2). Then log in, and type the following:

```
$ rm -rf .gnome-2
```

Then switch back to GUI mode (Ctrl+Alt+F7), and log in as usual.

111   Enable the Root User   ☐

Ubuntu loves to use sudo/gksu to dish out superuser powers, but you can permanently enable the root account so you can log into it.

Type the following, which will assign the root user a password and thereby activate it:

```
$ sudo passwd root
```

Then type a new password that you'll use in the future when logging in as the root user.

In the future, you can switch to the root user at the command prompt by typing su -. You won't be able to log in as root from the login window, however, unless you alter a login preference. Click System → Administration → Login Window, then click the Security tab, and put a check in Allow Local System Administrator Login. Then close the program, and log out and back in again as root (provide root as your username). Note that running a GUI as root is about as dangerous as it gets, but, then again, it's your computer!

If you don't want to enable the root user but would still like to switch to the root user account on occasion, Ubuntu can accommodate you; see Tip 83, on page 131.

112 Quickly Create Graphical Text Banners

Tip 219, on page 244, discusses using the figlet command-line tool to create ASCII banners of words, but if you want to quickly create text banners as a image file, perhaps for use on websites or presentations, you can use GNOME's font preview tool. It isn't really designed for this, but the appropriation of existing commands is the beauty of Linux!

You need to specify the text, plus which font to use (including its full path) and the output filename. The following will create a banner saying 'Ubuntu Kung Fu' using the Arial font contained within my Windows partition, outputting a file called banner.png:

```
$ gnome-thumbnail-font --text 'Ubuntu Kung Fu' '/media/disk/WINDOWS/ ←
Fonts/ARIAL.TTF' banner.png
```

Obviously, you should ensure your Windows partition is mounted (by selecting its entry on the Places menu) before running any command using fonts contained in its file system.

113   Securely Erase Data

There are a handful of situations where securely erasing data can be useful. If you're about to sell a computer or even if you're about to dispose of it, it makes sense to completely wipe the hard disk.

Simply deleting the files isn't good enough because they can still be recovered using specialized software. Instead, you must overwrite the entire disk with junk data.

In addition to wiping entire storage devices, you occasionally might want to wipe a file on your existing hard disk that contains personal data so that it can't be recovered, either deliberately or accidentally.

Ubuntu's shred can help in both situations. It simply overwrites a file (or hard disk/removable storage) over and over again with random data so that the original data isn't recoverable (even by extremely specialized data recovery agencies, or so it's claimed by shred's creators).

Wiping Storage Devices

Let's say you want to securely erase the data on a USB key stick so that it can't be recovered. You would follow these steps:

1. First you must find how Ubuntu refers to the USB stick on a technical level. To do so, insert it so that its icon appears on the desktop, and then make a note of its name. Then open a terminal window, type mount, and look for the line in the output what refers to the USB keystick. For example, on my test PC, the keystick's label (name) was KINGSTON, so I picked out the following line (this line has been truncated for brevity):

   /dev/sdb1 on /media/KINGSTON type vfat (rw,nosuid,nodev, ...

   I then made a note of /dev/sdb (note that the number at the end should be dropped; it refers to the partition on the USB key stick, and we intend to wipe the entire thing, regardless of partitions).

   It's very important you get this step right because there's no going back if you make a mistake! shred is irreversible.

2. After this, unmount the USB key stick by right-clicking it and selecting Unmount Volume.

3. Then, at the command prompt, type the following:

```
$ sudo shred -v /dev/sdb
```

It's *vital* you replace /dev/sdb with what you discovered earlier! This is one situation where typos can be disastrous.

After this, shred will wipe the key stick. It will probably take a long time to complete, but you'll see a progress report onscreen every few seconds.

By default, shread overwrites the data twenty-five times, but you can speed up the process by using the -n command option, which tells shred how many times to overwrite. Unless you're expecting the CIA to come and visit, a value of -n1 should be good enough for most of us (the full command then becomes sudo shred -v -n1 /dev/sdb).

When the USB key stick has been erased, you'll need to reformat it, because the format component of the disk was part of that securely erased. This can be done by following the steps in Tip 44, on page 93.

Essentially the same method as described here can be used to wipe a hard disk, but this time you must use Ubuntu's live distro mode on the install CD so that the hard disk isn't mounted. Boot from your Ubuntu install CD on the computer whose disk you want to erase, and select Try Ubuntu from the boot menu. When the desktop appears, open a terminal window, and type the following (this assumes the computer has one hard disk fitted; note that you should remove any type of removable storage device before issuing this command, such as USB key sticks):

```
$ sudo swapoff
$ sudo shred -v /dev/sda
```

Note that this wipes the *entire* hard disk—not just Ubuntu! If a Windows partition is on there too, it will also be shredded. To wipe a floppy disk, replace /dev/sda with /dev/fd0.

Wiping Files

Wiping files rather than entire disks is simply a matter of specifying the file, this time adding the -u command option.[20]

---

20. If you read the shred manual, you'll see a warning that when completely shredding files on journaled file systems—such as the ext3 system used by Ubuntu—some trace of the file might be left behind. However, this is an issue only for ext3 file systems that use the data=journal mode. Ubuntu uses the data=ordered mode, which allows shred to completely destroy files.

For example, let's say you wanted to destroy *partypicture.jpg* beyond recovery:

```
$ shred -v -n1 -u partypicture.jpg
```

Note that there is no need in this case to precede the command with sudo because the file belongs to you.

114 Play Emacs Games

If you're a fan of this arcane text editor, you might be interested in the "hidden" games that help you take a break every now again. Start emacs, then hit Esc, and type x. Then type any from the following list: tetris, pong, snake, solitaire, gomoku, or doctor (an Eliza clone).

115 Fix Video Playback Problems

If you find video playback is distorted or jumpy, open a terminal window, and type gstreamer-properties. In the program window that appears, select the Video tab, and in the Plugin drop-down list beneath Default Output, select X Window System (No Xv).

If you run into problems with Totem video playback, you might be interested in installing an alternative media player; see Tip 231, on page 263.

116 Turn Any Text File into a PDF at the Command Line

There are a number of ways of converting a text file into a PDF at the command line. Perhaps the easiest is to "print" it to Ubuntu's PDF printer driver. The file will then be saved to the PDF folder in your /home folder. This tip uses the lp command, telling it which printer to use with the -d command switch:

```
$ lp -d PDF textfile.txt
```

For further PDF manipulation tips, see also Tip 168, on page 196; Tip 189, on page 218; Tip 215, on page 240; and Tip 258, on page 289.

117 Avoid Repetitive Strain Injury When Using Ubuntu

Although some might scoff at repetitive strain injury, it is a significant cause of workplace injury. To help avoid it, you might choose to install WorkRave, a GNOME applet[21] that includes timers to tell you when to take a break and then guides you through exercises to lessen the chances of RSI occurring. To install the program, simply search for and install workrave using Synaptic. Once installed, log out and back in again; then right-click a blank spot on the panel, and select Add to panel. Select WorkRave from the list.

WorkRave works on the principle of three separate break timers. The first is for *microbreaks*, which are short pauses of a few seconds every few minutes. The second are *rest breaks*, which occur maybe every hour. The third is the *daily limit*, which is intended to encapsulate your working day.

Each time a rest break comes around, a window pops up showing some exercises you should do, along with a countdown timer, which is designed to help you complete each. If you're too busy to do the exercises, simply click the Skip button. Whenever a microbreak is due, the icon on the panel will switch to a green bar to tell you.

The times for each break can be set by right-clicking the panel icon and selecting Preferences.

118 Uninstall Ubuntu

Yes, it's unthinkable, yet it might be desirable for users who have tried Ubuntu but found it's not for them. Therefore, knowing how to uninstall Ubuntu safely and cleanly, without data loss, is a must.

---

21. A version of WorkRave is also available for Windows. Visit the project website for more information: http://www.workrave.org.

When used on a dual-boot computer, the following steps will remove the Ubuntu partitions, before expanding the Windows partition to fill the empty space, and then restore the Windows boot loader. Bear in mind that these steps involve repartitioning, which you undertake at your own peril. You should certainly back up any vital data first.

1. To delete the Ubuntu partitions and enlarge the Windows partition, you'll need to boot from your Ubuntu CD and use Gparted. Select the Try Ubuntu option from the Ubuntu installer boot menu, and once Ubuntu is up and running, click System → Administration → Partition Editor.

2. Look for your Ubuntu swap partition in the list—it will probably be identified as linux-swap. Right-click it, and then select Swapoff from the menu that appears.

3. Select the main Ubuntu partition (it will be identified as ext3 in the list), right-click, and select Delete. Repeat with the linux-swap partition. Note that the two partitions might be in an extended partition (it will be identified as extended). You may need to select this too, and then select Delete.

4. Right-click the NTFS (Windows) partition, and select Resize/Move. Then, in the dialog box that appears, click and drag the right edge of the graphical representation of the partition until it fills the disk. Click the Resize/Move button. Then click the Apply button in the main Gparted window. Note that if you see an error during NTFS resizing, it's likely you didn't shut down Windows properly the last time you used it. Reboot into Windows, and run a chkdsk. Then repeat this step.

   Once the partition work is finished, reboot your computer using either your Windows XP or Vista CD/DVD, depending on the operating system installed. Note that it will not be possible to boot into Windows at this time—if you attempt to boot the hard disk, you will see an error.

5. If your computer is running Windows XP, when the installation CD's initial choices menu appears, hit r to get to the Recovery Console. Select your Windows partition when prompted, and enter the administrator password when prompted (if you didn't set an administrator password, just hit Enter).

Type the following commands, the last of which will reboot your computer:

```
C:\> fixmbr
C:\> fixboot
C:\> bootcfg /rebuild
C:\> exit
```

The bootcfg command will ask you to type a load identifier. This is the Windows boot menu entry and can be anything you want—"Windows" is a good choice. When prompted for OS Load Options, just leave the line blank, and hit Enter.

6. If you're running Windows Vista, choose your language settings and click Next when the installation dialog box first appears. Then click the Repair your computer option. Click the No button when asked if you want to automatically repair. Your Windows partition will then be detected. Once detection has finished, click the Next button and, in the ensuing screen, click the Command Prompt option. In the command prompt window that appears, type the following:

```
X:\Sources> bootrec /fixmbr
X:\Sources> bootrec /fixboot
X:\Sources> bootrec /rebuildbcd
X:\Sources> exit
```

Hit y when prompted after typing bootrec /rebuildbcd. Once the DOS box closes, click the Restart button.

7. You should now be able to boot into Windows.

There's one last thing to take care of—getting rid of the Windows boot menu we introduced when restoring the Windows boot loader. If you're running Windows XP, you will see this, and you might see it when running Windows Vista too. If running Windows Vista, right-click Computer on the Windows menu, and click Properties. Then click the Advanced System Settings link on the left. Alternatively, if you're running Windows XP, right-click My Computer on the Start menu, and select Properties. Then, regardless of which Windows version you're using, click the Advanced tab, and click the Settings button under the Startup and Recovery heading in the dialog box that appears. In the Default Operating System drop-down, select the entry for Windows, and ensure there's a check alongside the Time to display list of operating systems entry. Then reduce the time value to 0. Click the OK button, close the parent dialog boxes, and then reboot to test the settings.

119 Network Ubuntu, Mac, and Windows…Without Doing Anything

So, a Mac, Windows PC, and Ubuntu box walk into a bar and plug themselves into an Ethernet hub. And that's the end of the joke. From that point onward, without any configuration necessary, all three computers should be able to network with each other. This is because, in the absence of a DHCP/DNS server to assign network addresses, all the computers will default to the *Zerconf* system (known as *Bonjour* on Apple Macs and *Automatic Private IP Addressing* on Windows; sometimes it's also known as *link-local*). The machines will sort themselves out with an IP address somewhere in the 169.254 range (assuming all the computers are set to use IPv4 by default, which is very likely).

120 Access ISO Images As If They Were Disk Drives

The standard method of distributing Ubuntu as a full operating system is as an ISO image, which you can burn to disc and boot from. If you need to look into what's in an ISO image, you have a number of choices. The first is to right-click the image file and select Open with "Archive Manager". The slight issue with this approach is that opening larger ISO files (DVD-ROM images, for example) can take some time, as can extracting files. A better way is to mount the ISO image just like you would an actual disk. To do so, open a terminal window, and type the following (this assumes the file ubuntu.iso is in your /home folder):

```
$ sudo mkdir /media/ISO
$ sudo mount -o loop ~/ubuntu.iso /media/ISO
```

Note that the first command creates a mount point and doesn't need to be typed in the future. Once the ISO image is mounted, an icon for it will automatically appear on the desktop.

To unmount the image, type sudo umount /media/ISO in the terminal window.

To learn how to create your own ISO backup images of virtually any physical CD/DVD, see Tip 203, on page 229.

□

121 Improve Ubuntu's Microsoft Office 2007 File Support

You might be aware of the scandal surrounding Microsoft's new Office 2007 file formats (also supported in Microsoft Office 2008 on the Apple Mac). Luckily, few people are actually using the file format right now, and the older .doc, .xls, and so on, file formats remain dominant. OpenOffice.org comes with the ability to open Office 2007 files but not save them, and to be truthful, it isn't very good at importing (at least not at the time of writing).

But there's a simple solution. The OpenOffice Ninja website offers the odf-converter-integrator package, which seamlessly converts files to and from Office 2007 format and integrates fully with OpenOffice.org so you can save and load files. You can download the Ubuntu package from http://katana.oooninja.com/w/odf-converter-integrator/download (select the "Ubuntu i386" version). Download to the desktop. To install, open a terminal window, and type the following (ensure all OpenOffice.org applications are closed):

```
$ sudo apt-get install libgif4 libungif4g
$ sudo dpkg -i ~/Desktop/odf-converter-integrator-chocolate_0.1.4-1. ↩
i386.deb
```

Obviously you should replace the filename on the dpkg line with that which you downloaded, because it's very likely the version number will have changed. Ensure you update the package frequently because the converter software is still being developed and improves all the time.

To configure OpenOffice.org to always save in Microsoft Office file formats, see Tip 249, on page 279.

122   Use a Friendly Version of vim

For reasons best known to Ubuntu developers, the version of the vim text editor that runs if you type vi at the command prompt isn't set up in the most user-friendly way. Backspace won't work, while the cursor keys aren't assigned properly and will cause letters to appear in INSERT mode. This can make editing difficult unless you're used to the specific vim keyboard shortcuts. To make vim act more like it should, you can install a better version using Synaptic—just search for and install the vim package (the package that supplies vim out of the box is vim-common). Configuration is automatic, and typing either vi or vim will start the improved version.

To install a GUI version of vim, see Tip 181, on page 211.

123   Get Around Partitioning Errors If Using Boot Camp on Macs

I wanted to install Ubuntu alongside OS X on my Apple MacBook. I tried to use Boot Camp, but it threw up an error about unmovable files and suggested I blank the hard disk and start again. I was a tad too busy to do that, so I booted Ubuntu in live distro mode (insert the CD, and hold down c when booting) and clicked System → Administration → Partition Editor. Then I resized the OS X HFS partition there. Of course, as with any repartitioning process, you should back up your data first. I also created the new ext3 partition using Partition Manager (remember that you shouldn't create a swap partition because it confuses Boot Camp) and then ran the installer from within live distro mode. The only other thing I had to remember was to set GRUB to install to /dev/sda at the end, rather than (hd0,0), which is default. After this, I could boot Ubuntu by holding down Alt during the boot chime and selecting Windows (see Tip 124, on the following page for a way of getting around this incorrect boot label).

Note that you should always attempt to resize the partition using Boot Camp, even if it's prone to failure, because this performs the additional invisible background task of configuring your Mac to dual-boot (Macs use an EFI boot system, rather than the standard PC BIOS). You will not be able to dual-boot if you simply use Gparted to shrink the Mac OS X partition without first using BootCamp.

124 Have Macs Correctly Refer to Ubuntu in Dual-Boot Mode

The Boot Camp provided by Apple to allow dual-booting on Macintosh computers is designed for Windows. The Macintosh boot menu that appears when you hold down Alt during boot confirms this—even if you install Ubuntu, it will still read "Windows." There are some ways around this using OS X's own tools, but none is satisfactory. The easiest way to get around it to install rEFIt (http://refit.sourceforge.net), a third-party Mac boot manager. This shows a nice graphical boot menu each time you start up, complete with the correct icons and terminology for Linux partitions. You can install it from within OS X or create a bootable CD and install it that way. Setup is automatic after installation, and no configuration is needed. Just reboot to see the effect.

If you want to uninstall REFIt, remove the efi folder in the root of the OS X file system. Then start OS X's System Preferences, select Startup Disk, select your Mac OS disk in the list, and then click the Restart button. To choose between OS X and Ubuntu in the future, hold down the Alt key after hearing the boot chime.

125 Sleep, Ubuntu, Sleep!

The sleep command is usually used in shell scripts, but it can be useful in simply delaying day-to-day commands typed at the prompt. As its name suggests, it causes the prompt to pause for a set period before executing any more instructions. Inserted before another command, it can cause the computer to pause before executing that command. For example, the following will cause the computer to shut down (switch to run level 0) in thirty seconds:

```
$ sudo sleep 30s; sudo telinit 0
```

Note that this particular example works only because the computer "remembers" the sudo powers used with the first command (sleep), so when they're called by the second command (telinit 0), they're still relevant. In this particular case, if the pause were longer than 160 seconds (two minutes; the sudo grace period), then the command wouldn't work. To learn about how to extend the sudo pause, see Tip 47, on page 99.

126 Instantly Create an HTML Slideshow of Photos

Use Synaptic to install igal. Once installed, copy all the pictures you want to make into a slideshow into one folder. Then switch to that folder, and type igal. It's as simple as that—there's no need to specify the files. The necessary HTML files for a slideshow will be created automatically, and all you need do is upload all the files to your website. The main file igal creates is index.html, and you might want to rename this to something like slideshow.html to avoid overwriting your website's index.html file. You should also be aware that igal creates thumbnails of the images as hidden files (files preceded by a period), and these will need to be uploaded to the website too. To view then in a Nautilus file-browsing window, click View → Show Hidden Files.

There's no reason why the slideshow will work only online. You could also email the whole folder full of images plus HTML to others as a single compressed file and instruct them to double-click index.html when they've decompressed the folder. The slideshow will then open in their browser.

If all you want to do is instantly view a folder full of photos as a slideshow, see Tip 208, on page 233.

127 Reveal the Desktop

Like it or loathe it, Windows has a lot of useful productivity features. One of those is the Show Desktop icon that appears in the Quick Links toolbar and allows users to instantly minimize all windows in order to access the desktop. Ubuntu includes its own variation at the bottom left of the screen, but it's more useful to hit the keyboard combination that does the same thing: Ctrl + Alt + d. If you have the desktop effects activated, everything will slide out of the way to the edges of the screen. Otherwise, it'll simply be like everything has minimized to the taskbar. Hitting the combo again will cause the windows to reappear in their original positions.

☐ | 128 | Set Hard Disk Power-Saving

Ubuntu has a powerful raft of power management features, accessible through System → Preferences → Power Management, but you might notice one missing if you're used to Windows or OS X: hard disk spin downtime. This is where the hard disk powers down after a period of inactivity. When data is requested after this, it spins up again, although there is sometimes a momentary pause while this happens.

It's possible to set your hard disk to spin down under Ubuntu in order to save power and/or wear and tear (particularly on a computer left on most of the time), but you'll need to edit a configuration file. Follow these steps:

1. The configuration file containing the settings is hdparm.conf, so open it in Gedit by typing the following into a terminal window: gksu gedit /etc/hdparm.conf.

2. Look for the line that reads #spindown_time = 24, and remove the hash from the beginning of the line so it reads simply spindown_time = 24.

3. Alter the spindown_time time to any value you want. Each number is five seconds, so the default setting of 24 equates to 120 seconds (24 x 5 = 120 seconds). However, a value greater than 240 changes things—beyond 240, each unit equals 30 minutes. So, a value of 241 will spin down the disk after 30 minutes, a value of 242 will spin down the disk after 60 minutes, and so on. Setting the line to read spindown_time = 241 is a good choice, because the disk will spin down after 30 minutes of inactivity.

4. Save the file when you've finished, and reboot for the changes to take effect.

Remember that this doesn't mean the hard disk will spin down thirty minutes after you stop using the computer. It means it will spin down thirty minutes after *all hard disk access has ceased*. Often Ubuntu will do things like flush its caches or run anacron jobs in the background, meaning the hard disk can't spin down until thirty minutes after these jobs have finished.

To stop the hard disk spindown, edit the hdparm.conf once again, and put a hash (#) before the spindown_time line. Then save the file, and reboot the computer.

For laptop power-saving tricks, see Tip 5, on page 53, and Tip 106, on page 147.

129 View the GNOME Desktop Version

You might find that some software you want to install requires a particular version of the GNOME desktop to function correctly. To find out the version number, click Help → About GNOME. For instance, the default version shipped with Ubuntu Hardy Heron (8.04.1) is 2.22.2.

To learn the Ubuntu version number, see Tip 62, on page 112.

130 Avoid GNOME Startup Errors

Every now and again I see the following error message when booting into GNOME: "There was an error starting the GNOME Settings Daemon." To avoid it appearing in the future, I clean out my /tmp folder, which contains temporary files. Start by logging out so that you're back at the login screen. Then switch to a virtual terminal (Ctrl+Alt+F2), and log in. Then type sudo telinit 1. This will switch to the first run level and shut down the graphical subsystem. On the menu that appears, select the root - Drop to root shell prompt option, and then type the following (exactly as written—be careful not to mistype!):

```
# rm -rf /tmp/{*,.*}
# reboot
```

Once your system has restarted, log in as usual. Some suggest that disabling IPv6 can also avoid GNOME startup errors—see Tip 60, on page 111.

☐ ### 131 Use FTP Under Ubuntu

When it comes to FTPing into a site, there's a wealth of choice under Ubuntu. You can use Firefox, the Nautilus file manager, or the command line.

Firefox

To use Firefox, simply type the address into the address bar, remembering to precede it with ftp:// rather than http://. Once you're connected, Firefox lets you drag and drop files onto the desktop (or Nautilus windows), but you can't *upload* files to a site.

If the FTP site requires a username/password, you will be prompted for it, or you can also supply it within the URL in the form username:password@address, for example:

```
ftp://keir:mypassword@ftp.example.com
```

Nautilus

Using Ubuntu's default file manager provides perhaps the most fuss-free and capable choice of FTP client and allows drag and drop of files to and from the server (that is, download and upload). To access a site, click any Nautilus file-browsing window, and click Go → Location. Then type the site address, remembering to include the ftp:// prefix. Once connected, you'll be prompted for your username/password, if applicable, and you'll be able to have Nautilus remember it for future access.

Following connection, the FTP site is treated like any other mounted file system, and an icon will appear on the desktop. To disconnect from the site, right-click the desktop icon, and select Unmount Volume. One handy tip is to create Nautilus bookmarks of FTP directories you access frequently. You can do this by clicking Bookmarks → Add Bookmark or just hitting Ctrl+d, as in Firefox. Once the bookmark is clicked upon in the future, Nautilus will connect automatically, as if the folder concerned were on your own computer or the local network.

Command-Line FTP Tool

The third method of FTPing provided by Ubuntu is to use the command-line ftp tool. You can connect to a site by typing the following:

```
ftp ftp.example.com
```

Obviously, you should replace ftp.example.com with the address of the FPT site. After this, you'll be prompted for your username (just hit [Enter] if it's the same as your Ubuntu login) and then your password.

After connection, ftp works mostly the same as a standard command-line prompt. ls can be used to list files, cd can be used to switch folders, and so on. The two unique but essential commands are get and put, which download and upload specified files, respectively.

Typing an exclamation mark (!)[22] will give you a shell session on your computer for quick file operations. To return to the ftp program, type exit (*don't* type ftp—that will start a *new* FTP session!).

Another useful command is help, which lists the available commands. You can then use help to ask for information about a specific command: help pwd. Once you've finished your uploading/downloading work, type quit to disconnect from the site, and quit the ftp program.

If you long for a Windows-like FTP experience of using a program such as FTP Explorer or CuteFTP that shows the site contents within a single window, then give Gftp a try. Use Synaptic to search for and install the gftp-gtk package. Once installed, this can be found in the Applications → Internet menu.

To learn how to set up your own personal FTP server, see Tip 226, on page 255.

132 Switch to Old-Fashioned Tree View in Nautilus

☐

Remember how file manager windows used to show files on the right and show a tree view of the file system on the left? This made it easy to hop from place to place in the file system.

---

22. An exclamation mark (!) is known as a *bang* in Linux-speak. You'll often hear it referred to as such in Linux documentation.

To switch back to this way of working with Nautilus, click the Places drop-down above the left pane, and select Tree. By default you'll see only folders listed in tree view. To have files listed too, click Edit → Preferences, and remove the check from Show only folders under the Tree View Defaults heading in the dialog box that appears.

For more Nautilus tricks, see Tip 72, on page 118; Tip 85, on page 132; Tip 165, on page 194; Tip 104, on page 146; Tip 144, on page 178; Tip 261, on page 292; Tip 272, on page 302; and Tip 295, on page 333.

133 Kill Any Crashed Program

When a Linux users wants to get rid of a crashed program, he kills it—literally. The kill command is used for this purpose, but it needs the program ID (PID) number to work. This can be discovered using the pgrep. For example, let's say Firefox has crashed and won't respond to requests to quit. Open a terminal window, and type the following:

```
$ pgrep firefox
```

A three- or (more likely) four-digit number will be returned—something like 7198. All you need then do is type the following:

```
$ kill 7198
```

You might also try the killall command. This lets you specify the program name—killall firefox, for example.

The kill command has a more ruthless brother, designed to click and kill GUI programs: xkill. Just type the command from a terminal window, and after the cursor has changed to a cross, click the crashed program. It will be terminated instantly. If you decide to change your mind, right-clicking anywhere will cancel xkill. Bear in mind that xkill can also terminate components of the GNOME desktop, so if the panel stops responding, for example, it can be used.

134 Increase the Number of Documents Remembered by Gedit

☐

You can give Gedit the memory of an elephant when it comes to the recent files listed on its File menu. Open gconf-editor, navigate to /apps/gedit-2/preferences/ui/recents, and change max_recents on the right to virtually any number you want. About 10 is a sensible number, but 20 or 30 are possible.

For more Gedit tips and tricks, see Tip 93, on page 138; Tip 10, on page 59; and Tip 155, on page 188.

135 Utilize All of a Sound Card's Features

☐

Out of the box, Ubuntu gives access to only a fraction of your sound card's functionality. For example, if you have a four-point surround sound system, the mixer window—accessible when you double-click the volume control icon on the desktop—won't show a fader for the rear channels. To utilize all your sound card's useful functions, including the surround sound feature, double-click the desktop volume icon, and in the mixer window that appears, click Edit → Preferences. Then select the faders and/or switches you want to appear on the main mixer window. An example is shown in Figure 3.24, on the next page.

To learn how to adjust the volume from the command line, see Tip 76, on page 122.

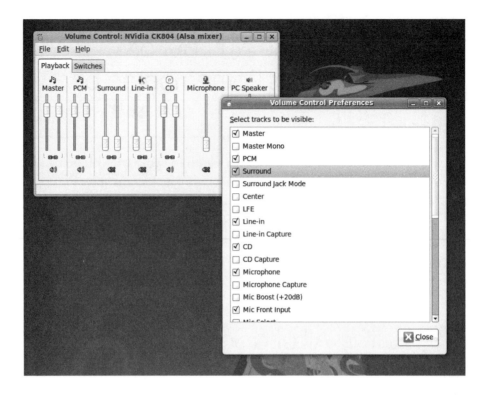

Figure 3.24: ACTIVATING A SOUND CARD'S FULL FEATURE RANGE (SEE TIP 135)

136   Monitor Network Speed

Sometimes it's useful to be able to see the speed of data transfers across the network or Internet. To do so under Ubuntu, install the netspeed package. This is a GNOME applet that shows both upload and download speeds (represented by up and down arrows, respectively). Once installed, you can activate it by right-clicking a blank spot on the panel, clicking Add to panel, and selecting the *second* Network Monitor entry in the list (it will have a description that reads "Netspeed Applet").

If the applet seems to show no throughput, right-click it, select Preferences, and then, in the dialog box that appears, ensure the correct network device is selected in the Network device drop-down list. You can discover the network device that's providing your connection by right-clicking the NetworkMonitor icon at the top right of the screen, clicking Connection Information, and looking at end of the Interface line.

If you're the kind of person who likes to monitor your network speed, you're probably the kind of person who likes to know their IP address too. See Tip 255, on page 287.

137 Make the Command Prompt Colorful

This is a simple tweak that adds a little color to the command prompt so that it's easier to pick amongst a lot of output.

Open your .bashrc file in Gedit (gedit ~/.bashrc), and add a new line at the bottom that reads as follows:

```
PS1='${debian_chroot:+($debian_chroot)}\[\033[01;32m\]\u@\h\[\033 ↩
[00m\]:\[\033[01;34m\]\w\[\033[00m\]\$ '
```

Your fingers will probably ache after typing that! Check to ensure you've typed it correctly, and then save the file. From now on, all command prompts will be in color, in both terminal windows and virtual consoles.

Changing the color scheme is a little complicated. Look at the previous command line, and pick out 01;32m and 01;34m. The first numbers refer to the coloring of the username@hostname component of the prompt, and the second refers to the path listing that comes after the colon (:).

Possible values are as follows:

```
Style
00 -- Normal (no color, no bold)
01 -- Bold

Text color
30 -- Black
31 -- Red
32 -- Green
33 -- Yellow
34 -- Blue
35 -- Magenta
36 -- Cyan
37 -- White
```

Background color
```
40 -- Black
41 -- Red
42 -- Green
43 -- Yellow
44 -- Blue
45 -- Magenta
46 -- Cyan
47 -- White
```

It doesn't matter in which order the numbers are written, and you can supply more than two (in other words, 01;34;43m). For example, to change the prompt to a magenta background with white text for the username@hostname component and green text for the path component (without bold in both cases), you could change the line to read as follows:

```
PS1='${debian_chroot:+($debian_chroot)}\[\033[45;37m\]\u@\h\[\033 ↩
[00m\]:\[\033[32m\]\w\[\033[00m\]\$ '
```

To simply make the entire prompt bold without any colors so that it's simply easier to spot in a long list of output, set the values at 01:

```
PS1='${debian_chroot:+($debian_chroot)}\[\033[01m\]\u@\h\[\033 ↩
[01m\]:\[\033[01m\]\w\[\033[00m\]\$ '
```

Bear in mind that bold text does not appear on virtual consoles. You should also check any color schemes you set against the black background of the virtual console—a common mistake is to set colors that just aren't visible against anything other than the white background of the GNOME Terminal window.

138 Make Windows Permanently Available

Do you find it annoying that, after booting, your Windows partition must be manually selected from the Places menu? Me too. To ensure Windows is always mounted, you'll need to add an entry to the /etc/fstab file, as follows:

1. Mount your Windows partition (click its entry on the Places menu), and then open a terminal window. Type mount. Look for the line that includes /media/disk, and look at the front of the line. It should read something like /dev/sda1. Make a note of this.

2. Create a permanent mount point for the Windows partition by typing sudo mkdir /media/windows.

3. Open the fstab file for editing by typing gksu gedit /etc/fstab. Add a new line at the end that reads as follows:

```
/dev/sda1 /media/windows ntfs-3g rw,defaults 0 0
```

If necessary, replace /dev/sda1 with what you discovered earlier. Then reboot. From now on, your Windows partition will always be available whenever you boot, and an icon should appear on the desktop at all times. If you want to mount the partition read-only (very wise), replace rw in the previously shown line with ro.

You will not be able to unmount the Windows partition in the usual way by right-clicking its icon and selecting Unmount volume. To do so, open a terminal window, and type sudo umount /media/windows.

If you want to return to the old way of having to select your Windows partition before it mounts, simply follow the previous instructions to edit the /etc/fstab file, and remove the new line you added. Then save the file, and reboot your computer.

139 Give the Boot Menu Wallpaper

☐

Ubuntu's boot menu is ugly and looks like it's straight out of 1985. It doesn't have to be this way. Ubuntu uses the GRUB menu software, and that's capable of having a graphical backdrop that can be any picture. However, you'll need to shrink the picture and reduce its color level. Because of this need to simplify the image, graphical designs tend to work better than photographs (I noticed that cartoon images work well too—pictures from *The Simpsons* are a particularly good choice!).

1. Choose a picture, and then load it into the GIMP (right-click, and select Open With → Open with "GIMP Image Editor"); you might like to know that the default Ubuntu desktop wallpapers are stored in /usr/share/backgrounds. You should select a picture that's roughly in 4:3 ratio, such as a digital camera snap. Don't select very tall or broad images—they won't work.

2. Right-click the image in GIMP, and select Image → Scale Image. In the Width box, type 640, and hit the [Tab] key. The Height box should then automatically change to 480. If it doesn't, click the

small chain icon to the right of the Width and Height boxes so that it changes to a broken chain icon. Then enter 480 into the Height box. Once done, click the Scale button.

3. Right-click the image again within GIMP, and select Image → Mode → Indexed. Ensure Generate Optimum Palette is selected, and then type 14 into the Maximum Number of Colors box. Then click the Convert button. The picture might now look ugly, but such a low color count is all the GRUB boot menu allows. You might want to try an alternative simpler image if you don't like what you see. A number of nice Ubuntu-themed ready-made boot menu wallpapers are available for download from https://wiki.ubuntu.com/ Artwork/Incoming/Hardy/Alternate/Grub.

4. Right-click the image again within GIMP, and select File → Save As. Give the file a name in the Name box, and use the .xpm file extension. You might save the file as bootwallpaper.xpm, for example. Bear in mind that GIMP automatically detects the file type it should save the file as from the file extension. Click OK to select the default alpha values, if prompted.

5. Open a terminal window, and type the following (this assumes the file was saved to the desktop):

```
$ sudo mkdir /boot/grub/splashimages
$ gzip ~/Desktop/bootwallpaper.xpm
$ sudo mv ~/Desktop/bootwallpaper.xpm.gz /boot/grub/splashimages
```

Replace bootwallpaper with the filename you chose.

6. Then open the boot menu file for editing in Gedit:

```
$ gksu gedit /boot/grub/menu.lst
```

Look for the line that begins ## ## End Default Options ##, and, after that, add a new line that reads splashimage=(hd0,4)/boot/grub/ splashimages/bootwallpaper.xpm.gz. As earlier, replace bootwallpaper with the filename you chose. For an example taken from my test PC, see Figure 3.25, on the facing page. Save the file, and then reboot to see the new wallpaper in action.

Note that the last step assumes your computer is dual-booting with Windows. If, however, Ubuntu is the only operating system on your computer, the line should read:

splashimage=(hd0,0)/boot/grub/splashimages/bootwallpaper.xpm.gz.

To remove the wallpaper, simply edit the menu.lst file, and remove the splashimage line you added.

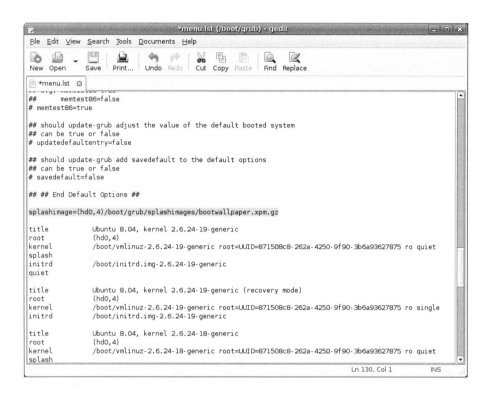

Figure 3.25: EDITING THE BOOT MENU CONFIGURATION FILE TO ADD A WALLPAPER ENTRY (SEE TIP 139)

140 Access All Removable Storage from the Command Line

Any storage device you insert or otherwise connect to from your computer, including digital cameras, MP3 players, USB memory sticks, network shared folders, and so on, will most likely be automatically mounted in one of two file system locations:

- The /media folder (this is where USB memory sticks usually get mounted).

- The .gvfs in your /home folder.[23] Note that this is a hidden folder

---

23. This book was written using Hardy Heron (8.04) as a base. This is the first release

that won't show up during normal file browsing. You must select View → Show Hidden Files within Nautilus to see it or use ls -a at the command line.

☐ | 141 | ## Reconfigure Your Graphics Card from the Ground Up

If Ubuntu just hasn't gotten it right when it comes to your graphics card and/or monitor, you can configure things manually. To do so, open a terminal window, and type gksu displayconfig-gtk. Settings relating to your monitor are located on the Screen tab, while you can change the graphics driver in use by selecting the Graphics Card tab. If you can't seem to get *any* driver to work, try clicking the Driver drop-down list and then selecting VESA from the Choose Driver by Name drop-down list. VESA is a kind of failsafe driver that uses only the most primitive parts of a graphics card and should allow you to get at least some kind of desktop visible, although performance will not be very good (video playback might stutter, for example).

Don't forget that if you have an nVidia card or certain ATI Radeon cards, you might want to select to use proprietary drivers. To do so, click System → Administration → Hardware Drivers. Then check Enable alongside the entry for your card, and once the driver installation has completed, reboot the computer. Often using a proprietary driver is the only way to get support for less usual screen resolutions, such as wide-screen settings.

---

of Ubuntu to use GVFS, a virtual file system layer. The goal of GVFS is to take care of all kinds of external storage so that everything is available in a uniform way to desktop users, but at the time of writing it's in its infancy and some devices—such as USB memory sticks—are still mounted in the old-fashioned way, in the /media folder. This is almost certain to change with the next release of Ubuntu.

142 Unlock the Package Database

□

Have you ever received either of the following errors at the command prompt when trying to install software?

```
dpkg: status database area is locked by another process
```

Or

```
Could not get lock /var/lib/dpkg/lock - open (11 Resource temporarily
unavailable)
Unable to lock the administration directory (/var/lib/dpkg/), is
another process using it?
```

What it means is that another software installation application is open, probably Synaptic or Update Manager. Only one program can install software at any one time. You'll need to close any others to continue.

143 Administer Ubuntu Using a Web Browser from Any Computer (or Operating System)

□

Webmin is some fun software designed to let a user administrate a system using a web browser. The web browser can be running in the computer itself, on another computer on the same network, or even on the Internet (provided the network is configured correctly). Webmin is geared around server configuration, but it still offers one or two tools for more humble users.

Unfortunately, it isn't contained within the Ubuntu software repositories and must be downloaded from the Webmin site. Additionally, several dependencies must be manually taken care of. Start by visiting http://www.webmin.com/download.html, and download the Debian package (if an Ubuntu package is available, download that instead, but at the time of writing both Debian and Ubuntu packages were combined).

Open a terminal prompt, and type the following, which will install the dependencies needed by Webmin:

```
$ sudo apt-get install libnet-ssleay-perl libauthen-pam-perl libio ↩
-pty--pty-perl libmd5-perl
```

Then to install the Webmin package, type the following (assuming it's been downloaded to the desktop):

```
$ sudo dpkg -i ~/Desktop/webmin_1.420_all.deb
```

Obviously, you should replace the filename with the one you downloaded.

Once installation has completed, Webmin is ready to use immediately. To access it from your own machine, open a web browser, and type the following address:

```
https://localhost:10000
```

To access it from another computer, you'll need to know your computer's IP address. This can be discovered by right-clicking the NetworkManager icon, selecting Connection Information, and looking at the IP Address line in the dialog box that appears. For example, the computer I installed Webmin into had the IP address of 192.168.1.6, so to connect from my Apple MacBook computer, I open the Safari web browser and type the following into the address bar:

```
https://192.168.1.6:10000
```

Regardless of how you connect, the first time you do so you will be warned about an invalid security certificate. This happens because Webmin uses the encrypted https:// web browser protocol, which relies on security certificates that are issued by a handful of Internet agencies. Because getting one of these certificates is impractical for every installation, Webmin generates its *own* certificate for the purposes of allowing https:// connections.[24]

Therefore, on each machine you use to access Webmin, you must tell the web browser to either ignore the seemingly insecure certificate or add an exception, as in the case of Firefox under Ubuntu—click the Or you can add an exception link when the warning dialog box appears, and then click the Add Exception button. Then click the Get Certificate button in the dialog box that appears, and then click Confirm Security Exception, as shown in Figure 3.26, on the next page.

After this, you'll see a username and password login. Type your standard Ubuntu username/password combination, and you should be

---

24. If you get hold of a digital certificate or already own one for the machine that Webmin is installed on, you can configure Webmin to work with it instead of its own self-generated certificate. Once it's installed, click Webmin on the left of the window and then Webmin Configuration. Then click the SSL Encryption icon, and click the Upload Certificate tab.

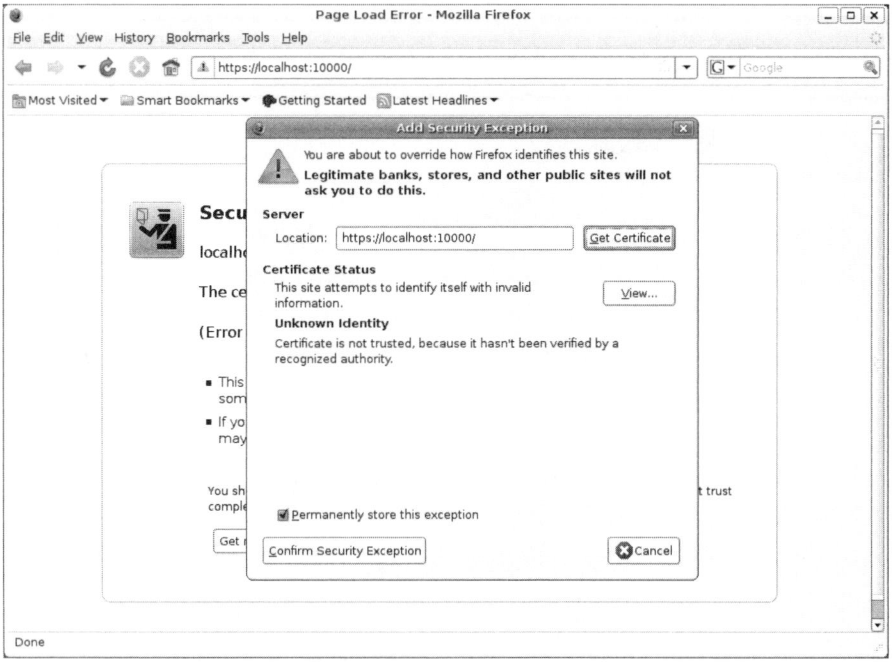

Figure 3.26: ADDING A SECURITY EXCEPTION FOR WEBMIN (SEE TIP 143)

presented with Webmin's dashboard. On the left are the system admin-istration categories from which you can choose. You can choose to add users, for example, by clicking the System link and selecting Users and Groups. You can edit the book loader menu by clicking the Hardware link and selecting GRUB Boot Loader. You can even run shell commands by clicking Others and then Command Shell.

Remember that, if you have activated Ubuntu's firewall (see Tip 37, on page 82), you'll need to add an outgoing rule to allow Webmin to be accessed by computers on the network. Bear in mind too that if you have a computer that directly connects to the Internet (that *isn't* behind a NAT firewall, such as that provided by a broadband router), then your Webmin login screen will be accessible by the entire Internet. You should ensure that you keep Webmin up-to-date if this is the case, to keep on top of potential security vulnerabilities.

☐ **144** Give Nautilus Windows Their Own Wallpaper

You can apply a colored or textured background to Nautilus windows by clicking Edit → Backgrounds and Emblems and then clicking and dragging your choice on top of any open Nautilus window. To get rid of it, click and drag the Reset icon on top of a Nautilus window.

To use your own image for Nautilus wallpaper, you must copy it to the /usr/share/nautilus/patterns folder and then add it to the Nautilus Backgrounds and Emblems selection dialog box. To do this, first copy the image to the relevant location using sudo powers:

```
$ sudo cp image.jpg /usr/share/nautilus/patterns/
```

Replace image.jpg with the filename of your image. Then open the Backgrounds and Emblems dialog box, as described earlier, and click the Add a New Pattern button. Your new image should be listed as one of the choices, so double-click it to add it to the choices of wallpaper in the Backgrounds and Emblems dialog box. Then select it in the main dialog box. Note that the wallpaper will be tiled—there is currently no way to center or stretch wallpaper in Nautilus windows.

For more Nautilus tricks and tips, see Tip 72, on page 118, Tip 85, on page 132; Tip 165, on page 194; Tip 132, on page 165; Tip 104, on page 146; Tip 261, on page 292; Tip 272, on page 302; and Tip 295, on page 333.

☐ **145** Create an Encrypted File Store Accessible from Any Operating System

Tip 250, on page 280, explains how to encrypt individual files under Ubuntu, but if you spend time on many different computers and operating systems, it might be worth creating an encrypted file store that you can copy to, say, a USB stick and carry around with you. An encrypted file store is a single file that is then mounted by the system and accessed as a virtual disk drive. When you've finished, you unmount it, thus "locking" the store so that nobody can access it without typing the password.[25]

TrueCrypt is open source software and runs on Ubuntu, Windows, and Mac OS X. It's extremely easy to use, and it's very simple to create as many encrypted file stores as you need.

Installing TrueCrypt

Start by downloading TrueCrypt from http://www.truecrypt.com. Select the Ubuntu x86 .deb release. You might also choose to download the versions for any other operating systems you'd like to use your new file store under.

At the time of writing, the Ubuntu release is supplied in a TAR archive, which must be first uncompressed. Additionally, a dependency package must be installed from the Ubuntu repositories. The following commands, to be typed into a terminal window, first install the dependency, then extract the TrueCrypt .deb file, and lastly install it (these instructions assume the file was downloaded to the desktop):

```
$ sudo apt-get install dmsetup
$ tar zxf ~/Desktop/truecrypt-6.0a-ubuntu-x86.tar.gz
$ sudo dpkg -i truecrypt-6.0a/truecrypt_6.0a-0_i386.deb
```

Obviously, you should replace the filename with the one you downloaded. It's likely the folder into which the .deb file is extracted will also be different.

Creating an Encrypted File Store

Once TrueCrypt is installed, you can start it by typing hitting Alt+F2 and typing truecrypt. The following instructions explain how to create an initial encrypted file store:

1. The first step is to create your initial encrypted file, known as a *volume*. So, click the Create Volume button. A wizard will appear. Ensure Create a file container is selected, and click Next. (Note that

---

25. It's possible to create a so-called traveler version of a TrueCrypt file store, which means the computer you attach the USB memory stick to doesn't need to have True-Crypt installed. For more information, see http://www.truecrypt.org/docs/?s=traveler-mode. Of course, another method of doing this is to simply carry around the installation file for TrueCrypt on the same USB memory stick, so you can install it where you need.

the second option, Create a volume within a partition/device, might seem to suit our needs better, but creating a container file allows the encrypted file store to be transferred easily from one USB key stick to another, if need be; thus, it's the best choice here.)

2. Next, select the type of volume you want to create. The default choice of Standard TrueCrypt volume is fine. You might want to investigate the Hidden TrueCrypt volume option at some point, but it has a specific purpose and adds some complications. When done, click Next.

3. In the Volume Location text field, enter where you want to create the encrypted file store. If you plan to create it on your USB keystick, you should click Select File, click the Browse for other folders link, and then click its entry in the Places list on the left. Don't forget to type a filename in the Name text field in the file-browsing dialog box once you've navigated to the mount point. Give the filename the extension .tc. This isn't essential but will enable you to double-click the file store to open it in Windows and Mac OS X. Once done, click the Save button to close the file-browsing dialog box, and click Next in the wizard to move to the next step.

4. You'll be invited to choose the encryption algorithm you want to use. As you select from the drop-down list, the description will change to show the pros and cons of each choice. AES is a good choice for most uses. You can also change the hash algorithm if you want, but there shouldn't be any need to do this. Once done, click Next.

5. Now you'll be prompted to enter the size the archive. If you've selected a USB stick, you'll be told how much free space is available. You can't enter fractions of a GB/MB, so to enter 1.9GB, for example, you would need to select MB from the drop-down list and type 1945 into the Volume Size text box (bearing in mind that there are 1024MB in 1GB). Once done, click Next.

6. After clicking Next, you'll be invited to choose a password for the archive. As always, a good password involves both lowercase and uppercase characters and should be as long as you can make it while making it possible to remember. Avoid clichéd phrases or anything else that might be easily guessed. Click Next when done.

7. You'll now be asked to choose the file system for the file store. FAT is the best choice because it's understood by Windows, Mac OS X, and Ubuntu. Click Next when you've made your choice.

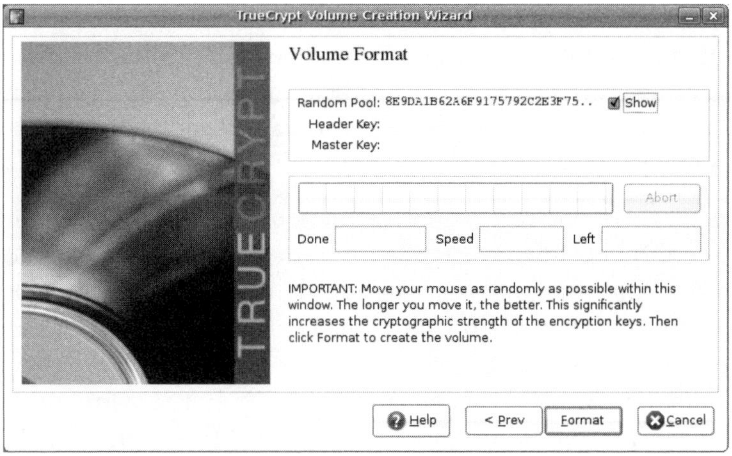

Figure 3.27: GENERATING RANDOM DATA FOR TRUECRYPT (SEE TIP 145)

8. When you click Next, you'll move to the file store creation screen. However, first you must create some random data for the encryption process. As strange as it might seem, this is done by waving the mouse pointer around within the TrueCrypt program window! So, do this for a few seconds (for an example taken from my test PC, see Figure 3.27), and then click the Format button. After this, the file store will be created. This might take some time! Once it's done, click Exit.

Accessing the File Store

After creating the file store, you must mount it so it's accessible. Follow these steps to do so and to configure your computer to do so in the future:

1. Start TrueCrypt if it isn't already running, as described earlier, and in the main TrueCrypt dialog box, select 1, under the Slot heading.

2. Click the Select File button. Navigate to your new file store using the file-browsing dialog box, and click the Open button. Back in the TrueCrypt window, click the Mount button. You'll immediately be prompted for its password, so type it. Then a dialog box will appear asking you to type your Ubuntu login password, because the mount procedure needs superuser powers. After this, a new icon should appear on your desktop offering access to the

encrypted file store, as if a new drive had been connected to the system. Double-clicking the icon opens a Nautilus window showing its contents, and you can drag and drop files to it, just like any removable storage device. You can close the TrueCrypt program window.

3. Once you've finished using the file store, open the TrueCrypt dialog box by clicking its notification area icon, select the mount in the list, and click the Dismount button. This will "lock" the file store. Then, if the file store is on a USB keystick, right-click its desktop icon, and select Unmount Volume. Note that the file store will be automatically dismounted when you log out or shut down, provided TrueCrypt is running (you'll know if this is the case because the notification area icon will be present).

4. One useful tip is, when the file store is mounted, to click Favorites → Add Selected Volume in the TrueCrypt window. From then on, you can quickly mount the file store by right-clicking the True-Crypt notification area icon and selecting Mount All Favorite Volumes.

5. To unlock a file store when it's double-clicked so that TrueCrypt doesn't need to be started manually each time, right-click a file store file, and click Properties. Then, in the dialog box that appears, select the Open With tab, and click the Add button. In the new dialog box that appears, click the Use a custom command fold-down chevron, and in the text field type truecrypt %. Then click the Add button and the Close button in the parent window. Note that this will work only if, as described earlier, you ensure all file store files you create have the file extension .tc. To subsequently lock the file store, you'll need to start TrueCrypt and use the Dismount button, as described earlier. Rebooting or shutting down the computer will also lock the file store.

☐

146 Find Out How Much Disk Space Is Available

As with Windows, you can find out how much space is free on a disk (including removable storage devices such as USB memory sticks) by clicking Places → Computer, right-clicking the drive in question, and selecting Properties. To do the same at the command line, type df -h. The -h command option is necessary to provide "human-readable" figures (that is, figures in megabytes, gigabytes, and so on, rather than in bytes).

147 Make Ubuntu Blue (or Dark Gray or Dark Brown)

□

Use Synaptic to search for and install the blubuntu-look package, and you'll get a complete theme based around the color blue. Once the packages are installed, right-click the desktop, and select Change Desktop Background. Then select the new blue wallpaper. Click the Theme tab, and select the new Blubuntu option. You'll need to log out and then back in again for the changes to fully take effect, but before doing that, click System → Administration → Login Window, and in the dialog box that appears, click the Local tab. Then select the radio button alongside Blubuntu in the list, click the Background Color box, and manually select a pleasant shade of blue from the color wheel (this color will form the background when the desktop is loading). Then log out and back in to see the full effect.

If you would like a glossy black/dark gray finish to your windows, use Synaptic to install the ubuntustudio-theme package. Then select Ubuntu Studio from the theme chooser (System → Preferences → Appearance).

If you're using Ubuntu 8.04 (Hardy Heron) and want to use the dark brown theme slated for inclusion in Ubuntu 8.10 (at least at the time of writing), use Software Sources to add the following repository:

deb http://ppa.launchpad.net/kwwii/ubuntu hardy main

and then do a system update (System → Administration → Update Manager). Log out and back in again and then use the theme chooser (System → Preferences → Appearance) to select the NewHuman theme.

For additional tips that tweak the Ubuntu look and feel, see Tip 74, on page 120; Tip 21, on page 67; Tip 79, on page 127; Tip 199, on page 227; Tip 220, on page 246; Tip 274, on page 304; and Tip 289, on page 328.

☐

| 148 | **Use Versions of Ubuntu That Are Entirely Free Software** |

Ubuntu was created from the ground up to respect the ethics and purpose of the free software movement. However, the decision was made a few years ago to include a small quantity of proprietary software in the form of graphics and wifi drivers. This is seen as a stop-gap measure until usable open source alternatives are available. Additionally, some software—such as the Firefox web browser—is covered by trademark agreements that are more restrictive than advocates of true free software ideals would like.

Currently, there are two projects to distribute versions of Ubuntu that are completely—and strictly—free software. The first is GNewSense (pronounced *G-new-sense*), which, as its name suggests, is a project sponsored by the Free Software Foundation. An installable ISO image can be downloaded from http://www.gnewsense.org. The project's major releases tend to follow those of Ubuntu itself.

The other project is Gobuntu, which is officially supported by the Ubuntu Foundation.[26] Its releases trail a little behind the official releases, however, and it currently uses the text-mode (alternate) installer, rather than the live distro installer. It can be downloaded from http://cdimage.ubuntu.com/gobuntu/releases/, while more information can be found at http://www.ubuntu.com/products/whatisubuntu/gobuntu.

The Ubuntu install CD also includes an option that will cause the installer not to install proprietary drivers and also disable the restricted and multiverse software repositories that contain software of a nonfree nature. At the install CD boot screen, move the highlight using the cursor keys so that Install Ubuntu is selected, and then hit F6 twice. Then highlight Free Software Only on the menu that appears, again using the cursor keys. Hit Enter, then hit Esc, and finally hit Enter to start installation. Note that this doesn't remove software of questionable trademarking.

---

26. At the time of writing, it seems Gobuntu might be heading for the rocks. Mark Shuttleworth has suggested that effort should be invested in GNewSense instead.

You might also be interested in Tip 80, on page 127, which describes how to use the open source OpenSolaris remix of Ubuntu.

149 Install OpenOffice.org's Database Component

☐

OpenOffice.org Base—the database component of the venerable office suite—isn't installed out of the box. This is because it simply wouldn't fit on the install CD. This is a shame because Base offers a very simple and usable front end to database creation and maintenance, just like Microsoft Access. To install Base, use Synaptic to search for and install openoffice.org-base. Once installed, you'll find it on the Applications → Office menu.

150 Monitor Your Computer's Temperature and Fan Speeds

☐

Some people just like to have a virtual dashboard on their computer, showing the temperature their computer is running at, along with the speed of fans in the computer. If you have a high-performance computer, this can be very useful in diagnosing crashes because of overheating. To see this kind of information in Ubuntu, use Synaptic to search for and install sensors-appplet. Once done, reboot your computer. When the desktop reappears, right-click a blank spot on the panel, click Add to panel, and then select Hardware Sensors Monitor from the list.

The information used by sensors-appplet is supplied by kernel modules, and not all computers are fully compatible. You'll know if you see patently false information (such as temperature readings of zero), although you might first check to ensure the applet is viewing your hardware configuration correctly—right-click the applet, click Preferences, and then click the Sensors tab.

To monitor your CPU load or alter the CPU speed on the fly, see Tip 240, on page 273 and Tip 106, on page 147, respectively.

151 Print Multiple Photos on One Sheet of Paper

Got a lot of pictures to print but not a lot of paper? To print small pictures, with many to a page, use GNOME Photo Printer—use Synaptic to search for and install gnome-photo-printer; it can be found on the Applications → Graphics menu once installed.

Start by clicking and dragging photos onto the GNOME Photo Printer program window (ensure the Files tab is selected). Then click the Layout tab, and select the size you'd like each photo to be. Very small sizes are possible using the Custom option. The aspect ratio of each picture will be preserved, so you needn't get the exact dimensions right here. Once done, click the Print Preview button to see how it all looks. You might find you're able to get more pictures into a single page by switching to landscape—click the Paper tab, and select the option beneath the Page orientation drop-down list. To really cram pictures onto a page, try reducing the margin sizes too, under the Margins heading.

Once done, ensure the correct printer is selected in the Printer tab, and then click the Print button.

Of course, there's no reason why GNOME Photo Printer can't be used to print just two or four pictures on a sheet of paper for use in the likes of photo frames, provided the correct image size is set under the Layout tab.

152 Try Some Alternative Web Browsers

Konqueror, Epiphany, Seamonkey, and Midori are just some of the alternative web browsers available under Ubuntu that can make a good alternative to Firefox. All can be installed from Synaptic (search for epiphany-browser in the case of Epiphany).

Konqueror usually comes installed on versions of Linux using the KDE desktop. While most don't have any complaints about Firefox, Konqueror is said to be faster and more compatible with web standards.

Epiphany is officially the GNOME default browser and is built using the same Mozilla technology as Firefox, although most versions of Linux built using GNOME rely on Firefox instead. However, Epiphany mirrors the overall look and feel of the GNOME desktop and is a true GNOME application. For example, you can redefine the menu shortcuts by following Tip 254, on page 286, something you can't do with Firefox.

Seamonkey is the new name of the old Netscape Communicator browser suite, and as such, it includes an email client and news reader alongside a browser and even an HTML creation tool. If you were a fan of Netscape Communicator in its heyday, it's definitely worth trying.

Midori is a newcomer to the scene and uses the Webkit rendering engine, rather than Mozilla, for its web browsing back end. Webkit is used in Apple's Safari web browser and was originally based on Konqueror's KHTML engine, so it comes with a good pedigree. It's a good choice to use in the unlikely event that a page doesn't render correctly using Firefox.

Once installed, you can make any of these browsers the system default by clicking System → Preferences → Preferred Applications. Then, in the Web Browser drop-down list, make your choice. Now, whenever you click a link in an email (or similar), the alternative browser will start instead of Firefox.

153 Quickly Hide/Unhide Windows Using the Keyboard

Ubuntu can "roll up" windows to just their title bars (known as *shading*), but the function isn't activated by default. However, the function can be coupled to a keyboard shortcut so that you can quickly roll up a window to see what's behind it, before unrolling it again (for example, if you're typing something you've seen on a Firefox web page into a terminal window). To set this up, start Keyboard Shortcuts (System → Preferences), and scroll down to the Toggle Shaded State entry in the list. You'll need to use a keyboard shortcut not already in use and also one that you won't accidentally press. I find Ctrl + Alt + Space works pretty well, so click in the shortcut column alongside the entry in the list, and then hit the shortcut combination (that is, hit Ctrl + Alt + Space —don't type the words!). Then give it a try on the Keyboard Shortcuts window—

roll it up, and then roll it down! If you want to get rid of the shortcut, repeat the previous step to create a new shortcut combination for the entry, and hit Backspace (not Delete!).

154 Convert Images from One Format to Another at the Command Line

Although you can fire up the GIMP to convert an image from one format to another, it's something of a sledgehammer to crack a nut, and time-consuming too. An easier way is to use the Imagemagick software. You'll need to use Synaptic to install it first, however (search for and install the imagemagick package). Once installed, simply use the convert command. The command is intelligent enough to work out what you're trying to do from the filenames you give it. For example, the following will use Imagemagick to convert filename.jpg into a bitmap file:

```
$ convert filename.jpg filename.bmp
```

If you're converting an image into a JPEG file, which sacrifices image quality for file size, you might want to add the -quality command switch. Here you can set a value between 0 (poorest quality) to 100 (highest quality); better quality equates to larger file sizes. Most consider settings of between 60–80 good enough for most uses. The following will convert filename.bmp into a JPEG image with a quality setting of 80:

```
$ convert -quality 80 filename.bmp filename.jpg
```

For more command-line image conversion tips, see Tip 11, on page 60, and Tip 214, on page 239.

155 Significantly Expand Gedit's Functionality

In my humble opinion, Gedit is one of the most amazing text editors in the world. It goes far beyond the usual confines of editors, not least because it's extensible—it utilizes a plug-in structure. Amazingly, not all the plug-ins it comes with are enabled by default, and you can enable more by clicking Edit → Preferences and then clicking the Plugins tab. Put a check alongside those you want to activate. If the plug-in has options you can configure, the Configure Plugin button will stop being gray. My favorites? Change Case is useful, as is Snippets, which lets you paste familiar chunks of text (particularly useful for programmers). Once a plug-in is activated, you'll most likely be able to access its functionality from the Tools menu in Gedit, although some, such as the Change Case plug-in mentioned earlier, add an entry to other menus (in this case, the Edit menu).

You can download even more plug-ins from http://live.gnome.org/Gedit/Plugins.

For other Gedit tricks, see Tip 10, on page 59; Tip 134, on page 167; and Tip 93, on page 138.

156 Make New Mail Windows Taller

Whenever I start a new mail in Evolution, the first thing I do is click and grab the resize handle and make it bigger. Maybe I just write a lot in my emails, but I realized I could avoid it happening in the future by tweaking a gconf-editor setting. Once the program has started, head over to /apps/evolution/mail/composer, and change the height key to something like 600 or 700, depending on the resolution of your screen (the value simply refers to the number of pixels). The changes take effect immediately—try creating a new mail to see what happens.

For more Evolution and general email hacks, see Tip 42, on page 90; Tip 7, on page 54; Tip 158, on the next page; Tip 172, on page 200; Tip 246, on page 277; and Tip 260, on page 291.

157 Avoid Making Badly Burned CD-R/RW Discs

Some CD-R/RW drives use so-called BurnProof technology to avoid buffer underrun errors that result in unusable discs. This will probably be activated by default in the drive's hardware, but you might as well make the GNOME desktop attempt to activate it, in case it isn't. To do so, start gconf-editor, navigate to /apps/nautilus-cd-burner, and then put a check in the burnproof box.

To learn how to activate the equally useful overburn mode of CD-R/RW drives, see Tip 27, on page 72.

☐

| 158 | Import Email Messages from Outlook and/or Outlook Express |

If you're a former Windows user with a huge Outlook archive (.pst file) packed full of messages and you would dearly love to import these into Evolution, then you're in luck. Evolution can't understand .pst files out of the box, but you can install Mozilla Thunderbird under Windows and then use it to import the .pst file. Thunderbird uses the industry-standard mbox file for its mail store, and you can then import this into Evolution under Ubuntu.

Here are the steps:

1. First you'll need to remove any password protection from the .pst file. You'll have to delve into Outlook's Tools → Options menu to do this. (On Outlook 2003, I clicked the Mail Setup tab and then clicked the Data Files button; after this, I clicked the Settings button and clicked Change Password. Then I left the new password fields blank.)

2. Still in your Windows system, download and install Thunderbird (http://www.mozilla.com/thunderbird). Quit Outlook, and during the first run of Thunderbird that happens immediately after installation, select to import from Outlook (and/or Outlook Express, if applicable).

3. Thunderbird should now list your Outlook messages. Now, within Thunderbird, click Tools → Account Settings, and look in the Local Directory text field. This is where your all-new mbox files are stored. Make a note of the location.

4. Boot Ubuntu, and mount your Windows partition by selecting its entry on the Places menu. Start Evolution, and then click File → Import. In the dialog box that appears, select Import a Single File.

Then click the Filename drop-down list to browse to the location you noted earlier (remember that your Windows partition will be mounted at /media/disk). The mbox files are in the Mail/Local Folders folder of the Thunderbird profiles folder. The mbox files have no file extension but will be simply called Inbox, Sent, Trash, and so on. Once you've selected the file, you'll be asked where you want to import the messages into within Evolution—Inbox, Sent, and so on. Once you click the Import button, the messages will begin to appear. You can repeat this step to import all the Thunderbird mbox files.

159 Use the Mac OS "Quit" Keyboard Shortcut

If you've just switched from Mac OS, you might be used to hitting ⌷Command⌷+⌷q⌷ to quit a program. Ubuntu prefers ⌷Alt⌷+⌷F4⌷ (like Windows), but using ⌷Command⌷+⌷q⌷ can be a hard habit to break.

Therefore, to bring this little piece of Mac to the Ubuntu world, open gconf-editor, head over to /apps/metacity/window_keybindings, and look for the close key in the list on the right. Then double-click the entry, and change it to read <Super>q. This will cause an open application to close when the Windows key plus ⌷q⌷ is hit (when a Mac keyboard is being used, the Command key equates to the Windows key). Try your new shortcut for the first time to close the gconf-editor window!

160 Switch to bash If sh Is in Use

Sometimes, particularly if things go wrong, you might find yourself dumped to the simple Bourne Shell (sh) command prompt in order to rescue the system. sh is pretty primitive, and depending on the version in use and how it's set up, it might not have useful features like ⌷Tab⌷ autocomplete. You'll know if this is the case because the prompt will probably be a simple dollar ($) or hash (#) sign. To switch to bash, just type bash. If that doesn't work, you may have to specify the exact path: /bin/bash.

To find out which shell you're currently using, type ps -p $$, and look under the CMD heading.

161 Instantly Edit a File When You're Viewing It in less

Have you ever been viewing a file in less and wanted to start editing it? Just hit [v]. This will open it in the nano text editor.

162 Access Ubuntu's Desktop from Any Computing Device

The Ubuntu Remote Desktop software (available via System → Preferences → Remote Desktop) is designed to let another computer take control of your desktop across a network or the Internet.

It's based on VNC, an established open source technology, and there are versions of the software for virtually every type of computing platform, including handhelds (and, of course, the various Windows and Mac OS operating systems). Just search Google for a version for your particular computer—because the original VNC is open source, there are many ports of the original. Beware that one or two organizations charge a fee for VNC, however.

TightVNC (http://www.tightvnc.com) is a good choice if you're running Windows, although a cross-platform Java version is also available. Chicken of the VNC (http://sourceforge.net/projects/cotvnc/) is considered a good choice for Mac OS X.

VNC usually comes in two separate components: server and viewer. To access a remote computer's desktop, you'll need the viewer program. To make your desktop accessible from another computer, you'll need the server component. Both are already installed on Ubuntu, although to activate the server component, you'll need to click System → Preferences → Remote Desktop and click Allow other users to view your desktop.

163 Remove the Annoying Delay When Installing Firefox Extensions

☐

If you install Firefox extensions (Tools → Add-ons with the Firefox program window), there will be a three-second delay before the Install Now button becomes active. This is there for a good reason—to ensure you don't just click it automatically without first reading what the dialog box says you're about to install. To eliminate (or just reduce) the delay, type about:config in Firefox's address bar, and click the I'll be careful, I promise button. Then, in the Filter text area, type security.dialog_enable_delay. Double-click the entry under the Value heading, and change it to read 0, for no delay, or perhaps 1000, for a one-second delay (the units are milliseconds).

164 View Technical Details of Your PC's Hardware

☐

GNOME Device Manager used to be a standard feature of Ubuntu but, for some reason, isn't any longer. You can still install it using Synaptic—search for and install gnome-device-manager. Once installed, you'll find it on the Applications → System Tools menu. To significantly enhance its usability, click View → Device Properties in the program window. This adds a second Properties tab to the display that shows the technical details about each application. In some ways it's an information overload, but it can prove vital when problem solving.

In most ways, GNOME Device Manager is similar to its Windows counterpart. The main difference is that it's purely an informational tool, with no ability to change drivers or configurations. The other difference is that just because hardware appears in the list under GNOME Device Manager doesn't mean it's set up for use under Ubuntu. GNOME Device Manager's list is produced by simply probing the hardware and reporting what it finds.

lspci and lsusb do a similar job at the command line. You can use the -v, -vv, and -vvv commands with lspci, depending on how much information you would like returned (-vvv providing the most information). lsusb takes a simpler -v command option if you require more information.

Also worth investigating for command-line hardware diagnosis is hwinfo, which you can install via Synaptic. This provides extremely detailed lists of hardware connected to the system, and it's usually best to pipe its lengthy output to a viewer application (hwinfo|less). hwinfo also takes the --short command option to reduce the volume of its output slightly.

165 Switch to Old-Fashioned "Spatial Browsing" Mode

Nautilus can work in two separate modes. The default, in which you see a toolbar and the window is "reused" to show the contents of each folder you double-click, is *browse* mode. The other mode is *spatial browsing*, and you might already be aware of how it works because it's how file-browsing windows used to work in the days of Windows 95—every time you navigate to a new folder, a new browsing window opens.

Some people swear by spatial browsing, although quite a few others find it annoying. If you want to try it, click any open Nautilus window, and click Edit → Preferences. Select the Behavior tab, and remove the check alongside Always open in browser windows. Then close all Nautilus windows, and open a new one. Note that spatial browsing Nautilus windows have an additional feature in the form of a drop-down list showing the current browsing hierarchy. This is found in the bottom left of the window, and it lets you both find out where you are in the file system and also change to a parent folder quickly and easily.

For more Nautilus tricks, see Tip 72, on page 118; Tip 85, on page 132; Tip 132, on page 165; Tip 104, on page 146; Tip 144, on page 178; Tip 261, on page 292; Tip 272, on page 302; and Tip 295, on page 333.

166   Clear the Package Cache

If you're running tight on disk space, you can try deleting the cache of package files. By default, the APT system keeps all the packages it has downloaded in case they're needed in the future. It's rare this is the case (and, anyway, assuming you have a decent always-on Internet connection, you can just download afresh if you need to do so).

To clear the package cache in Synaptic, click Settings → Preferences, and click the Files tab. Then click the Delete Cached Package Files button. To clear the cache from the command line, type the following:

```
$ sudo apt-get clean
```

167   Search man Pages

Whenever you read a man page, it's likely you'll be looking for a particular term, such as a command option. You can search by hitting the forward slash key (/) and typing your search query at the prompt that appears. Then hit Enter. The document will scroll to the example found, which will be at the top of the terminal window. Every other instance of the search term will now be highlighted. You can simply move through the document using the cursor keys or type n to jump straight to the next example of the search term (typing a slash once again also does this). Shift+n will search backward.

If you want to search for a character, you need to "escape" the character by typing a backslash, just like with filenames (see the sidebar on page 22). To search for the dollar symbol ($) in a man page, you would hit / to open a search prompt and then type \$.

If you want to search *all* man pages for a particular term, use the apropos command at the prompt. Let's say you wanted to search for any man page that discussed fonts. To do this, you could type the following:

```
$ apropos font
```

This will return the line from any man page that the search term is on, alongside the name of the man file.

If you're searching for a phrase, enclose it in quotes:

```
$ apropos "font name"
```

168 Convert a PDF to an Image

Not every computer has a PDF viewer, and not everybody likes handling PDF documents. Sometimes the best policy is to convert a PDF to an image. To do this, first install the imagemagick package using Synaptic, then open a terminal window, and type the following (this will convert filename.pdf to filename.png):

```
$ convert filename.pdf filename.png
```

You can specify a different file type by changing the file extension of the second file—to output bitmap files, for example, you could alter the previous example to read convert filename.pdf filename.bmp.

A separate image file will be outputted for each page of the PDF file, and they will be numbered sequentially from 1 onward (in other words, filename1.png, filename2.png, filename3.png, and so on).

For more PDF manipulation tips, see Tip 116, on page 153; Tip 189, on page 218; Tip 215, on page 240; and Tip 258, on page 289.

169 Use a Dial-Up Modem

Like all Linuxes, Ubuntu has spotty support when it comes to dial-up modems (those used to dial into ISPs over the phone line). Some work. Some don't. Generally speaking, those that work tend to be older models that connect via the serial port or newer, more expensive models that connect via USB (more expensive models have dedicated modem hardware, rather than relying on software drivers to handle the decoding, which is what causes problems for Ubuntu).

If your modem works, you can use the gnome-ppp software to connect/disconnect. It can be installed via Synaptic and, once it's installed, you'll find it on the Applications → Internet menu. When running it for the first time, click the Setup button, and then click the Detect button under the Modem heading in the dialog box that appears. Once done, click Close to return to the main dialog box, where you can enter your ISP's username, password, and phone number. Then click Connect to dial up.

When connected, gnome-ppp minimizes to the notification area. Right-click it to disconnect from the call.

170 Steal the Windows (or Mac OS) Fonts

Some Windows fonts are ubiquitous (Arial, Times New Roman, Verdana, and so on) to the extent that websites and business documents demand them. There are two ways of grabbing them for your Ubuntu system. The first, and easiest, is to use Synaptic to search for and install the msttcorefonts package. This will give you the Microsoft Core Web Fonts, which includes most of the popular ones. Note that during installation you'll be warned about needing to install Debian Font Manager. This can be ignored—just click Next when it appears.

The other way to get the fonts is to steal them from your Windows or Mac OS X installation. This is better in some ways because you can grab all the fonts included with Windows and Mac OS X (including some like Tahoma that aren't provided by the msttcorefonts package), as well as those installed subsequently by other applications, such as Microsoft Office.

Importing Fonts from Microsoft Windows

To import fonts if you dual-boot with Windows, follow these steps:

1. Access the Windows/fonts folder in your Windows partition—it's usually called something similar to Fonts and can be found in the Windows folder. Then, click View as List in Nautilus, and then click the Type heading to sort by file extension. [Shift]-click to select all the TrueType fonts; then right-click the selection, and select Copy. You can see an example in Figure 3.28, on the next page.

2. Use Nautilus to browse to your /home folder. Then right-click, select Create Folder, and type fonts as its name. Once it's created, double-click it. Then right-click anywhere in the empty space, and select Paste. Once the files have been copied across, return to your

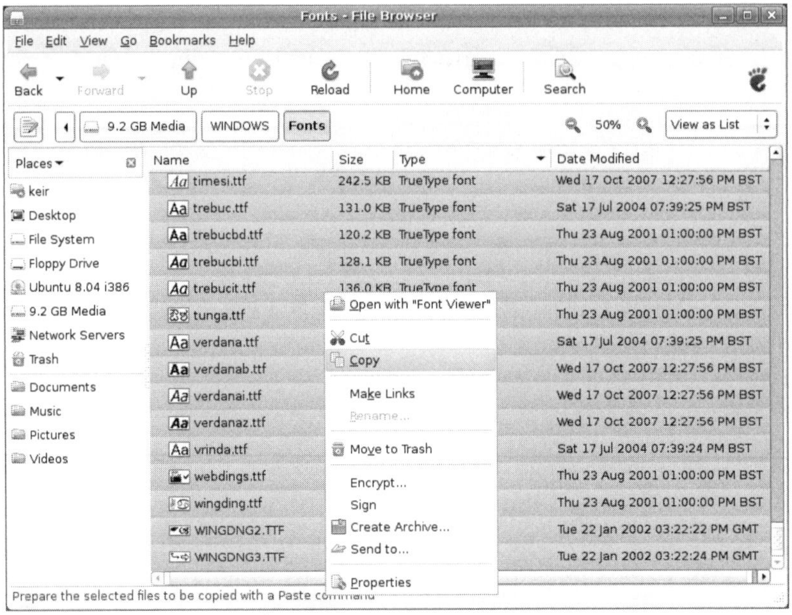

Figure 3.28: Selecting Windows fonts for importing into Ubuntu (see Tip 170)

/home folder, and rename the fonts folder to .fonts. Note that this makes it into a hidden folder—to access it in the future in Nautilus, you will need to click View → Show Hidden Files.

Your fonts will now be available in all applications, although you will have to restart any applications that are running (Firefox, OpenOffice.org, and so on) so they can make use of them.

Import Fonts from Macintosh OS X

To import fonts from your Mac OS X partition, a little more work is required. Generally speaking, Mac fonts are usually either in TrueType form (.ttf), as with Windows, or .dfont, in which case they must be converted using the fondu tool.

Here are the necessary steps:

1. The easiest method of importing your Mac fonts is to copy all the fonts into a new folder on your Ubuntu desktop and then process them, before installing them. Do this by mounting the Mac partition (selecting its entry on the Places menu) and copying the

contents of both /Library/Fonts and /System/Library/Fonts in the Mac partition to the new folder.

2. Use Synaptic to search for and install fondu. Once it's installed, open a terminal window, navigate to the new folder full of Mac fonts, and type the following to convert them:

```
$ fondu *
```

3. Open the new folder in a Nautilus window, click View as List, and sort the fonts by file extension (click the Type heading) so you can then select all the .ttf fonts by Shift-clicking. Once selected, right-click the fonts, and select Copy. Then follow the second step in the Windows instructions to create a .fonts folder into which you can copy the .ttf fonts.

When using Microsoft or Mac OS X fonts, follow Tip 21, on page 67, to switch Ubuntu to a different type of font rendering. I also found imported Mac OS X fonts looked better if I subsequently switched font hinting to either None or Slight (System → Preferences → Appearance; click the Fonts tab, and then click the Details button).

---

171   Use Unusual Characters or Symbols

If you write in foreign languages or just use unusual symbols in your work, you might have used Character Map under Windows. Ubuntu's equivalent is found on the Applications → Accessories menu. It works in pretty much the same way—double-click the letter(s) you want, and then click Copy. One useful tip is that right-clicking a letter enlarges it.

You can make the character map fill the screen, to aid in searching, by running gconf-editor, navigating to /apps/gucharmap, and putting a check in the fullscreen box. To quit the program when it's in full-screen mode, either hit Alt+F4 or click File → Quit.

By right-clicking a blank spot on the panel, selecting Add to panel, and selecting Character Palette from the list, you can have a constantly onscreen list of unusual foreign characters—useful if you often type in languages other than your own. Click the small down arrow to the left of the applet to change the selection of characters shown. Selections of characters are available for most languages.

| 172 | Encrypt and Sign Emails |

Some people like to digitally sign their emails. This means the recipient can be sure that the email is from them. Alternatively, or additionally, emails can be entirely encrypted so that only the recipient can read them—anybody who intercepts the message along its travels through the Internet will see only garbage.

Email encryption and signing works on the principle of a *key pair*. Two cryptographic keys are created by an individual—a private one that you keep secret and a public one that you share with others, either by giving them the details in a file or by uploading it to a public key server.

The two keys work in concert—effectively, anything encrypted with one can be decrypted only with the other. When used with email, this allows you to digitally sign using your private key. Those who have the public key can check the signature of the email, which could have been generated only by you and which is also based on the contents of the email, thus proving things weren't tampered with in transit. Alternatively, anybody with your public key can encrypt an email (and/or file) so that only you can decrypt it using your private key. If you have *their* public key, you can encrypt emails so that only they can read them.

The following steps show how to set up encryption, first by creating a key pair and then by configuring Evolution to use it (note that you can skip creating a key pair if you have already followed the instructions in Tip 250, on page 280).

Creating a Key Pair

Here's how to create a key pair (note that this needs be done only once):

1. Click Applications → Accessories → Passwords and Encryption Keys to start the Seahorse application, which is used to manage all encryption keys within Ubuntu.

2. In the program window that appears, click the New button. In the dialog box that appears, select PGP Key,[27] and click the Continue button.

---

27. Ubuntu and most other versions of Linux use the GNU Privacy Guard (GPG) software, which is an entirely free software version of the original Pretty Good Privacy (PGP) software. GPG uses the OpenPGP standard, just like PGP, so the two are entirely compatible.

Figure 3.29: CREATING A KEY PAIR (SEE TIP 172)

3. In the dialog box that appears, fill in the Full Name and Email Address fields. You must type both a forename and surname into the Full Name text field. In the Comments field, you can type a short description to describe who you are, such as your location or job. This can help avoid confusion if more than one person shares the same name as you or has a similar-looking email address. For an example, see Figure 3.29.

4. In the Advanced key options drop-down list, you can choose a different type of encryption, although the default choice of DSA Elgamal and 2048 bits is considered extremely secure and also flexible enough to meet most needs. Once done, click the Create button.

5. After this, you'll be prompted for a passphrase. Essentially, this is the password that you will need to decrypt emails others have sent to you. It's important you make the passphrase something hard to guess but also memorable enough so you don't forget it. The passphrase can include letters, numbers, symbols, and space characters.

6. After this, the key will be generated. This will probably take some time. Depending on the speed of your computer, it could take up to an hour.

7. Once it's finished, you'll need to export the public key so your email contacts can use it. To export it as a file so you can hand it to others on a floppy disk or USB key stick, simply select the new key, right-click it, and click Export Public Key. You'll be prompted to save a .asc file, so do so. Then simply pass this file onto friends or colleagues, and ask them to import it as a trusted key.[28]

8. Alternatively, you might choose to upload it to a public key server. This is like a worldwide phonebook of public keys. It certainly saves a lot of effort handing the key out to your contacts one by one. To do so, right-click the new key you created, and click Sync and publish keys. Then click the Key Servers button in the dialog box that appears, and in the new window, select an option from the Publish keys to drop-down list (pgp.mit.edu is a good choice). Click the Close button, then the Sync button in the original dialog box.

Signing Email

Once the keys have been generated, signing email using Evolution is easy. Just select the PGP Sign option from the Security menu in the Evolution new mail window. However, prior to this, you'll need to configure Evolution to use the key, as follows:

1. Start the Seahorse application (Applications → Accessories → Passwords and Encryption Keys), right-click your key, and select Properties from the menu that appears. In the dialog box that appears, click and drag to highlight the text alongside the Key ID heading. Then right-click the highlight, and select Copy.

2. Close Seahorse, and then start Evolution. Click Edit → Preferences, ensure Mail Accounts is selected in the window that appears, and double-click your email address on the right of the window.

3. In the dialog box that appears, click the Security tab, and then in the PGP/GPG Key ID field, paste the key ID you copied earlier. Click the OK button, and then click Close button in the parent window. After this, you should be able to sign messages.

---

28. Perhaps it goes without saying that your contacts will need some kind of PGP email setup before they can import your public key. Encryption programs are available for both Mac and Windows—just search Google. If they're using Windows, direct them toward http://www.gpg4win.org, which is an implementation of the same GPG software used under Ubuntu.

Encrypting Email

If you want to encrypt messages for other people within Evolution so that only they can read them, you'll need to import and trust their public keys and subsequently select to encrypt the emails in Evolution, as follows:

1. Start Seahorse (Applications → Accessories → Passwords and Encryption Keys), and click the Find Remote Keys button. In the dialog box, type the email address of the individual in the Search for keys containing text field. Then hit Search.

2. In the search results window, select any key you want to import, and click the Import button on the toolbar. Then close the search results window, and click the Other Collected Keys tab in Seahorse.

3. You should now physically check that the key was actually created by the recipient. Ideally, this should be done in person, or over the phone, and can be done by reading aloud the key ID to them—this is listed alongside the key and is eight digits. Try to avoid using email for this task because emails can be tampered with in transit.

4. If you are sure the key was generated by the individual, right-click it, select Properties, and then select the Trust tab. Then put a check alongside I have checked that this key belongs to…. You can also put a check alongside I trust signatures from…, which will mean that any further keys you import that have been trusted by your contact will automatically be trusted by you.

   It's also a good idea to click the Sign this key button, which will prompt you to state how well you trust the imported key. Once the information has been entered, the level of trust will be added to the key, and the whole thing will be signed using your own key. These details can then be uploaded to the key server and serve as part of the PGP *Web of Trust* system that helps prove the authenticity of public keys (for more details, see http://en.wikipedia. org/wiki/Web_of_trust). After this, the new key will now appear under the Trusted Keys in Seahorse.

5. Close the Properties dialog box. You should now find the imported key is in your Trusted Keys collection—ensure the Trusted Keys tab is selected to see this.

6. If an individual has handed you their public key file in person, perhaps on a USB memory stick or floppy disk, then click Key →

Import, and navigate to the key file. Then follow the previous steps to trust and sign the key, if desirable. Remember that emailing a public key is not a good way of exchanging keys, because the key may be tampered with (or swapped with another) in transit.

7. Switch to Evolution, and click Edit → Preferences. Ensure Mail Accounts is selected on the left of the window that appears, and double-click your email address on the right. In the dialog box that appears, click the Security tab, and put a check the box alongside Always trust keys in my keyring when encrypting. This option will let you send encrypted email to a recipient even if you haven't signed their key, as explained in the previous step (if you intend to sign all keys you import, then this can be skipped). Then click OK and Close in the parent dialog box.

8. After this, to encrypt emails for that recipient in Evolution, click Security → PGP Encrypt in the new mail window. If you see an error message about a "broken pipe," it's likely you don't have that recipient's public key or you possess it but have not signed it. Check the details and try again.

173 | Get a Nice Trash Can on the Desktop

By default, Ubuntu keeps the desktop clean. I think that if your desktop isn't cluttered with icons, then you're not human (and may possibly be a robot). To add the usual Trash, Computer, Network Servers, and other icons to the desktop, start gconf-editor, and head to the /apps/nautilus/desktop entry. Then, on the right side, put a check alongside trash_icon_visible, home_icon_visible, and so on. The new desktop icons should appear immediately.

For more useful desktop organization tips, see Tip 104, on page 146, and Tip 256, on page 288.

174 Create .zip Files Using Maximum Compression

When you right-click a file or folder and select Create Archive, File Roller steps in to shrink things down. However, it will use only "normal" compression for ZIP files. This is for a reason—not all operating systems are compatible with the more aggressive "maximum" compression, and it can also take quite a bit longer to crunch/uncrunch files. Yet the savings in file size can be worthwhile, and the truth is that both Windows and Mac OS X are fine with maximally compressed files.

To switch File Roller to use maximum compression by default, start gconf-editor, and navigate to /apps/file-roller/general. Then change the compression_level key to read maximum. The changes will take effect straightaway whenever you next opt to compress a file.

To learn how to add RAR archive support to Ubuntu's compression tool, see Tip 16, on page 63.

175 Create an Ubuntu "Updates" CD/DVD

If you are installing Ubuntu afresh on more than one computer, your Internet connection can start to feel the strain as each computer attempts to download and install available updates. There are a handful of solutions, but perhaps the simplest is to set one of your new Ubuntu computers to cache the update package files and then burn the cached package files to a CD/DVD for manual installation on any other computers.

Of course, this technique can also be used if you have just installed Ubuntu on just one computer and want to create an "emergency" archive of updates, although bear in mind that the sheer frequency of

Ubuntu updates means it will become out-of-date very quickly.[29] Here's what to do:

1. Before you let the first computer update, start Synaptic on that computer, and enable full package caching. Click Settings → Preferences, click the Files tab, and ensure Leave all downloaded packages in the cache is selected. Then close Synaptic, and allow Update Manager to update the system as usual (you'll find Update Manager on the System → Administration menu if you want to force an update; hit the Check button when Update Manager starts to refresh the package lists).

2. Once the updates have downloaded and installed, select CD/DVD Creator from the Places menu, and then open another Nautilus window (Places → Home Folder). Using that window, browse to /var/cache/apt/archives/. Copy all the files ending in .deb to the Nautilus CD/DVD Burner window. Then click the Write to Disc button. Insert either a CD or DVD-R/RW, depending on the total file size of the packages.

3. On the computer(s) that is to be updated, copy all the packages from the freshly burned CD/DVD disc to an empty folder, and then type the following (this assumes the packages have been copied to a folder called packages on the desktop):

```
$ sudo dpkg -i ~/Desktop/packages/*.deb
```

Once the command has completed (it will take some time, and you will see a lot of output scroll past; this is harmless), you can delete the folder containing the packages.

4. If you want, you can now delete the cached packages from the first computer by following Tip 166, on page 195.

---

29. I once created a disc of updated packages for use on several computers I was installing Ubuntu upon. In the five minutes it took me to burn the disc and install the packages on one of the new computers, a new set of updated packages were released, and Update Manager subsequently popped up to tell me.

176 Stop Ubuntu "Graying Out" Stalled Program Windows Quickly

If you have desktop effects enabled, Ubuntu will "gray out" program windows that it thinks have either crashed or stalled. This can be a useful visual indication that something has gone wrong, but the delay before it happens—five seconds—is just too quick. Programs like Synaptic have a habit of pondering their next action for slightly longer than that, and that can cause them to "gray out."

You can alter the timeout by editing a setting using gconf-editor. Simply navigate to /apps/compiz/general/allscreens/options, and change the ping_delay key to 10000. This will change the "graying out" delay to ten seconds (10,000ms). For fifteen seconds, change the setting to 15000.

177 Get a High-Quality (and Free) Command-Line Word Processor with Microsoft Word

If there's one piece of software the Linux world seemingly lacks, then it's a good-quality command-line word processor (which is to say, one that works entirely within a virtual console or a terminal window). There are some excellent text editors, of course. There are even some text editors with word-processor-like features. However, there are none that include the likes of easy formatting tools or built-in spell checking.

The solution? Download and install an old DOS version of Microsoft Word that is now offered for free from Microsoft's website. You can then use the DOSBox software to run it. It really does work! (But you can't print—at least not unless you want to hook up your old dot matrix printer...).

Here's how to get it all working:

1. Use Synaptic to install dosbox. This is a DOS emulator and virtualization program primarily designed for old games, but we're going to use it to do some magic.

2. The first thing to do is create a virtual hard disk for DOSBox by creating an empty folder in your /home folder—you can call it anything, but drive_c is a good a name as any.

3. Download the old DOS version of Microsoft Word.[30] It's freeware nowadays and is just over 3MB in size.

4. Copy the downloaded file into your virtual hard disk folder using Nautilus. Then start DOSBox (Applications → Games), and connect to the virtual hard disk you created earlier by typing mount C foldername, replacing the foldername with the name of the folder. Then switch to the new hard drive by typing C:.

5. Still in the DOSBox window, type Wd55_ben.exe to uncompress the installer. You'll see a few errors about files that already exist. Just ignore the errors—overwrite or don't overwrite. It's up to you.

6. Once the decompression has finished, type setup.exe to run the installer. Work through the installation options. Don't let Word alter your system settings or add a new mouse driver—DOSBox takes care of all that for you.

7. Once installation has finished, type word.exe to run Word. See it in action in Figure 3.30, on the next page. It's still a useful bit of software for basic word processing tasks.

Every time you start DOSBox, you'll need to remount the virtual hard disk, and this can be annoying. To avoid this, start DOSBox, and type CONFIG -writeconf dosbox.conf. This will write out a configuration file. Quit DOSBox, open the new config file in Gedit (gedit ~/dosbox.conf), and add the following two lines to the end of the file:

```
mount C foldername
C:
```

Again, you should replace foldername with the name of the virtual hard disk folder you created earlier.

If an old DOS version of Microsoft Word is still too high-tech for you, see Tip 221, on page 247, although if you like your new DOS adventures and want to expand it into playing some classic DOS games, see Tip 281, on page 314.

---

30. http://download.microsoft.com/download/word97win/Wd55_be/97/WIN98/EN-US/Wd55_ben.exe

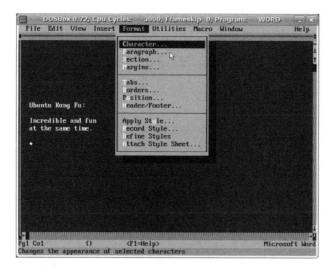

Figure 3.30: MICROSOFT WORD RUNNING IN DOSBOX (SEE TIP 177)

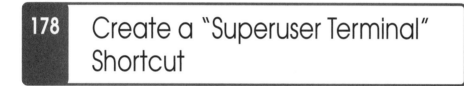

178 Create a "Superuser Terminal" Shortcut

Some versions of Linux offer a "superuser terminal," which, when run, automatically logs you in as the root user so you can perform system administration tasks unhindered (you'll need to enter your password when the terminal program is first run, of course). There's little doubt that, if you have a lot of tasks to do, this can be a useful thing.

To create your own superuser terminal shortcut, right-click the desktop, and select Create Launcher. In the Name box of the dialog box that appears, type Terminal (superuser). In the Command box, type gksu gnome-terminal. A suitable desktop icon will be automatically added (a guy flashing an ID card!), but by clicking the icon preview, you can choose your own. Leave the Comment field blank, and click the OK button. Then test your new shortcut by double-clicking it.

To add the shortcut to a menu, start the Main Menu program (System → Preferences). In the Main Menu program window, select which of the menus (Applications, Applications' submenus, System → Preferences or System → Administration) you'd like the new shortcut to appear on. Do this by selecting them in the Menus pane on the left side. Then drag and drop your new launcher to the Items pane on the right. In my opinion, the new launcher is perhaps best stored on the System → Administration menu, along with other programs that are used to administer the system and require root powers. Once the menu entry has been created, you can delete the desktop launcher if you want.

179 Find Out Who You Are!

If you use more than one user account under Ubuntu, it can sometimes be confusing to remember who you are logged in as and which user accounts are logged in at the current time (am I still logged in as user franko on virtual console two...?). To find out who you're currently logged in as, type whoami. To find out which user accounts are currently logged in, type users (bear in mind that your username might appear more than once because every virtual console login and open terminal window counts as a login). To find out which groups your user account belongs to, type groups.

180 Install Ubuntu Partner Software

Every now and again Canonical (Ubuntu's corporate sponsor) partners with various proprietary software companies to bring their products to Ubuntu. Examples in the past have included Real, the company behind the RealPlayer software, and Panda Security, which offers an antivirus program for Ubuntu. To gain access to this software, first enable third-party repositories—click System → Administration → Software Sources, and click the Third-Party Software tab. Then put a check in the first line—http://archive.canonical.com/ubuntu hardy partner. Click the Close button, and agree when the program advises that you need to reload the software list.

Then, to browse and install the partner software, click Applications → Add/Remove, and in the Show drop-down list select Third party applications. Put a check in the box alongside any you want to install, and then click the Apply Changes button.

181 Use a GUI Version of vim

☐

If you're a fan of the respected vim text editor, then you might be interested in Gvim, which is a version of the vim text editor with an added GUI. To install it, use Synaptic to search for vim-gnome.

The program doesn't add itself to any of Ubuntu's menus but can be run by typing gvim at the command prompt. Once it's up and running, you can use it just like any other version of vi/vim, typing a colon to enter commands and switching to text insert mode by hitting ⟦i⟧. However, the menus and icon bar offer access to all the usually hidden vi/vim features, as well as some new ones. Gvim is primarily built for programmers and offers the like of syntax highlighting and the ability to compile straight from the program window, but the fact it offers a GUI way of working and luxuries such as GUI file open/save dialog boxes should make it appeal to everybody!

182 Rescue a Crashed GUI

☐

Occasionally I find that a GUI program crashes and seems to lock up the desktop. If this happened under Windows, I'd be reaching for the reset button on the case, but Ubuntu is different. I'm able to switch to a virtual console and kill the errant program from there. Then, when I switch back to the GUI, everything is usually fine again.

If a similar thing should happen to you, first switch to a virtual console by pressing ⟦Ctrl⟧+⟦Alt⟧+⟦F2⟧. Then use the following command, substituting *programname* for the command-line name of the program that's crashed (tip: you can try to discern what the command-line name might be by typing the first part of what it's likely to be and using ⟦Tab⟧ autocomplete to get the rest):

```
$ killall programname
```

To learn more about killing programs, see Tip 133, on page 166.

☐

183 See a Quote of the Day Whenever You Log In

Back in the Unix days of old, having a quote-of-the-day (QOTD) appear whenever you logged on was considered the height of fashion. Sadly, it's no longer as popular, but it can still be fun and is easy to enact in Ubuntu.

Have a Quotation Appear at the Command Prompt

Here are the steps to have a QOTD appear whenever you log in at a virtual console or open a terminal window:

1. Start by using Synaptic to install signify.[31] This is a simple program that outputs lines from a text file whenever it's used. It's designed primarily for email signatures but doesn't have to be used that way.

2. Once it's installed, open Gedit, and create a new file called .signify in your /home folder. Then head off to your favorite site that's full of pithy or funny quotations. I recommend http://coolsig.com, but bear in mind that, as with all quotation sites, some of the quotations are mildly sexually suggestive. Ideally you should find a series of quotations that you can cut and paste and that are separated by blank lines between them. Avoid any quotations that include percentage or dollar signs, because they're interpreted differently by Signify and can cause problems.

3. Cut and paste the quotations into the new Gedit document. At the top, create a new line that reads % {. At the bottom of the file, so it's the last line, add % }. Between each of the quotations, on a line of its own, add % |. Each quotation can run across multiple lines and will be distinct from the next, provided it's separated by % |.

---

31. Actually, if you don't want to install and configure Signify, then there's no need. Out of the box, Ubuntu includes a similar program called fortune with ready-made mottos, literary quotations, and jokes. To use it instead of Signify, substitute fortune in the place of signify in Tip 183.

Here's what a file containing just four quotations might look like:

```
% {
A fanatic is one who can't change his mind and won't change the
subject.
-- Winston Churchill
% |
All the people like us are We, and everyone else is They.
-- Rudyard Kipling
% |
Now is the time for all good men to come to the aid of the party.
% |
And therefore as a stranger give it welcome.
There are more things in heaven and earth, Horatio,
Than are dreamt of in your philosophy.
Hamlet (Act 1, scene 5)
% }
```

4. Save the file, and then open .bashrc in your /home folder for editing (in a terminal window, type gedit ~/.bashrc). At the end of the file, add a new line that reads, simply, signify. Then save the file.

Whenever you log in at a virtual terminal or open a terminal, one of your quotations will appear at the top of the screen above the command prompt or at the top of the terminal window.

Have a Quotation Appear Whenever You Log In to Your Desktop

There's one final trick. To make your quotation of the day appear in a dialog box whenever you log into the Ubuntu desktop, follow these steps, which will create a new script and make it run each time the desktop starts (these steps assume you've followed the previous steps to install Signify and have created a hidden .signify file containing quotes):

1. Start Gedit, and create a new file called .qotd in your /home folder. Then type the following into it:

```
#!/bin/bash
# Pop-up a dialog box showing output from signify
zenity --info --title "Quote of the day" --text "$(signify)"
```

2. Save the file and close Gedit. Open a terminal window, and type the following to make the new script executable:

```
$ chmod +x .qotd
```

3. Click System → Preferences → Sessions. Click the Add button in the dialog box that appears. In the Name field, type Quote of the day. In the Command field, type /home/username/.qotd, replacing

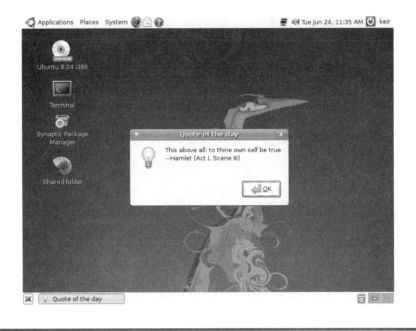

Figure 3.31: A QOTD MESSAGE APPEARING AFTER LOGON (SEE TIP 183)

username with your username. Leave the Comments field blank. Close all the dialog boxes, and log out and in again to see the results of your effort. For an example taken from my test PC, see Figure 3.31.

☐ | 184 | # Make GNOME System Monitor Appear When Ctrl+Alt+Delete Is Hit

Windows NT, 2000, and XP all bring up the Windows Task Manager application when Ctrl + Alt + Delete is hit. Under Ubuntu, this key combination brings up the shutdown window. If you want to switch to the Windows way of working and start GNOME System Monitor each time Ctrl + Alt + Delete is hit, follow these instructions:

1. Start by removing the existing key binding. Click System → Preferences → Keyboard Shortcuts, and scroll down to the entry under

the Desktop heading that reads Log out. Click Ctrl+Alt+Delete on the right side of the window, and once it's highlighted, hit the `Backspace` key. It should now read Disabled. Close the Keyboard Shortcuts window.

2. Start gconf-editor, navigate to /apps/metacity/keybinding_commands, and double-click the command_1 key. In the Value box of the dialog box that appears, type gksu gnome-system-monitor. Then hit OK. Now navigate to /apps/metacity/global_keybindings in gconf-editor. Look for the key that reads run_command_1, and double-click it. In the Value text field of the dialog box that appears, type the following (type the actual words, including the enclosing angle brackets— don't hit the actual keys!): <Control><Alt>Delete.

After this, Gnome System Monitor should start whenever you hit `Ctrl`+`Alt`+`Delete`. Unlike with Windows, you will be prompted to type your administrator password. Bear in mind that Gnome System Monitor will be running with full administrator privileges. You can kill any program by right-clicking its entry in the list on the Processes tab and selecting Kill Process.

185 Change Your Computer's Name (Hostname)

When you first installed Ubuntu, you were offered the chance to set the Ubuntu hostname, which is what appears at the command prompt and is also how your computer is identified should you activate services such as file sharing.

You probably ended up with something like john-desktop. To change the hostname to something more exiting, you'll need to edit both the /etc/hosts and /etc/hostname files. This is best done in run level 1 (rescue mode), when practically no other software is running.

Here are the steps required:

1. Log out so you return to the login screen, and then switch to a virtual console. Log in, and type sudo telinit 1. This will switch you to rescue mode. At the text menu that appears, use the cursor keys to select Root - drop to root shell prompt, and hit `Enter`.

2. Type nano /etc/hosts. Identify your hostname within the file (it will most likely be on the second line), and change it to what you want. Remember that hostnames involve only letters and/or numbers and no spaces. You should also steer clear of symbols. When you've finished making your edits, hit Ctrl+x to quit the program. Type y to save the modified buffer (in other words, save the file), then hit Enter to actually save the file, and quit the program.

3. Repeat the previous step, this time editing the /etc/hostname file. This file contains *only* the hostname. Change it to exactly what you typed earlier (it must be completely identical!). Then save the file, and quit nano.

4. Reboot the computer by typing telinit 6.

When the computer reboots, you should find that your hostname has changed. If the computer shares files with other computers, they may find that any shortcuts they created to the shared resources on your computer no longer work. They will now have to re-create them afresh by browsing for your computer as if you had just started sharing folders.

186 Reduce the Wubi Boot Delay

If you've used Wubi to install Ubuntu into your Windows file system, you'll be used to seeing the Windows boot menu, from which you can either choose Windows or choose Ubuntu. If you're an impatient type, you might like to know you can reduce the number of seconds this menu appears.

To do so under Windows Vista, right-click Computer on the Start menu, and select Properties. Then click Advanced System Properties in the window that appears. If you're using Windows XP, right-click My Computer on the Start menu, and click Properties. Then, in either operating system, click the Advanced tab, and, under the Startup and Recovery heading, click the Settings button. Ensure there's a check alongside Time to display list of operating system, and alter the time value to whatever you want.

Don't change the value to zero! This will mean the menu won't appear.

For more Wubi tips, see Tip 19, on page 65, and Tip 217, on page 242.

187 Swap Around the Minimize, Maximize, and Close Buttons

☐

I don't know why you'd want to do this, unless you're an inveterate tweaker (or maybe a migrating Mac OS X user), but to reorder the minimize, maximize, and close buttons, fire up gconf-editor, head for the /apps/metacity/general entry, and look for the button_layout entry. Simply rearrange the order of menu:maximize,minimize,close to the order you want. For example, to have the close button at the left of the arrangement, you'd change it to read menu:close,maximize,minimize. The changes will be instant.

The colon (:) between menu and the other words serves a specific purpose. Anything to the left of the colon appears on the left of the window bar, and anything to the right of the colon appears on the right. This is why the maximize, minimize, and close buttons appear on the right, and the menu button appears on the left. With this in mind, to create a Mac OS X–like arrangement, you could change the key to read close,minimize,maximize:menu.

Should you want to return things to normal, change the key to read menu:minimize,maximize,close.

188 Add an Uber-Start Button to Ubuntu

☐

In Tip 209, on page 234, I explained how to add a Windows Start-like button to your panel. If you want to investigate an interesting development based on the Start button concept, use Synaptic to install gimmie. Once it's installed, right-click a blank spot on the panel, select Add to panel from the menu that appears, and then select Gimmie from the list.

As you can see, Gimmie adds four new buttons to the panel: Linux, Programs, Library, and People. Each button provides access to a different aspect of your computer's functionality or your online life. Linux gives access to the file system, including removable storage devices. By clicking the Settings button, you can also administer your computer. Programs provides access to installed software—the submenus off the Applications menu are listed as buttons on the left. Library provides access to not only your documents but also to music and movies, arranged in the order you last accessed them. Finally, People ties into Pidgin to show who is currently online or who you've recently chatted to.

Give Gimmie a trial. It has all the hallmarks of being one of those radical ideas that might just change the way you use your computer.

☐ **189 View Technical Details of PDF Files**

To learn nearly every technical detail of a particular PDF file, including what software outputted it, its page size, and its creation date, use the pdfinfo command at the terminal: pdfinfo filename.pdf. If for any reason you want to know what fonts a PDF uses, use the pdffonts command: pdffonts filename.pdf.

For more PDF tips, see Tip 116, on page 153; Tip 168, on page 196; Tip 215, on page 240; and Tip 258, on page 289.

☐ **190 Connect to a Remote Computer As If You Were Sitting in Front of It**

SSH is a method of remotely accessing a computer as if you were sitting in front of it. All the data between the two computers is sent encrypted, and SSH is considered a very secure way of working. It's also very simple to use.

The steps required to install ssh and make a connection are as follows:

1. Start by using Synaptic to install openssh-server on the computer to which you intend to connect. This computer is known as the *remote* computer. The computer from which you intend to make the connection is known as the *local* computer. If it's running Ubuntu, or indeed almost any version of Linux (and also Mac OS X), it already has the software installed to connect to a remote computer.

2. Once the software is installed on the remote computer, on the local computer open a terminal window (or switch to a virtual console), and type the following:

```
$ ssh username@address
```

Obviously, you should replace username and address with details specific to your setup. The username should be for an account on the *remote* computer. address can be an IP address or the fully qualified domain name of the computer, if it has one—if you're just connecting across a local network, then it's unlikely this will be the case.

For example, to connect as user keir on a computer with an IP address of 192.168.1.13, I would type the following:

```
$ ssh keir@192.168.1.13
```

If you need to find out the IP address of the remote computer, move over to it, and right-click the NetworkMonitor icon. Then select Connection Information, and in the dialog box that appears, read the four sets of numbers alongside the IP Address heading.

3. Upon the first connection, you'll be warned that "the authenticity of the host can't be established." This is not an issue, so answer yes to the question of whether you want to carry on connecting. After this, you'll be prompted for the password of the user account you're logging into, so type it.

4. And then you'll be logged in to a standard shell session on the remote computer. Remember that the command-line prompt tells you the current username you're logged in under and also the name of the host you're logged into.

When you've finished, just type exit to log out of the remote computer and end your SSH session.

You can even run graphical applications across an SSH connection. To do so, use the following command to connect to the remote computer:

```
$ ssh -X username@address
```

Once connected, you can start any graphical application by typing its name. For example, to start Gedit, you would type gedit, as shown in Figure 3.32, on the following page. Always remember that, although the program appears on your computer, it's actually running on the remote computer. If you were to start OpenOffice.org Calc and run complex

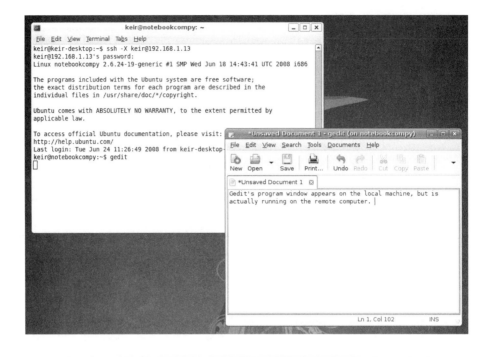

Figure 3.32: RUNNING GUI APPLICATIONS ACROSS A REMOTE CONNECTION (SEE TIP 190)

calculations, the remote computer would be the one doing the number-crunching. It then tells the computer you're sitting in front of how to draw the program window.

An additional feature of SSH connections is that you can also transfer files. This is done using the SFTP command at the prompt, which is part of the larger SSH suite of software and which works much like the FTP command (see Tip 131, on page 164). You can also transfer files using Nautilus. Open a Nautilus window, and click Go → Location. Then, in the Go To text field, type sftp://address, replacing address with the details you discovered earlier. You'll then be prompted for the username and password of the remote computer. Once entered, you'll be browsing the remote machine's files and can copy/delete files at will.

191 Change Ubuntu's System Sounds ☐

Ubuntu doesn't make as heavy use of sounds as some other operating systems, but there are still some in use—when you log in, you hear the familiar music at login, for example.

To change the system sounds, do the following:

1. Click System → Preferences → Sound, and then click the Sounds tab. As you can see, there are entries for just about any significant system event, such as an error dialog box appearing, but most aren't used by default. By clicking the drop-down entry in the list, you can select from a variety of default sounds or click Select sound file to choose your own.

   Ubuntu understands any sound file in .wav format. As you'll see from the file chooser dialog box, there are already quite a few sounds to choose from, and an additional small but basic sound theme can be found in the purple folder.

2. New sound themes can be downloaded from http://www.gnome-look. org (click the Systemsounds link on the left). Any downloaded sound themes should be copied across to their own folder in /usr/share/ sounds. Because this is a root-owned folder, you will have to do this with administrator powers—type Alt+F2, and type gksu nau- tilus. Then move the new files. Don't forget to close the Nautilus window immediately afterward because otherwise you might for- get and use it to accidentally wipe protected files.

3. Some sounds are distributed as Ogg or MP3 files, which need to be converted to .wav files before Ubuntu can use them (and before you copy them to /usr/share/sounds). To do this, you can use the SoundConverter program, which can be installed using Synaptic (search for and install the soundconverter package). Once the pro- gram starts (it will be added to the Applications → Sound & Video menu), click Edit → Preferences, and then select WAV from under the Type of result? heading. Then click the Close button. After this, click the Add File button on the toolbar to locate the Ogg/MP3 files, and then click the Convert button to write out converted .wav files.

To turn off the annoying beep that sounds whenever you hit a wrong key, see Tip 98, on page 142.

☐

192 Move Around the Command Line Like a Pro

Seeing a true expert use the command line can be a dazzling experience. The cursor leaps from word to word, and commands are executed in milliseconds. It's a strong reminder that the command prompt is by no means more primitive than more recent GUI developments. However, being a whiz at the command line doesn't take that much experience. It just needs know-how.

To jump from word to word, hold down `Ctrl`,[32] and use the left and right arrow keys. To jump to the beginning of the line, press `Ctrl`+`a`. To jump to the end, press `Ctrl`+`e`. `Ctrl`+`u` will delete everything "behind" the cursor, back to the dollar prompt. Try it to see what happens. `Ctrl`+`k` does the opposite—it deletes everything from the cursor to the *end* of the line. `Ctrl`+`w` and `Alt`+`d` do the same with any word the cursor is in the middle of—`w` deletes everything before the cursor to the beginning of the word, while `d` deletes everything to the end of that particular word. `Alt`+`Backspace` deletes the entire word behind the cursor. If you make a mistake while deleting anything using `Alt`+`Backspace` (or any of the other delete keyboard combinations mentioned here), hit `Ctrl`+`y` to restore it. `Ctrl`+`l` will clear the screen (although previous commands will still be viewable by scrolling the terminal window).

☐

193 "Scroll" a Virtual Console

One benefit of using a terminal window over a virtual console is that the terminal window records just about everything you type, along with the output. It's just a matter of scrolling the window. However, a little-known fact is that the virtual console has a similar feature, although its memory isn't quite as large. To scroll up or down, type `Shift`+`Page Up` or `Shift`+`Page Down`.

---

32. In man pages and other technical documentation, `Ctrl` is often indicated by a caret symbol (^) or by the letter C. `Alt` is often referred to by the letter M, which stands for "meta" (a relic of older keyboard types used in Unix days).

For yet more virtual console-related productivity tips, see also Tip 46, on page 98; Tip 179, on page 210; Tip 18, on page 65; Tip 198, on page 226; Tip 207, on page 232; and Tip 233, on page 267.

194   Do Math at the Command Line

Sometimes it can be handy to do simple math at the command prompt. The built-in bc command is the front end to an "arbitrary precision calculator language," and if you work or study in a field involving mathematics, it's well worth reading its man page to find out how it works. Yet, as powerful as it is, it can also be used for more trivial calculations at the command line.

To use it, type bc at the prompt. Then type in the math you want to work out, using the +, -, * (multiply), and / (divide) symbols. For example, to work out what 200 multiplied by 133 is, you would type 200*133 and then hit Enter.

By default there are no decimal places, but this can be changed by typing scale=8, which will return results with up to eight decimal places (like a standard calculator).

When you've finished, hit Ctrl+d to quit bc.

Using bc interactively can be annoying for quick sums, so you can create a small shell script that takes math as an input and then run it through bc in noninteractive mode. Effectively, this is like creating your own command that will do simple math.

Start Gedit, and start a new file called calc. Type the following into it:

```
#!/bin/bash
# Run input through bc for simple math purposes
scale='scale=8;' # No of decimal places for result
math=${scale}$@
echo $math|bc
```

Save the file, and close Gedit. Then mark the script as executable, and then copy it to the /usr/bin folder so that it will be available for all users, as follows:

```
$ chmod +x calc
$ sudo mv calc /usr/bin/
```

After this, the script can be used from the command line, in a way similar to this:

```
$ calc 203+99/16
```

This will add 203 and 99 and then divide by 16, returning a result of 209.1875.

To learn how to convert hexadecimal to decimal, and vice versa, see Tip 211, on page 236.

☐ **195   Create Keyboard Shortcuts That Use the Windows Key**

If you've tried to define your own keyboard shortcuts using the program on the System → Preferences menu, you'll have noticed that it doesn't let you use the Windows key (the keys to the left and right of the spacebar that usually have the Microsoft Windows logo on them). The Keyboard Shortcuts program sees the Windows key as just any other key, like a letter and number, so you can't combine it with any other keys to create a combination.

But a solution isn't far away. Click System → Preferences → Keyboard, and then click the Layouts tab in the window that appears. Then click the Layout Options button, and in the new dialog box that appears, click the small arrow alongside Alt/Win Key Behavior. Then select the radio button alongside Super is mapped to the Win-keys, click the Close button, and then click the Close button in the parent dialog box.

You can now use the Keyboard Shortcuts program, as mentioned at the start of this tip, to define new shortcuts involving the Windows key.

You can also make certain programs start on key combinations, including the Windows key and/or the Alt and Ctrl keys. Let's take as an example having Nautilus open in Computer view when Windows+e is pressed, a useful keyboard shortcut you might be familiar with when using Windows. The first thing to do is define the command you want to run in this instance, so start gconf-editor, navigate to /apps/metacity/ keybinding_commands, and double-click the command_1 key on the right. In the Value text field of the dialog box that appears, type nautilus computer://.

To define the actual keyboard shortcut, switch to /apps/metacity/global_keybindings in gconf-editor, and double-click the run_command_1 key. In the dialog box that appears, type <Super>e.

After this, you can quit gconf-editor and test your new shortcut. Nautilus will open in Computer display mode whenever you hit `Windows`+`e`.

Any command can be typed into the command_1 key in gconf-editor, as described earlier, with virtually any arguments or options. Additionally, up to twelve command keys are available in gconf-editor, as described earlier, along with corresponding run_command keys, where keyboard shortcuts can be defined.

You might notice that, even though you enable the Windows key as described earlier, some options in the Keyboard Shortcuts program just don't seem to work when a Windows key is used in their shortcuts, even though using `Ctrl` or `Alt` seems to work fine. It's not clear why this is, but you can use gconf-editor to alter existing keyboard shortcuts so they work with the Windows key.

Most can be found by navigating to /apps/metacity/global_keybindings and /apps/metacity/windows_keybindings—just double-click the key relating to the shortcut, delete the contents, and type the new keyboard combination. <Super> can be combined with <Shift>, <Alt>, and <Control>, in any number of combinations.

If you want to include the cursor keys in any shortcut combinations, just type Left, Right, Up, or Down. For example, to cause Nautilus to start in Computer mode, as described earlier, when `Windows`+`Cursor Left` is hit, you would change the value of run_command_1 to read <Super>Left. <Home>, <End>, <Insert>, <Delete>, and <Pause> are also available for use and correspond to the keys above the cursor keys on a standard desktop PC keyboard. `Page Up`, `Page Down`, and `Scroll Lock` must be written as <Page_Up>, <Page_Down>, and <Scroll_Lock>.

196 Create a Text File Without a Text Editor

Often creating a quick text file is necessary. The following will do the job without running any external programs other than those built into the command line. You can type what you want, including line spaces.

Obviously, replace textfile.txt with any filename you choose. Once you've finished entering the data, hit $\boxed{\text{Ctrl}}$+$\boxed{\text{d}}$ to save the file:[33]

```
$ cat > textfile.txt
```

To subsequently process the words you have typed, see Tip 221, on page 247.

197	Turn Off the OpenOffice.org Splash Screen

OpenOffice.org applications can take some time to start, and during that period, the splash screen stays on top of all other windows. To turn off the splash screen so you can get on with other tasks while OpenOffice.org starts, open a terminal window, and type the following to open the OpenOffice.org central configuration file:

```
$ gksu gedit /etc/openoffice/sofficerc
```

Change the line that reads Logo=1 to read Logo=0. Save the file. The changes will take effect the next time you start OpenOffice.org.

For more OpenOffice tips and tricks, see Tip 121, on page 158; Tip 149, on page 185; Tip 249, on page 279; Tip 295, on page 333; and Tip 308, on page 351.

198	See Which Virtual Console You're Working At

If you have a number of virtual consoles running at the same time, it can become confusing to know which of them—1 to 6—you're currently

---

33. $\boxed{\text{Ctrl}}$+$\boxed{\text{d}}$ sends an "end-of-file" (eof) message, thus ending input and causing the file to be saved. Some other commands use $\boxed{\text{Ctrl}}$+$\boxed{\text{d}}$ too, and if you read their man pages, they will say something like "...to terminate input, send eof." Because it effectively tells bash that you've finished your input, $\boxed{\text{Ctrl}}$+$\boxed{\text{d}}$ is also a quick way of logging out of a virtual console or terminal session.

switched into. To find out, just type tty. The result will be something like /dev/tty2, and the number at the end refers to the virtual console number.

For additional virtual console-related productivity tips, see Tip 46, on page 98; Tip 179, on page 210; Tip 193, on page 222; Tip 18, on page 65; Tip 207, on page 232; and Tip 233, on page 267.

199 Periodically Change the Desktop Wallpaper

Adding a bit of variety to the desktop experience is always good, and you can use Drapes to rotate the desktop background to a different image at a predefined interval or whenever the icon it adds to the notification area is clicked.

It can be installed by using Synaptic to search for and install drapes. Once installed, run it by starting a command-line prompt (or by hitting Alt+F2) and typing drapes. Upon first running, Drapes will add a notification area icon at the top-right of the screen. Right-click this and select Preferences. Once the Drapes dialog box appears, click the General tab, and check Start Desktop Drapes on start.

After this, you can add whatever wallpapers you want by clicking the Display tab and clicking the Add button. Navigate to where your wallpaper images are stored (if you want to add the Ubuntu defaults, navigate to /usr/share/backgrounds), and use Shift-select to select many files at once. Then click Open. After this, they will all be imported into Drapes and will added to the list of wallpapers to be periodically used as desktop backgrounds. They will be sorted and categorized according to size upon being imported, but you can ignore this. To vary the timing, click the General tab, and change the slider under the Timing heading.

For other wallpaper-related enhancements to Ubuntu, see Tip 139, on page 171; Tip 144, on page 178; Tip 1, on page 50; Tip 237, on page 270; and Tip 290, on page 328.

200 Get Warned When sudo Powers Hang Around

When you type your password to run a system administration application, the system remembers the authorization for a short time. If you then run another application that requires authentication, you won't be prompted for your password. This is both good and bad: it's good because it makes life easier but bad because, sometimes, the password prompt serves as a warning that the software might do drastic things to the system.

Tip 47, on page 99, explains how to eradicate the period that sudo hangs around, but as an alternative, you can make a warning dialog box appear each time a GUI application runs when it would ordinarily require authentication.

Open gconf-editor, and head over to /apps/gksu. Look for display-no-pass-info on the right of the screen, and put a check in it. The change will take effect immediately.

For additional sudo/password-related enhancements, see Tip 271, on page 301, and Tip 78, on page 126.

201 Add a "Similar Words" Sidebar to the Dictionary

This tip makes the Dictionary application return words that have similar spellings to the one you asked it to look up, such as permutations of the word. Start Dictionary (Applications → Accessories → Dictionary), and click View → Sidebar. Note that the sidebar will need to be moved because it squashes the Dictionary program window by default—click and drag its handle to do so.

202 Add Drop Shadows to Screenshots

☐

Taking screenshots of your Ubuntu desktop is easy—simply press `Print Screen` (or `Alt`+`Print Screen` to capture the currently active window). You can automatically add a stylish drop shadow to screenshots by loading gconf-editor and looking up /apps/gnome-screenshot. Then change the border_effect key so that it reads shadow. To add a slight black outline, type border instead. Screenshots are saved as PNG files with a transparent background, so the shadowed screenshot can be used against virtually any background in a document or website.

To disable the automatic addition of drop shadows or black borders, should you want, change the border_effect key to read none.

203 Create a Backup ISO Image of Almost Any Physical CD/DVD

☐

Backing up valuable CDs or DVDs is always a good idea. Ubuntu includes a tool that can back up just about any CD or DVD, whether it contains data, music, or video (copy-protected games console DVDs will not be backed up, however). It outputs ISO images, similar in nature to the ISO images that are used to distribute Ubuntu. They're simply large files containing a verbatim (uncompressed) copy of the disc contents.

To create your own ISO images, right-click the disc's desktop icon, select Copy Disc, and then, in the dialog box that appears, select File image from the Copy disc to drop-down list. When you click the Write button, you'll be prompted for a filename to save the disc as.

If you ever need to burn the ISO to a disc, right-click it, and select Write to Disc. Alternatively, see Tip 120, on page 157, which explains how to mount an ISO image as if it were a physical disk drive on your computer.

204 Change Firefox's Spell-Checker Language

Firefox includes a handy spell checker that will ensure anything you type into text boxes is correct. Any incorrect words are underlined in red. The problem is that it defaults to American English, which can be annoying for the British, Canadians, Australians, and those of other primarily English-speaking nations. The solution is easy—just visit http://addons.mozilla.org/en-US/firefox/browse/type:3, and then click the Install link alongside your language of choice. After Firefox has restarted and the next time it highlights a word it thinks is misspelled, right-click the word in question, click Languages in the menu that appears, and select your choice from the list. This will then become Firefox's default. Note that it's possible to have many different spell-check languages installed and to switch between them this way.

For additional Firefox-related tips, see Tip 7, on page 54; Tip 55, on page 108; Tip 64, on page 113; Tip 69, on page 117; Tip 163, on page 193; Tip 212, on page 238; Tip 213, on page 238; and Tip 285, on page 322.

205 Take Full Control of PulseAudio Sound Output

Ubuntu 8.04 Hardy Heron introduces a new sound subsystem to Ubuntu: PulseAudio. Amongst other things, this is designed to give fine-grained control over audio output—the sound from each application can be adjusted manually, for example (useful if you want to turn down the audio from a Flash animation without also turning down the MP3 music playing).

Unfortunately, the other Ubuntu audio control tools are lagging a little behind. The PCM component of the main volume control window that appears when you right-click the volume control and click Open Volume Control no longer controls application audio output, This means it's no longer possible to adjust the output of, say, Totem Movie Player against the volume of the CD player.

An interim solution until this is fixed is to use Synaptic to search for and install PulseAudio Volume Control (its package name is pavucontrol). Once installed, it can be run by typing pavucontrol into a terminal window, and once up and running, any application that's currently outputting audio will appear on the Playback tab.[34]

To have the PulseAudio Volume Control start instead of the standard GNOME volume control utility when the desktop volume icon is double-clicked, type the following to open the relevant configuration file into Gedit:

```
$ gksu gedit /usr/share/applications/gnome-volume-control.desktop
```

Look for the line that reads Exec=gnome-volume-control, and change it so it reads Exec=pavucontrol. Then save the file.

From now on, whenever you right-click the volume control applet and select Open Volume Control, or simply double-click the volume icon, the PulseAudio Volume Control will open instead. Note that the older volume control program can still be run by typing gnome-volume-control into a terminal window.

---

206 | Use the Command Prompt to Sleep, Hibernate, Shut Down, or Reboot

Assuming that your computer uses ACPI (virtually all computers do that have been made in the past five years), typing any of the following commands into a terminal window or virtual console will cause Ubuntu to enter sleep mode, hibernate (suspend to disk), shut down and switch off, or reboot. Bear in mind that if you installed Ubuntu using Wubi, hibernate isn't possible.

---

34. To have Firefox appear on the Playback tab of PulseAudio Volume Control when playing back Flash animations/games, it's necessary to install the libflashsupport package.

To hibernate, type the following:

```
$ sudo /etc/acpi/hibernate.sh
```

To put Ubuntu into sleep mode (enter a low-power mode, but leave the computer switched on and able to resume at a keystroke or after hitting the PC's power button), type the following:

```
$ sudo /etc/acpi/sleepbtn.sh
```

To cause Ubuntu to shut down, save your data, and close your applications; then type the following (there are *no* warning dialog boxes with this command!):

```
$ sudo telinit 0
```

To reboot Ubuntu, again save your data and close your applications, because there are no warning dialog boxes, and type the following:

```
$ sudo telinit 6
```

To learn how to do all of the previous with a single mouse-click, see Tip 227, on page 259.

207 Mirror Commands and Output Across Different Terminal Windows

To have one terminal window mirror the contents of another, first start a screen session in one of them. screen effectively allows you to create a command-line login that's independent of any actual terminal windows or virtual consoles (so if the terminal window quits, the command-line login will still be running in the background). To start it, simply type screen. Then open another terminal window, and *attach* to the currently running screen session by typing screen -x. Now try typing something to see what the effect is.

To *detach* from the screen session, in either or both terminal windows, type [Ctrl]+[a], and then hit [d]. Note that if you detach in both terminal windows, the screen session will still be running in the background. To quit it, you must reattach to it (type screen -r) and hit [Ctrl]+[d] (or just type exit at the prompt).

This trick works in a virtual console too—you could start a screen session in a terminal window and have it mirrored at a virtual console prompt by attaching to it using screen -x.

By combining this tip with an SSH remote connection (see Tip 190, on page 218), not only can you create a command login using screen that will persist on the remote computer even if the SSH connection is lost (which is useful if running commands that take some time to complete or if you're using a flaky connection), but you can create a setup whereby what you type is mirrored on the remote computer in a terminal window—just ask the user sitting in front of the remote computer to open a terminal window and type screen -x, once you've started screen in the SSH session. This provides an excellent way of remote teaching.

208 Instantly View a Load of Images as a Slideshow

☐

To instantly view all the images in a particular folder as a slideshow, just type eog -f *.jpg. This uses the Eye of GNOME default image viewer built into Ubuntu (eog), and the -f command option switches it to full-screen mode. To move through images, use the left/right cursor keys, or hit the spacebar. To quit the slideshow, hit Esc, and then quit Eye of GNOME.

Unfortunately, at the command line it isn't possible to specify how long each slide is shown for, but this can be done when the slideshow is up and running by hitting Esc to leave full-screen mode and then clicking Edit → Preferences, clicking the Slideshow tab, and changing the Switch image after value.

The previous command assumes that the images concerned are JPEG images. If you specify a wildcard to indicate any file (eog -f *), Eye of GNOME will be confused by nonimage files and throw up an error. You can get around this by using *brace expansion* to specify all potential image formats, as follows:

```
$ eog -f *.{jpg,tif,bmp,gif,png}
```

But this can be hard to remember and annoying to type. You might consider turning the command into an *alias*—see Tip 259, on page 290—

but perhaps a better solution is to use Synaptic to install mirage. This is an alternative image viewer that's almost identical to Eye of GNOME, but it lacks the problems mentioned earlier. To use it to create an instant slideshow in any folder (even one that contains files that are not images), just type mirage -f -s *.

To create an HTML slideshow of images, see Tip 126, on page 161.

209 Use a Windows-Style Start Button and Taskbar

Ubuntu uses a dual-menu system, whereby the Applications, Places, and System menus are always visible at the top of the screen, and an application's menus appear below. This isn't the most efficient use of desktop space, and you can add a single Windows-like Start button to access Ubuntu's software and off which can be found the Places, System → Preferences, and System → Administration menus.

The following steps explain how to combine the top and bottom panels of Ubuntu into one to create a similar arrangement to Windows:

1. Start by pruning the top panel of any features you don't need. This is necessary to save space. For example, Ubuntu activates the Fast User Switcher by default (look for your username at the top right of the screen), even if the system has one only user account. To remove it, right-click it, and select Remove from Panel. You might also choose to make the time and date display take up less space—right-click it, select Preferences, and uncheck Show the date. After this, you can find the date by hovering the mouse cursor over the time display.

2. Right-click a blank spot on the top panel, and select Add to Panel. In the dialog box that appears, look for Show Desktop, and click the Add button. Do the same with Window List, Deleted Items, and Workspace Switcher. Once done, leave the Add to Panel dialog box open but move to the next step.

3. Right-click anywhere on the Applications Places System menu text, and click Remove from Panel. Then return to the Add to Panel dialog box, and select Main Menu. Click Add, and then close the Add to

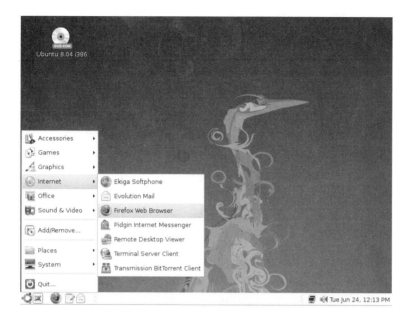

Figure 3.33: ADDING A WINDOWS-LIKE START BUTTON AND PANEL ARRANGEMENT (SEE TIP 209)

Panel dialog box. You will now have a Start-like button. Look for the icon—it will be the circular Ubuntu logo.

4. You can now delete the bottom panel. Right-click it, and select Delete this Panel. Then click and hold the top panel, and drag it down to the bottom of the screen (assuming you want it at the bottom—many people prefer to have it at the top).

5. Now you can move everything on the main panel to where you'd like it to be. To do so, right-click each item, and select Move. If Move is grayed out, you'll need to uncheck Lock to Panel. If some icons are locked, you won't be able to move anything past them, so it's a good idea to first ensure *everything* is not locked. If you'd like to add a dividing line between certain elements on the panel, right-click a blank spot on it, select Add to Panel, and in the dialog box that appears, select Separator. This can be handy in order to clearly separate the new Start-like button from its neighbors.

The previous steps reproduce a Windows 95–like Start menu, which is vertical, with submenus coming off it. For an example taken from my test PC, see Figure 3.33, on the previous page. For something closer to the Windows XP/Vista Start menu, complete with separate areas for recently accessed documents and applications, use Synaptic to search for and install gnome-main-menu. Once installed, right-click a blank spot on the panel, click Add to panel, and select the *second* Main Menu entry in the list (it will have the icon of a monitor rather than the Ubuntu icon; if it doesn't appear to be in the list, log out and back in again).

210 Change Your Password

When it comes to changing your login password, you have two options. The first is to use the Users & Groups item on the System → Administration menu. When it starts, click the Unlock button, then highlight your username in the list, and click Properties. In the Password section of the dialog box that appears, type the new password in the User password and then the Confirmation text boxes. Then hit OK. The changes take effect immediately.

The alternative (and less involved) is to open a terminal prompt and type passwd. Type your old password, and then type the new password twice. If there are other users on the system, you can change their passwords here too—just type sudo passwd username, replacing username with a username. Note that you won't be prompted to type the old password first in this case.

211 Convert Hex to Decimal (and Vice Versa)

Tip 194, on page 223, explained how bc can be used to create a script that can do simple math at the command line. As mentioned, bc has many features. One of the many other things it can do is convert decimal to hex, and vice versa (if you're wondering what hex is, you might want to skip this particular tip). To convert from decimal to hex, start bc by typing bc at the command line, and then type obase=16. Then type the number you want to convert.

To convert hex to decimal using bc, start bc, and type ibase=16. Then type the hex number, ensuring that A, B, C, D, E, or F are all typed in uppercase.

When you've finished, hit Ctrl + d to quit bc.

As with the earlier tip, a simple script can be created to carry out the conversion at the command line. To create a script that converts decimal to hex, open Gedit, and create a file called dec-to-hex. Then type the following:

```
#!/bin/bash
# Take hex input and run it through bc for decimal output
option='obase=16;'
convert=${option}$@
echo $convert|bc
```

Save the file, and close Gedit. Then mark the script as executable, and then copy it to the /usr/bin folder so that it will be available for all users, as follows:

```
$ chmod +x dec-to-hex
$ sudo mv dec-to-hex /usr/bin/
```

After this, the script can be used from the command line similar to this:

```
$ dec-to-hex 255
```

To create a similar homemade command that converts hex to decimal, repeat the previous steps, but call the new script hex-to-dec, and in the third line of the script, type option='ibase=16;' instead. You will need to change the comment on the second line too, so it explains what the script does. Then follow the instructions to mark the script as executable, and copy it to /usr/bin, substituting the different filename for dec-to-hex. The new command can then be used from the command line in the same way (for example, hex-to-dec FFC21A).

Ubuntu's default Calculator application (Applications → Accessories) can also convert between hex and decimal. To do so, select Scientific on the View menu. Then, if you want to convert a decimal number to hex, type it, and click the Hex radio button. To convert a number from hex to decimal, select the Hex radio button. Then type the hex number, and click the Dec radio button.

212 Quickly Save Pictures on Websites

Did you know that if you click and drag a picture on a website to your desktop, it will be automatically copied across? Unfortunately, this doesn't work if the picture is also a link—in that case, a new file will be created that, when double-clicked, opens the link in the web browser. This also works in reverse with a new Evolution email—drag the image onto a blank spot of the new email text area, and it will be automatically attached.

For additional Firefox-related tips, see Tip 7, on page 54; Tip 55, on page 108; Tip 64, on page 113; Tip 69, on page 117; Tip 163, on page 193; Tip 204, on page 230; Tip 213; and Tip 285, on page 322.

213 Quickly Send Web Links by Email

Nearly all of us spot links whilst browsing that we want to send to friends. Usually we have to cut and paste the email address into a new email, which can take quite a few steps. An easier process is, within Firefox, to click File → Send Link. This will create a new email with the link in the body of the email and a suitable subject line. All you have to do is fill in the address.

If even that sounds like too much trouble, install the Email This! Firefox extension from https://addons.mozilla.org/en-US/firefox/addon/3102. This is better in some regard because it lets you also send text from the web page. Once it's installed (and Firefox has restarted), highlight the relevant text in the page, and then right-click anywhere in it. Select Email This!, and then select Mail-To This! (Windows/OS-X/Linux). This will create a new Evolution email with the link in the body of the mail, along with the highlighted text and the subject filled in automatically. If you don't want to send any text from the page, just right-click without first highlighting.

214 | Sharpen Images at the Command Line

If you followed Tip 154, on page 188, and Tip 11, on page 60, you'll already have come into contact with Imagemagick. This command-line program can do just about anything to images, and you can learn more about it by viewing its man page (man imagemagick) or viewing its website: http://www.imagemagick.org/script/convert.php.

Perhaps one of the most useful functions it can perform, besides file format conversion and resizing, is to sharpen an image. Almost all images look better when sharpened, particularly if they're being shrunk for use in printing or use on websites. To sharpen an image, use the -sharpen command option with convert. The possible values to be used range from .1 up to 3. A value of around 1 gives good results.

The following will sharpen an image:

```
$ convert -sharpen 0x1 filename.bmp filename_sharpened.bmp
```

That's *zero* after sharpen and before x. Obviously, you should replace filename.bmp with the source image and replace filename_sharpened.bmp with a name suitable for the new sharpened image.

Imagemagick can also be used to process lots of images at once (known as *batch processing*), although in that case the mogrify command must be used instead of the convert command. For example, to sharpen all the images in the current folder, type the following:

```
$ mogrify -sharpen 0x1 *
```

Note that the original files will be overwritten with sharpened versions of themselves, so you might want to make backups first. mogrify can also be used in place of convert in the aforementioned tips to shrink/enlarge lots of images at once or convert lots of images from one format to another.

215 View PDFs at the Command Line

If you want to view a PDF, simply use the evince program: evince file-name.pdf. This will open a program window showing the PDF file.

If you actually want to look at the PDF within the terminal window (or maybe in a virtual console), you'll first need to convert it to text. To do this, use the pdftotext program: pdftotext filename.pdf. This will create a .txt file containing the contents of the PDF. To view it, use the less command: less filename.txt.

To extract the images from the PDF, use the pdfimages command. You'll need to specify the filenames for the pictures and also the -j command option to ensure the photographic images are outputted as JPEG. For example, the following:

```
$ pdfimages -j filename-pdf pictures
```

...will extract the images as JPEGs and give them filenames beginning with pictures. So, the first might be pictures-001.jpg, the second pictures-002.jpg, and so on.

You can also convert PDFs to images by following Tip 168, on page 196. For other PDF tips, see Tip 116, on page 153; Tip 189, on page 218; and Tip 258, on page 289.

216 Run Windows Programs Under Ubuntu

You might have heard about Wine, the software that re-creates much of the Windows infrastructure under Linux so you can run some Windows software (not, unfortunately, *all* Windows software; newer titles in particular tend to be nonstarters. For details of the success or otherwise of particular Windows programs, see http://appdb.winehq.org).

There isn't space in a quick tips book like this to explain how to use Wine, but here are some tips:

- Wine can be installed by using Synaptic to search for and install the wine package. It's strongly advised you install the msttcorefonts

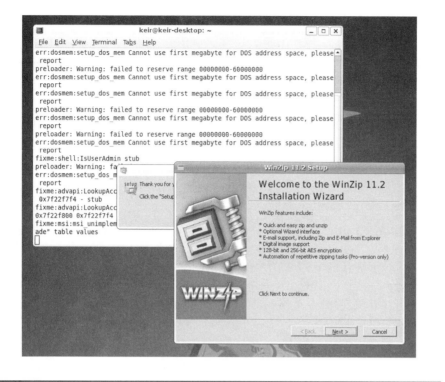

Figure 3.34: Installing Windows applications using Wine (see Tip 216)

package to install the Windows fonts and also the nas package, which provides enhanced sound support. However, Ubuntu versions can be a little behind the main Wine release, so you might want to add the official Wine repositories—see http://www.winehq. org/site/download-deb for details. However, don't assume that the newest version is always the best; sometimes newer releases break compatibility with some Windows programs. Often you upgrade at your peril!

- To run a Windows program, just download it (or insert the CD/ DVD), and then precede its installation program filename with wine. For example, to run the WinZip installer, I simply typed wine winzip112.exe. For an example, see Figure 3.34.

- Wine creates a whole fake C:\ drive when it's first run, but it's hidden within your /home folder. To access it, type cd ~/.wine/.drive_c. Then, to run any program, for example those from the Program Files folder, once again precede their .exe filenames with wine. Remember that filenames including spaces need to be enclosed in quotation marks, for example: wine ".wine/drive_c/Program Files/Internet Explorer/iexplore.exe".

- If a Windows program prompts you to reboot, you don't actually have to reboot! Instead, issue the wineboot command at the terminal.

- Bear in mind that Wine likes to provide lots of debug feedback in the form of worrying messages when it runs any Windows program. You can ignore this.

- The program Wine Doors (http://www.wine-doors.org) makes setting up and using Wine much easier and provides a centralized GUI configuration program that will walk you through installing certain Windows applications. For best results, this should be installed before Wine is used for the first time, so it can set up things correctly.

- Lots of software won't install unless Internet Explorer is installed. This can be done using Wine Doors. Installing Internet Explorer using Wine Doors will also install other useful Windows software, such as the DCOM98 system files, which helps many programs work under Wine.

- Wine can be difficult to get the most from, so you might be interested to hear that a handful of commercially sold versions are available that not only automate the installation of popular applications but also iron out some of the bugs that stop applications working. CrossOver Office (http://www.codeweavers.com) will let you run many Windows applications and games, including many recent examples (including versions of Microsoft Office up to Office 2003), while Cadega (http://www.transgaming.com) concentrates on games.

217 Uninstall Ubuntu If Wubi Has Been Used

If you want to uninstall Ubuntu and have used Wubi, resist the temptation just to delete the C:\ubuntu folder. This will remove the Ubuntu system files but leave behind the boot menu entry. Instead, browse to C:\ubuntu, and double-click Uninstall-Ubuntu.exe.

For other Wubu-related tips, see Tip 19, on page 65, and Tip 186, on page 216.

218 See a Visual Representation of File and Folder Locations

If you're new to the Ubuntu file system (or even an old hand), it can be easy to get lost while browsing the file system. As mentioned in Chapter 2, *An Ubuntu Administration Crash Course*, on page 5, the pwd can be used to get a quick reminder of the current folder, but you might also use the tree. First you'll need to install it using Synaptic—search for and install tree. Then just type tree at the prompt.

Here's what I saw on my test system when I typed the command within my /home folder:

```
.
|-- Desktop
|   |-- gnome-terminal.desktop
|   `-- synaptic.desktop
|-- Documents
|   |-- accounts08.ods
|   `-- brochure.pdf
|-- Examples -> /usr/share/example-content
|-- Music
|   `-- tom gold-magic.mp3
|-- Pictures
|   |-- barbecue.jpg
|   `-- disneyland.jpg
|-- Public
|-- Templates
`-- Videos
```

It should be obvious what's what here. The folders (Desktop, Documents, Music, and so on) are represented as branches on the virtual tree and the files (or subfolders) as subbranches. What you don't see here, and which is very useful, is that everything is color-coded according to the standard color-coding used at the prompt. Thus, folders are light blue, image files are purple, the MP3 file is green, and so on.

To see only folders, and not files within them (possibly more useful), use the -d command option: tree -d. To filter the results for a particular type of file or files with a particular name, use the -P command option. For example, to filter for .doc files, you could type the following:

```
$ tree -P *.doc
```

Or to filter for files that include disneyland in their name, you could type the following:

```
$ tree -P *disneyland*
```

As if all this wasn't enough, tree has a trick up its sleeve. It can output everything as a hyperlinked HTML file. This can be useful if you need to quickly create a directory listing of online files.

Let's assume that you have a website called http://www.example.com and the local folder that contains your local copies of the site is /home/keir/ website. The following command will output a file called index.html that contains a visual tree representation of the files contained within website, including hyperlinks to the files themselves:

```
$ tree -H http://www.example.com -T "Click a file to download" /home ↵
/keir/website/ > index.html
```

First we provide the URL the hyperlinks should be prefaced with. This could be a path on the server (for example, www.example.com/files; note that you must not include the trailing slash in the path). Then we provide the -T command option, which gives the web page a header—this can be anything you want, but steer clear of symbols like !, which have specific functions at the command prompt. After this, we provide the location of the files. Finally, we redirect output into the index.html file.

See also Tip 132, on page 165, to switch to a tree view in Nautilus.

219 Create Text Banners

Some tips in this book are useful. Some less so. Some are just fun. This tip is one of them.

Start Synaptic. Then search for and install figlet. Then type the following into a terminal window:

```
$ figlet "Ubuntu Kung Fu"
```

Figure 3.35: USING FIGLET TO CREATE A TEXT BANNER (SEE TIP 219)

For what I saw, see Figure 3.35. The output is built from symbols, letters, and other characters. There's even different fonts available—take a look in /usr/share/figlet. Any file with an .flf file extension is a font. To use a different font, just specify its name after the -f command option, without a file extension:

```
$ figlet -f lean "Ubuntu Kung Fu"
```

Believe it or not, figlet did have a serious use (well, actually, its older brother called banner did). In the days of shared dot-matrix printers and sheet-fed paper, the command was used to clearly indicate who had sent which print job. The banner text would appear at the start of any printed documents, so it was clear where the sheet output could be torn off.

I like to add a figlet command to the end of my .bashrc file so that figlet runs every time I log in at a virtual console or open a terminal window. Just type gedit ~/.bashrc to open the file in Gedit and add the entire command as a new line at the end. If you want a sentence to appear, as opposed to just a single word, ensure you enclose the sentence in quotation marks (that is, figlet -f small "Greetings Professor Falken").

You might want to take a look at the unfortunately titled toilet, which does exactly the same thing but with added color. Once it's installed, try the following:

```
$ toilet -f mono12 -F gay "Ubuntu Kung Fu"
```

☐ | **220** | # Use a Macintosh OS X–like Dock

Users of Mac OS X will be aware of the Dock, which forms the central hub around which programs can be launched and activated. Avant-Window-Manager is a faithful reproduction that includes several additional features, such as customization options. For an example of it in action, see Figure 3.36, on the next page. However, it works only if you have desktop effects enabled—see Tip 74, on page 120, for more information.

Use Synaptic to search for and install the awn-manager package. This will install Avant-Window-Manager and also a useful configuration program. Once installed, you can start Avant-Window-Manager by clicking its entry on the Applications → Accessories menu.

You'll need to start by adding some program launchers to it, so click and drag your favorite application icons from the Applications or System menus, and drop them onto Avant-Window-Manager. After this, you can launch the applications by simply clicking their icons. Note that Avant-Window-Manager effectively negates the need for a bottom panel, so you might choose to delete it (right-click, and select Delete This Panel). In fact, the functionality provided by the bottom panel interferes a little with Avant-Window-Manager because applications will minimize to it, rather than to Avant-Window-Manager.

To configure Avant-Window-Manager, click System → Preferences → Awn Manager. Amongst the options worth playing around with are the Look drop-down list on the Bar Appearance tab. Here you can select 3D Look to get a Dock more in style with Mac OS X Leopard.

To make Avant-Window-Manager start automatically each time you log in, click System → Preferences → Sessions, ensure the Startup Programs tab is selected, and click the Add button. Then type avant-window-navigator into both the Name and Command text fields. Leave the Comment field blank. Then click the OK button.

As mentioned, Avant-Window-Manager can be heavily customized. For further information, take a look at the program's wiki at http://wiki.awn-project.org, or post a message on the program's forums at http://awn.planetblur.org.

Figure 3.36: ADDING A MAC OS X-LIKE DOCK WITH AVANT-WINDOW-MANAGER (SEE TIP 220)

For other tips that add bling to the Ubuntu desktop, see Tip 21, on page 67; Tip 79, on page 127; Tip 147, on page 183; Tip 199, on page 227; Tip 74, on page 120; Tip 274, on page 304; and Tip 289, on page 328.

221 Process Words at the Command Line

No, this tip isn't a rehash of Tip 177, on page 207, which describes how to install Microsoft Word for use at the command line (yes, really).

Instead, this tip is a rundown of several useful text-processing tools available at the command line. The fact is that bash (and sh before it) predate the serious introduction of word processors. In fact, it could be argued that many word processing features evolved from text manipulation tools built into bash.

Start by consulting Tip 196, on page 225, to find out how to create a text file at the prompt with the minimum of fuss. Assuming you've now created a document, let's move on to look at the tools available to process it.

- Spell checking: As its name suggests, aspell is a spell checker. To use it, provide the filename of the text file to be checked after the -c option: aspell -c file.txt. Once it's running, you'll be presented with a list of alternatives for words that are misspelled. To select one, type the number next to its entry in the list. To skip that word, type [i]. To quit, type [x]. Bear in mind that the corrected file will overwrite the original once you've finished, although a backup of the file will be created with a .bak file extension.

To spell check a single word at the command line, use the look command: look mississippi, for example. If the word is in the list of results, then it's spelled correctly. If it's not in the list, then it isn't spelled correctly. Note that a long list of results might be returned because every permutation of the word will be returned. Search for cart, for example, and carton, cartographer, and others will be returned.

- Word count: wc stands for "word count" and, sure enough, can be used to count the words of a specified file (that is, wc textfile.txt). Three figures will be reported. The first is the number of lines, the second is the number of words, and the third is the file size (in bytes). Use the -w command option if you just want to know the number of words.

- Word wrap: You can make a document "word wrap" using the fold command. This sets carriage returns at the end of lines, so it isn't quite like the dynamic word wrap function you might be used to in word processors. Yet it's sometimes useful nonetheless. The -w command option is used to set the character count (per line) when the line should be broken. It is also advisable to add the -s command option to stop fold breaking words in half. The following will set a word wrap after approximately forty characters on each line, creating a new file called wrapped.txt with the changes within it:

```
$ fold -sw 15 file.txt > wrapped.txt
```

222 View a Calendar at the Command Prompt

You've probably already realized that clicking the time display at the top-right of the screen shows a calendar. To see the same kind of thing at the command line, type cal. Without any command arguments, it will show the dates for the current month. If you want the axis of the calendar reversed (days down the side, rather than across the top), type ncal instead. To see the dates for last month, this month, and next month, type cal -3 (for some reason, however, this particular command option doesn't work with ncal).

To see a calendar for a whole year, type the year straight afterward: cal 2010. To see a calendar for December of any particular year, type cal dec followed by the year (or you could type jan, feb, mar, and so on).

Both cal and ncal can be used to find out historical dates. To find out the day when the Declaration of Independence was signed, type cal july 1776. If you seriously need to know precise dates going back millennia, there might be issues with the Julian/Gregorian calendar switch—see cal's man page for details.

223 Repair Ubuntu File System Errors

On the whole, Ubuntu's file system is robust. I can honestly say that in my years of using Ubuntu I've never had to manually check the hard disk for errors. Even if the power has suddenly gone off, Ubuntu has booted correctly the next time with no data loss. This is helped by periodic disk checks that run automatically at bootup.

But if you need to manually check the disk, it's only a single command away. You'll need to boot from your Ubuntu install CD because it's not possible to check a file system while it's in use. Select Try Ubuntu from the install CD-ROM boot menu. When the desktop appears, open a terminal window, and type the following:

```
$ sudo fsck.ext3 -f /dev/sda5
```

This assumes that Ubuntu is installed alongside Windows on the hard disk. If it's the only operating system on the disk, replace /dev/sda5 with /dev/sda1.

If there are any errors, you'll be prompted to repair them. Usually you can agree to the repair.

To perform a surface scan for bad blocks in addition to a file system check, add the -c command option:

```
$ sudo fsck.ext3 -fck /dev/sda5
```

To fix the Windows (NTFS) file system from within Ubuntu, see Tip 38, on page 87.

224 Clone Your Ubuntu Installation onto a New Hard Disk

Just upgraded your system with a shiny new hard disk and want to make it your new book disk? Cloning Ubuntu to another hard disk is easy. In fact, Ubuntu provides tools to clone the entire hard disk— including the Windows partition, if there's one on there. This is the kind of fundamental task that Linux excels at, in fact.

Three things must be done. First, you must discover how Ubuntu refers to the hard disks. Second, you must install the ddrescue software and then use it to clone the disk. Third, once ddrescue has finished, you must use the Gparted utility to expand the disk partition(s) (assuming that the new disk is bigger than the old one, which is almost certainly going to be the reason for upgrading in the first place).

It's not a good idea to clone a hard disk that's in use (any more than it's a good idea to repair a car while it's being driven), so you must use your Ubuntu install CD's live distro mode. To carry out the following instructions, boot from your Ubuntu install CD, and select Try Ubuntu from the boot menu.

Note that *all* the following stages are carried out using the Ubuntu install CD's live distro mode. At no point in the process do you need to boot into your standard Ubuntu installation, apart from to test the cloned disk at the end.

Preparing to Clone

Before starting, it's a good idea to do three things in preparation. First, back up all valuable personal files to CD/DVD-R/RW disc, a USB key-stick, or an external hard disk. The instructions that follow involve drastic fundamental disk management and the possibility of data loss is present.

Second, it's a good idea to check the file system of the original hard disk for errors and possibly enact repairs. This can be done by following the instructions in Tip 223, on the previous page. Ideally, you should check the Windows file system for errors too. This can be done within Windows or by following the instructions in Tip 38, on page 87.

Third, remove any USB memory sticks, card readers, or other kinds of attachable storage, such as MP3 players or mobile phones. This will avoid confusion when partitioning.

After all this, open a terminal window, and type the following, which will scan the hard disks and list their partitions:

```
$ sudo fdisk -l
```

Here are the results from my test system:

```
Disk /dev/sda: 81.9 GB, 81964302336 bytes
255 heads, 63 sectors/track, 9964 cylinders
Units = cylinders of 16065 * 512 = 8225280 bytes
Disk identifier: 0x1c381c37

   Device Boot    Start      End      Blocks   Id  System
/dev/sda1    *        1     4742    38090083+    7  HPFS/NTFS
/dev/sda2          4743     9964    41945715     5  Extended
/dev/sda5          4743     9744    40178533+   83  Linux
/dev/sda6          9745     9964     1767118+   82  Linux swap/Solaris

Disk /dev/sdb: 120.0 GB, 120034123776 bytes
255 heads, 63 sectors/track, 14593 cylinders
Units = cylinders of 16065 * 512 = 8225280 bytes
Disk identifier: 0xb94838a4

Disk /dev/sdb doesn't contain a valid partition table
```

Two hard disks are listed in the results: look for the headings Disk /dev/sda and Disk /dev/sdb. I've put them in bold for you to see more clearly. Beneath each heading is technical information about the disk, and beneath that the partitions on that disk are listed.

It should be obvious that, on my test computer, /dev/sdb is the new hard disk because it has no partitions (it "doesn't contain a valid partition table"), while /dev/sda has the standard partition layout of an Ubuntu system so is clearly the old disk. Yours will probably be very similar, if not identical.

Look for the reference to your new hard disk, and make a note of it. In my case, I make a note of /dev/sdb. Then type the following to start the cfdisk partitioning program, which we'll use to write an initial partition table to the disk:

```
$ sudo cfdisk -z /dev/sdb
```

If necessary, replace /dev/sdb with the details of the new hard disk you discovered earlier. All you have to do when cfdisk starts is type [W] (note that's [Shift]+[w]) and then type yes to write a blank partition table. Then hit [q] to quit cfdisk. Don't worry about the handful of minor errors that are reported—these can be ignored.

Cloning the Disk

Now that we have this information, we can install ddrescue and use it to clone the disk. This needs to be installed because it isn't a default system tool. Although the computer is running the Ubuntu install CD live distro mode, it's still possible to install additional software from the online repositories. However, before doing this, it's necessary to enable the Universe software repository (of course, you will need to use NetworkManager to get online too, if you haven't already). Click System → Administration → Software Sources, and put a check in the box alongside Community-maintained Open Source software (universe). Then click the Close button, and agree to refresh the list of software when asked.

After this, type the following command at the prompt to install ddrescue:

```
$ sudo apt-get install gddrescue
```

After this, the ddrescue command is used as follows—first we specify the old hard disk, and then we specify the new hard disk. The -v command option is added to ensure ddrescue provides a status report as it progresses:

```
$ sudo ddrescue -v /dev/sda /dev/sdb
```

It's *extremely* important that you ensure you get the old and new disks in the right order. Otherwise, you might well overwrite the data on your old disk!

Once the cloning has finished—it will probably take an hour or maybe more, depending on the size of the original hard disk—you should shut down the computer, remove the old disk (you must disconnect the old disk before you can continue!), and boot from the cloned copy to test things. Remember that Windows XP/Vista might object to a new hard disk as part of its "Windows Genuine Advantage" system, and you might have to revalidate online. Of course, Ubuntu will work fine without any such worries.

Assuming everything works correctly, you can move onto the next step: expanding the partitions to take advantage of the larger hard disk.

Expanding the Partitions

Before attempting to expand the partitions, it's a good idea to check that your Ubuntu partition's file system is sound. To do this, boot into the Ubuntu install CD's live distro mode as before. Open a terminal window, and type the following to perform a disk check (these steps assume that Ubuntu is installed alongside Windows on your hard disk in the standard configuration):

```
$ sudo fsck.ext3 -f /dev/sda5
```

Once this has completed, close the terminal window and click System → Administration → Partition Editor.

What happens next depends on your requirements. If you just want to expand the Ubuntu partition, follow these steps:

1. In the Partition list, right-click the linux-swap entry, and select Swap-off. This will stop Ubuntu's live distro mode from accessing the swap partition so that it can be moved on the hard disk.

2. Before anything else can happen, the extended partition that contains Ubuntu must be resized. Right-click the extended entry in the list, and select Resize/Move. In the dialog box that appears, change the Free Space Following (MiB) box to read 0. Then hit Tab. This will cause the partition to be expanded to fill the space. Hit the Resize/Move button when done. Bear in mind that no changes are carried until the Apply button is hit, which you will do after making all the changes to the disk's partitions.

3. Right-click the linux-swap partition once again, and select Resize/Move. In the dialog box that appears, click and drag the graphical representation of the partition to the end of the free space (in other words, click and drag it to the right of the graphical display). After this, the Free Space Following (MiB) box should read 0. Click Resize/Move.

4. Back in the main GParted program window, right-click the ext3 entry in the list, and select Resize/Move. Click and drag the right-most edge of the partition in the graphical representation so that it "grows" to fill the free space. Eventually the Free Space Following (MiB) box will read 0. When this is the case, click the Resize/Move button.

5. Finally, click the Apply button on the main GParted toolbar. Then click Apply in the dialog box that appears, and sit back and wait

while the partitions are moved and resized. If you want to see what's happening, click the small arrow alongside Details in the Applying pending operations dialog box.

6. When GParted has finished, close the program, and then open a terminal window. Type the following, which will once again check the Ubuntu partition for errors (and, again, these steps assume that Ubuntu is installed alongside Windows on your hard disk in the standard configuration):

```
$ sudo fsck.ext3 -f /dev/sda5
```

If there are any errors, you'll be prompted to repair them. Usually you can agree to the repair.

After the file system check, you can reboot your computer from the new hard disk. You should find the Ubuntu partition is now larger.

If you want to resize your Windows partition too, these steps are still relevant. However, you will have to move the swap and ext3 partitions, as well as the extended partition containing them, before resizing the NTFS partition.

If you want to dispose of the old hard disk or pass it on to somebody else, be sure to securely wipe it, as described in Tip 113, on page 151. However, don't do so until you're 100% sure your new cloned copy is working correctly (I usually wait at least a week or two to ensure the copy works fine before doing anything to the old disk).

225 | Create a Boot Log to Help Solve Startup Problems

As a sibling of Unix, Ubuntu includes software to log just about everything (generally speaking, log files are stored in /var/log). The main kernel log can be viewed by typing dmesg into a terminal window, and most other log files can be viewed by clicking System → Administration → System Log.

But, if you're using Ubuntu 8.04 (or a handful of releases prior to this), you won't be able to log boot-time messages (for example, the stopping and starting of background services).[35] This is because the system software that does this—bootlogd—isn't compatible with the Upstart component of Ubuntu and has been deliberately disabled. As a workaround for Hardy Heron (8.04), you can install a hacked version of bootlogd put together by a member of the Ubuntu community. This is strictly untested, however, and might be buggy. It should be used only if it's vital that you see boot-time messages to solve a problem.

Start by downloading the file linked to from this bug report: https://bugs.launchpad.net/upstart/+bug/98955/comments/34. Then issue the following commands at the terminal to install the software (these commands build the package from the source code you downloaded and ensure that some vital dependencies required for building packages are installed too; the commands assume the file has been downloaded to the desktop):

```
$ cd ~
$ sudo apt-get install devscripts build-essential fakeroot
$ tar zxf ~/Desktop/bootlogd_2.86.02.tar.gz
$ cd bootlogd-2.86.02
$ debuild -us -uc -b
$ sudo dpkg -i ../bootlogd_2.86.02_i386.deb
```

From now on, and after rebooting, you'll find a log of the startup messages in the /var/log/bootmsg file. This can be viewed using Gedit or by using less at the command prompt: less /var/log/bootmsg.

It might be wise to remove bootlogd when you have diagnosed your boot-time problem to avoid future incompatibilities. To do so, type the following:

```
$ sudo dpkg -r bootlogd
```

226 Install a Personal FTP Server for File Sharing

Setting up Ubuntu's file-sharing component, as described in Tip 28, on page 73, is perhaps the best method of making files available to

---

35. Startup messages are usually hidden by the Ubuntu splash screen/progress bar but can be made visible by editing the /boot/grub/menu.lst file and removing quiet splash from the end of the line relating to the Ubuntu entry.

others across a network. However, the underlying technology—known as SMB/CIFS—is not very reliable. Network shares sometimes mysteriously disappear, only to reappear minutes later. Sometimes a computer stubbornly refuses to connect, even though everything is set correctly. Often there are long pauses.

A more robust method of sharing files on your Ubuntu machine is to install a personal FTP server. This is less secure than SMB/CIFS,[36] but if you're working on a private network protected by a NAT and/or firewall device, then it should be fine (most broadband routers use NAT). Every operating system available right now (Windows XP/Vista, Mac OS X, and other versions of Linux) can natively connect via FTP, without installing additional software.

Here are the necessary steps to install and configure a personal FTP server—these steps also activate anonymous access, so no username or password is required:

1. Start by installing vsftpd using Synaptic.

2. During installation, vsftpd creates a new dummy user account—ftp—where the shared files will be stored. However, before any file sharing can happen, a container folder must be created within the dummy account's /home folder. To do this, open a command prompt, and type the following:

```
$ sudo mkdir /home/ftp/Shared\ files
$ sudo chmod a+rwx /home/ftp/Shared\ files
```

3. Open vsftpd's config file in Gedit: gksu gedit /etc/vsftpd.conf. Look for the following lines in the file, and remove the hash (#) before them (for an example of the edited file with the relevant lines highlighted, see Figure 3.37, on the facing page):

```
write_enable=YES
anon_upload_enable=YES
anon_mkdir_write_enable=YES
```

4. After this, save the file, close Gedit, and type sudo /etc/init.d/vsftpd restart to restart the vsftpd with the new settings. It will automatically start each time the computer boots.

---

36. FTP servers send everything—including usernames and password details—unencrypted across the network. Thus, passwords could theoretically be "sniffed" by malign interests. Ideally, we would create an SFTP server for Tip 226, on the previous page, but, unfortunately, Windows XP/Vista does not natively support SFTP.

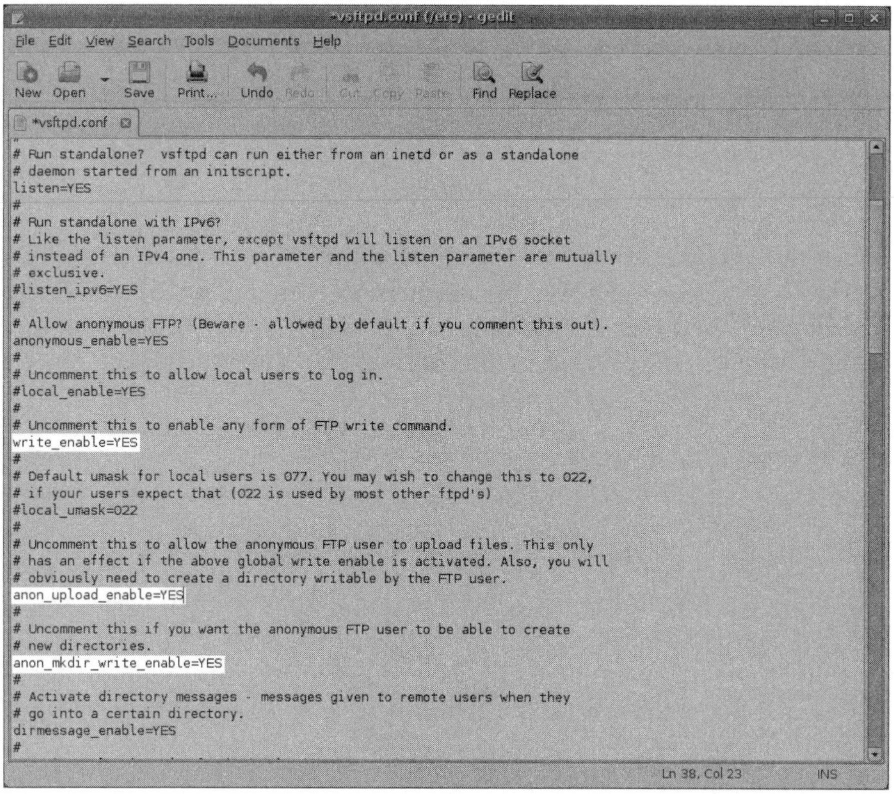

Figure 3.37: CONFIGURING VSFTPD (SEE TIP 226)

To access the new shared folder on your computer, click Places → Connect to Server, and in the Server field, type localhost. Then click the Connect button. After this, you can create a Nautilus bookmark for future access—click Bookmarks → Add Bookmarks in a Nautilus window, or hit Ctrl+d.

To access the shared folder from other computers, you'll need to tell the users of the computers the IP address of your Ubuntu computer. To discover this, right-click the NetworkManager icon, and select Connection Information. Then look for the IP Address line in the dialog box that appears. You will see four numbers separated by periods. On my test computer, I saw 192.168.1.13.

- Windows: Open a My Computer window, and in the Address bar, type ftp://address, replacing address with what you discovered earlier. Then right-click, and drag the Shared files folder to the desktop, and when you let go of the mouse button, select Create Shortcut Here. From now on, the desktop shortcut can be used to access the shared folder contents, even after a reboot.

- Mac OS X: By default, Macs can access an anonymous FTP only in read-only mode. To do this, open Finder, and then click Go → Connect to server. In the Server Address text field, type ftp://address, replacing address with what you discovered earlier. A Finder window will open showing the contents, but this can be closed. A desktop icon will also appear for the new FTP connection. Right-click it, and select Make alias. Use this new desktop shortcut whenever you want to connect in the future.

  To get read/write access to your new FTP server, Mac users will need to install MacFusion. Head over to http://www.sccs.swarthmore.edu/users/08/mgorbach/MacFusionWeb/; then download and install MacFuse and MacFusion. Launch MacFusion after installation, and click its icon at the top right of the screen. Then select Quick Mount and then FTP. In the dialog box that appears, type an easily remembered name into the Name field (something like Ubuntu shared will do) and the IP address you discovered earlier into the Server field. Then click OK. From now on, click the relevant entry after clicking the MacFusion icon.

- Other Ubuntu computers: Right-click the desktop, and select Create Launcher. In the Name text field, type something memorable—anything will do (maybe "Shared folder on Bob's computer"). In the Command field, type nautilus ftp://address, replacing address with the address you discovered earlier. Then click OK. Use this shortcut in the future whenever you want to connect. Alternatively, if you don't want to have a desktop shortcut, you can connect once and then create a Nautilus bookmark. Then delete the shortcut.

  You might also want to check out Tip 131, on page 164, which describes the cornucopia of FTP tools provided under Ubuntu.

227 Shut Down, Reboot, Hibernate, or Sleep Ubuntu with a Single Click

By creating desktop shortcuts to the terminal commands mentioned in Tip 206, on page 231, you can create one-click shutdown, reboot, hibernate, or sleep commands (although you'll need to enter your root password each time). You can do this by creating a launcher on the panels.

To create a panel launcher, right-click a blank spot on a panel, and select Add to panel. Then select Custom Application Launcher, and click the Add button. This will open the Create Launcher dialog box. It doesn't really matter what you type in the Name field of this dialog box. Something like Hibernate will do fine, assuming you're creating a Hibernate shortcut, of course. In the Command field, type any of the following, depending on what you'd like the shortcut to do (the function of each command is mentioned in parentheses after each command—there's no need to type that part):

```
gksu telinit 0 (shutdown)
gksu telinit 6 (reboot)
gksu /etc/acpi/hibernate.sh (hibernate)
gksu /etc/acpi/sleepbtn.sh (sleep)
```

Select an appropriate icon by clicking the icon preview button, and then click OK.

Note that, aside from the password prompt, there is no confirmation of any of these actions (and recall that the password prompt might not appear if you're in the sudo/gksu grace period—see Tip 47, on page 99, for details on how to change this). Before clicking any buttons that you create, be sure to save your work and also close open applications.

228 Delete Files Rather Than Trash Them

As you probably know, to delete a file (or files), you can right-click it and select Move to the Deleted Items folder or just drag it to the Trash icon at the bottom right of the screen. The only problem with this is that the files stick around in the trash until you opt to empty it, and this can present security issues with sensitive data.

To genuinely delete a file, rather than trash it, select it, and then press Shift+Delete. You can also add a Delete option to the menu that appears when you right-click a file by opening gconf-editor, heading over to /apps/nautilus/preferences, and checking the enable_delete key. This will do the same thing—permanently delete the file.

Currently, it's not possible to deactivate Ubuntu's trash function so that files are automatically genuinely deleted, no matter how you choose to delete them. To get around this, you can create a simple script that empties the trash and then make it run periodically as an hourly scheduled task (a personal cron job).

Start by creating a new file in Gedit called .emptytrash in your /home folder (bear in mind this file will be invisible because the filename is preceded with a period). Type the following into it:

```
#!/bin/bash
# Empty the GNOME trash by deleting the two relevant folders
rm -rf /home/username/.local/share/Trash/{files,info}/
```

The script works by deleting the two folders that contain and index the trash files within the GNOME desktop. Once the folders are deleted, new empty versions are automatically re-created by GNOME the next time the trash facility is used. A more elegant solution is possible, but this script has the benefit of being quick and thorough. Obviously, you should replace username with your own username. Then save the file, quit Gedit, open a terminal window, and mark the new script as executable, as follows:

```
$ chmod +x ~/.emptytrash
```

After this, add a job to your personal cron file by typing crontab -e. This will open your cron file in the nano text editor. Use the cursor keys to select a new line at the bottom of the file, and then type the following, which will cause the script to periodically run one minute past the hour while Ubuntu is up and running:

```
1 * * * * /home/username/.emptytrash
```

Again, you should replace username with your own username. Once done, hit Ctrl+x to quit nano, type y, and then hit Enter to save the buffer (save the file).

Note that Ubuntu's desktop Trash icon might still indicate it's full even though it's been emptied in this way.

229 Yank a USB Stick Even If You're Told You Shouldn't

You probably know by now that you shouldn't just pull a USB key stick out of a Ubuntu computer. This can cause data loss. Instead, you must right-click the desktop icon and select Unmount Volume. However, sometimes you might see an error message along the lines of "An application is preventing the volume from being unmounted." If you have no applications open, this can seem confusing.

The error message isn't just referring to applications. Any Nautilus window that's currently browsing the memory stick will have to be closed, and if you're browsing the USB memory stick contents from the terminal, then you'll need to cd away from that particular folder (that is, cd ~ to return to your /home folder). Then try again to unmount the key stick.

230 Rename Many Files at Once (aka Bulk Rename)

Have you ever been out with your digital camera and then returned home to find yourself with lots of files with names like IMG_0159.jpg, IMG_0160.jpg, IMG_0161.jpg, and so on? And have you then gone through one by one renaming them to something relevant? Well, there's no need to ever do that again because Ubuntu can come to the rescue!

There are a handful of ways of bulk renaming files at the command line, but many are quite involved, and you'll need to remember a chain of commands. To save the effort, use Synaptic to install purrr (that's pu, followed by three r's!). This is a GUI application that allows simple bulk renaming. Once installed, you'll find the program on the Applications → Accessories folder.

1. Start by clicking and dragging the files from a Nautilus window onto the Files section of Purrr. If you intend to bulk rename the files with sequentially increasing numbers, it's important to first sort them into the right order before dragging across—possibly the best way of doing this is to click View → View as List in Nautilus and then click the Date Modified heading to sort by the time the files were created (this is ideal for digital photographs). Alternatively, you might click the Name heading if the filenames can be sorted alphanumerically. Then Shift-click to highlight many files at once and drag them into the Purrr window.

2. In the Name template text field, you need to type the basic format of the new filenames. For example, if the pictures were all taken at Disneyland, you might type that. You'll see the effect on the new filenames as you type, although they won't actually be renamed until you hit the Rename button.

3. There are a handful of useful special inserts you can make into the filename. Typing [N] causes the original filename to be added to the renamed files, while [C] adds a sequential number count. [E] causes the file extension to appear (necessary if [N] isn't used).

   Here's an example. The following, when typed into the Name template box, will cause all the files to be named Disneyland, followed by a sequentially increasing number, and then followed by the original file extension:

   ```
   Disneyland [C].[E]
   ```

   Try it to see what happens. The [C] (count) operator can be further configured. A single comma inserted after C, followed by a number, sets the start number for the count. For example, [C,400] will start the count at 400. For an example from my test PC, see Figure 3.38, on the facing page. Two commas causes the count to skip numbers as it counts upward. For example, [C,,4] will name the first file with 1, the second with 5, the third with 9, the fourth with 13, and so on. In other words, +4 each time.

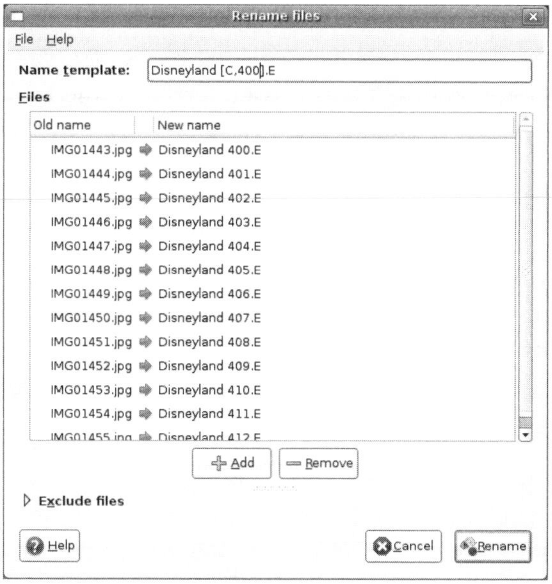

Figure 3.38: BULK RENAMING FILES USING PURRR (SEE TIP 230)

Three commas causes the count to be "padded" with zeros, and the number of zeros is specified by the number that follows. [C„3] will cause the count to start at 001, then 002, then 003, and so on. When the count reaches double or triple figures, the padding zeroes will disappear (that is, disneyland_009.jpg, disneyland_010.jpg...disneyland_099.jpg, disneyland_100.jpg, and so on).

4. Once you've typed your selection, hit the Rename button to carry out the renaming.

231 Get an Alternative Media Player

Once upon a time, Linux simply wasn't very capable when it came to multimedia playback. But times have changed, and nowadays the typical user is spoiled for choice. There are essentially two well-established choices available to the Ubuntu user, above and beyond the built-in Totem: Mplayer and VLC. Alongside Mplayer and VLC, the curious Ubuntu user can also install Kaffeine, which is the default media player of the KDE desktop. Kaffeine works well under Ubuntu, but it's really built to fit in with wider KDE functionality and also requires some extensive additional configuration when first installed.

Mplayer and VLC are entirely self-contained media players, meaning that they don't rely on external media frameworks provided by desktop environments.[37]

The benefits of using a different media player are found largely in the fact that Totem is very much a work in progress and its competitors are simply more mature. This manifests itself in things such as multimedia playback in web browsers, where personally I find Totem's browser plug-in lacking.

Because Mplayer and VLC are free to try, there's no reason not to give either a whirl. The following are more details about them. The following descriptions are some notes about how to configure each application to be the Ubuntu default for multimedia file playback.

Mplayer

Mplayer has claimed to be the granddaddy of all Linux media-playing applications and has been around since the early days. Since then, it has matured into possibly the most well-equipped media player application available for Linux (or Unix, bearing in mind Mplayer is open source).

In actual fact, Mplayer is a command-line program, but it's nearly always installed with a GUI front end, and that's how most people use it. To install it, just search Synaptic for mplayer. To make Mplayer the default application for browser-based audio/video playback, you should also install mozilla-mplayer. Once installed, Mplayer can handle just about any kind of mainstream audio or video format, including Windows Media, Real, DivX, and others. You'll find it on the Applications → Sound & Video menu. Once started, Mplayer usually shows two

---

37. Both GNOME and KDE utilize multimedia frameworks that effectively split the playback and decoding of video or audio into separate tasks that are handled by different programs. GNOME uses the Gstreamer framework, while KDE uses Xine. The benefit of a framework approach is that creating multimedia playback applications is simplified, and configuration (and initial setup) for the user is also simplified because it needs to be done only once. Of course, this being Linux, there's no reason why GNOME can't use Xine or KDE can't use Gstreamer, if that's beneficial to the user. For example, Tip 66, on page 115, discusses how to install a version of Totem that uses Xine, because Xine has better DVD playback capabilities (at the time of writing).

program windows: the video window and the transport (controls) window. To configure its options, right-click anywhere on either window, and choose from the pop-up menu that appears. To change technical settings (advised only if you know what you're doing, because Mplayer lets you tweak just about everything), click the Preferences option.

Mplayer's video window can be resized by clicking its edges. Mplayer's interface can be changed, and interface designs are known as *skins*. Select the Skin browser option in the right-click menu to choose between three default options provided out of the box. More skins can be downloaded from http://www.mplayerhq.hu/design7/dload.html—once you have downloaded them, place the unpacked files into the /usr/share/mplayer/ skins/ folder.

Some addition configuration might be required if you find that video playback results in a blank screen with only audio playback. Start Mplayer (Applications → Sound & Video → Mplayer Movie Player), and then right-click anywhere in the transport controls window. From the menu that appears, click Preferences, and after clearing the warning dialog box about changes not taking place until you restart, click the Video tab. Then select an alternative from the Available drivers list. If your computer has a 3D driver installed (you'll know this if desktop effects are activated), you can experiment with the gl or gl2 options. However, others will want to try the X11 option.

VLC

VLC and Mplayer are similar because both are self-contained applications that play back multimedia files, although VLC hasn't yet gotten 100% support for the playback of the RealPlayer audio/video format. However, VLC has a trick up its sleeve—streaming and file format conversion (the latter is commonly known as *transcoding*). For example, if you download a Windows Media (WMV) movie file and want to convert it to DivX, VLC will be able to help. Or you could download a file on one computer and stream it across the network (or even the Internet!) for other computers to watch.

To install VLC, search for and install the vlc package. For an example of VLC in action, see Figure 3.39, on the following page. If you want VLC to handle playback in the Firefox web browser, you should also search for and install mozilla-plugin-vlc. Once the application is installed, you'll find it on the Applications → Sound & Video menu. Most options can

Figure 3.39: VLC (see Tip 231)

be found on the program's menu, and a handy tip is to click Settings →
Extended GUI, which will provide video- and audio-tweaking controls.

To convert video or audio to a different format or stream across a network, click File → Wizard. Then follow the wizard through, selecting
the options you need (to convert a video, click the Transcode/Save to file
option). When prompted to select an input, click Existing playlist item to
convert/stream the currently playing file.

To configure either Mplayer or VLC as the default for multimedia file
playback, right-click any multimedia file (such as an .avi file), and select
Properties. Then click the Open With tab in the dialog box that appears,
and check the radio button alongside your player application. If the
application isn't listed, click the Add button, and locate it in the list
that appears.

This configuration will need to be done for all file types you want the
media player to automatically play back (.mp3, .wmv, and so on).

232 Compare Two Files to See Whether They're Different

☐

Sometimes you might be working on a file with a colleague and be sent a version with the same filename as one you already have. But how do you know whether that version has been updated? You can check the file size, but that's not 100% reliable—your colleague may have added data but also removed an equal amount.

There are two simple methods for quick file comparison at the command line. The first is to use the md5sum command, which outputs a unique 32-digit number based on the contents of the file. You'd then compare the md5sum output for each file side by side (one tip is that I usually compare a few digits from the start and a few from the end—if these are the same, then it's extremely likely the rest will be too). To use the command, just type md5sum filename1 and then md5sum filename2.

md5sum falls down a little on larger files, because it can take a while to generate the checksum. Another trick is to use the diff command. Just type diff filename1 filename2. If there's no difference, there will be no output. If there is a difference, you'll see one of two things: the message that "binary files filename1 and filename2 differ," which is likely if you're comparing, say, Word documents. Alternatively, the screen will fill with text, showing the difference between the files on a line-by-line basis. This is likely to happen only if diff thinks that the file is plain text (or, indeed, if the file actually is plain text, in which case you could redirect the output into a file for viewing later: diff filename1 filename 2 > changes).

233 Use the Mouse at the Virtual Console (complete with Copy and Paste)

☐

This is a neat hack that brings a block cursor to virtual console windows so that text can be easily copied and pasted. Just use Synaptic to install gpm. Once installed, open a terminal window, and type sudo /etc/init.d/gpm start to get the program running. In the future, gpm will start automatically on bootup.

Then switch to a virtual console to see the fruits of your labor. You should now have a block mouse cursor that moves around the screen. You can highlight text in the usual way. To paste it, click the middle mouse button (on most mice, this is the scroll wheel button; if your mouse has only two buttons, the right-click button will paste the text).

Some software that offers text-mode menus also respond to mouse clicks in this way. Check the command's help output to see whether a special command option is needed to support gpm.

234 See a Progress Display as the Desktop Loads

Many programs have *splash screens* when they start that give useful progress updates or just something to stare at while the hard disk grinds away. The GNOME desktop used with Ubuntu also has one of these, but it's disabled by default (at least in 8.04 Hardy Heron; some earlier releases had a splash screen). To activate it, fire up gconf-editor, navigate to /apps/gnome-session/options, and put a check along-side show_splash_screen.

To be honest, GNOME tends to start so quickly on my system that I only ever glimpse the splash screen, but there have been one or two situations where GNOME has gotten "stuck" while starting up, and the splash screen has given me valuable information about which component was causing the problem (as part of its display, the splash screen cycles through the system components that are being activated).

To personalize the splash screen, see Tip 237, on page 270.

235   Get Free-of-Charge Ubuntu CDs   ☐

If you have a friend who wants to try Ubuntu but is scared off by the process of downloading an ISO image and burning their own CD, direct them toward Ubuntu's ShipIt service (https://shipit.ubuntu.com/). They can then register to get sent a free copy of the latest Ubuntu release. Delivery might take up to ten weeks, however, so it might be quicker to simply burn a CD yourself and mail it to them. However, ShipIt will deliver a CD worldwide, and you can also order more than one CD if, for example, you want to hand out discs to colleagues or maybe even strangers![38] Sometimes a professionally manufactured CD is more convincing than a hastily burned CD-R with a handwritten label....

236   Make the GNOME Terminal Window Translucent   ☐

This tip gives GNOME Terminal windows an impressive graphical look and feel. Once it's made translucent, you'll be able to "see through" GNOME Terminal windows to the following desktop. This is mostly useless but looks great.

Start GNOME Terminal, click Edit → Current Profile, click the Effects tab, and select the Transparent background radio button. The changes will take effect immediately. You might want to click and drag the slider more toward Maximum to increase the opacity from the default setting because it leaves a distracting amount of the background visible.

To learn how to further customize the terminal look and feel, see Tip 25, on page 71, and Tip 137, on page 169.

---

38. One of the technical reviewers of this book, John Southern, regularly rents stalls at computer fairs to hand out free Linux install CDs. When pioneering Linux outfit Red Hat first started, it attended various shows and gave away Linux CDs, although it made a healthy profit selling hats, T-shirts, and other promotional items. This is the inverse of the usual approach, where promotional items are given away and the product is sold!

☐

237 Automate the Downloading and Installation of New Theme Components

Any Ubuntu user worth their salt knows about personalization. By clicking System → Preferences → Appearances, you can change just about any aspect of Ubuntu's look. You might also have discovered the http://art.gnome.org website, which offers many more widgets and wallpapers for download.

But downloading and installing new themes can be a time-consuming pain. Wouldn't it be nice if you could see a preview and then just click once to both download and install? As I'm sure you've probably guessed, *Ubuntu Kung Fu* has found a solution, and its name is GnomeArtNg (short for *Gnome-Art Next Gen*). This is a program that provides a front end to the http://art.gnome.org website in a desktop window and shows thumbnails of themes (or theme components). You can then click to download and install the items in which you're interested.

Unfortunately, Gnome-Art Next Gen isn't yet provided in the Ubuntu repositories, so you must download and install it manually. Start by visiting http://developer.berlios.de/projects/gnomeartng/. Click the Download link alongside the Packages heading (not Source or Binaries!). Then click to download the latest .deb file. Save the file to the desktop. Then issue the following command in a terminal window to install the software:

```
$ sudo dpkg -i ~/Desktop/gnomeartng-0.5.1-all.deb
```

Obviously, you should replace the filename with the one you downloaded. Once installed, the program will appear on the Applications → System Tools menu. When it first runs, the program will automatically download the latest thumbnails from the http://art.gnome.org/ site. This takes some time to complete and will happen each time you click the selection tabs in the program window. However, it needs to be done only once in each case—after this, the information is merely updated with any new components that have become available.

Running down the left side of the program window are the various categories of GUI items that can be personalized. Clicking each will show previews in the main program window of each component. To download, install, and activate any of them, simply select them, and then click the Apply button. In some cases, additional options are available—in the case of wallpapers, you can set whether the wallpaper centers on screen or is stretched, for example. If these options are available, they will be listed above the Apply button.

See also Tip 21, on page 67; Tip 79, on page 127; Tip 147, on page 183; Tip 199, on page 227; Tip 220, on page 246; Tip 274, on page 304; Tip 74, on page 120; and Tip 289, on page 328.

238 Burn Ubuntu CD Images (ISOs) Using Windows—for Free

There's a curious chicken-and-egg situation for Windows users who want to try Ubuntu. Although Ubuntu itself is fully conversant with the ISO image format, by which Ubuntu installation CDs are distributed across the Internet, ISO files are completely foreign to Windows. So, how does a migrating Windows user burn an ISO image?

Sure, they might have software like Nero installed, which can burn ISO images. However, if they don't, they face paying quite a lot of money to buy it.

I recommend Windows users who want to burn ISOs without buying any additional software download and install ISO Recorder from http://isorecorder.alexfeinman.com/. This is free of charge for personal use.

Once the program is installed, just right-click any ISO image, and select Open With → ISO Recorder. You can then burn straightaway or click the Properties button to set the burn speed (bear in mind that ISOs have a habit of not burning correctly at faster speeds).

To check the md5sum figure of the downloaded ISO before burning, download the Windows version of the md5sum command, which is available from http://etree.org/md5com.html. To use it, open a DOS prompt (Start → Run, and type cmd), and then navigate to where md5sum.exe has been saved to. Type md5sum, and then click and drag the ISO image onto the DOS window to complete the path and filename components. Then hit Enter.

☐

239 Quickly Create Links to Files, Folders, and/or Applications

There is a curious feature missing from the GNOME desktop that Ubuntu relies upon: quick and easy shortcut creation. For example, suppose you want to create a desktop shortcut to your Documents folder. You can right-click it and select Make Link, but this won't work with all folders because the new link is created within the parent folder, and you might not have permissions to write there (this can be an issue when creating links to system programs in the /usr/bin folder, for example). You can create a desktop launcher that redirects to the folder or file, but this is annoyingly long-winded and involves working your way through a dialog box.

A solution to this problem is built into GNOME. It's just hidden. Simply middle-click the folder or file, drag it to where you want the shortcut to be, and then select Link Here from the menu that appears when you release the mouse button. This will create a new link to the folder or file. On most modern mice, the middle mouse button is the scroll wheel, which doubles as a third mouse button.

The type of link created is a *symbolic link*, which isn't just a GNOME desktop shortcut. It will also work at the command line too.[39]

To create a symbolic link at the command line, type ln -s, specifying the original file and then the new link name (including paths, if necessary). For example, the following will create a link to the Gedit text editor (which lives in the /usr/bin folder) on the desktop and call it Text Editor; this command assumes you're currently browsing your /home folder:

```
$ ln -s /usr/bin/gedit "Desktop/Text Editor"
```

---

39. There are two types of links offered by the Ubuntu file system—symbolic links and hard links. Symbolic links are like shortcuts created within Windows—they're very small files that "point" toward another file (or folder). However, the link file exists at the file system level, unlike those in Windows, which are actual files. In contrast, a hard link is a little like copying the file, except the actual data isn't copied. Instead, an additional "pointer" is made for the file. In other words, two (or more) files share the same block of file data. Hard links introduce some complexity into proceedings and have a very specific use, so in most cases it's best to stick with symbolic links.

After this, the link will act just like the original file—double-clicking it will start Gedit. It's worth pointing out for the nervously inclined that deleting the shortcut won't delete the original file.

240 Monitor CPU Usage ☐

Keeping an eye on CPU load can be a good way of spotting whether something is going wrong on your computer—if the system is doing nothing in particular but CPU usage is at 99%, then it's likely a program is in the process of crashing.

A variety of CPU load applets are available under Ubuntu, and each goes about the task in a different, often entertaining, way. Perhaps my favorite is bubblemon, which shows CPU usage as a vessel of bubbling liquid. If it boils, your computer is busy! You'll find it listed in Synaptic. Once installed, log out and then back in again, and then right-click a blank spot on the panel. Select Add to panel, and select Bubblemon from the list. A good way to test the new applet is to drag a window around quickly—this taxes the CPU so should cause some virtual bubbles to rise.

Worth investigating if you'd like to take an opposing approach is cpufire-applet, which, as its name suggests, shows CPU load as rising licks of flame. It can be installed via Synaptic and configured in the same way as bubblemon—after logging out and back in, add the CPU Fire applet, as described earlier, by right-clicking the panel.

As entertaining as they are, neither applet offers much concrete information. Ubuntu's built-in System Monitor applet is much in the same vein and provides only a graph of CPU activity across time. To see actual numbers, you'll need to use Synaptic to search for and install the hardware-monitor applet. Once it's installed, log out and then back into Ubuntu. Right-click a blank spot on the panel, click Add to panel, and select Hardware Monitor from the list. The applet is very small, and you might just notice it where you initially clicked on the panel. By default it shows a graph of CPU activity. To see percentage figures, right-click it, select Preferences in the menu that appears, and after selecting the Viewer tab, click the Text radio button. If your computer has a dual-core processor, hardware-monitor will report the speed of both cores, and this can mean the display gets quite cramped. Therefore, you might want to click the drop-down list under the Font heading of the Viewer tab and select a smaller point size (maybe 8 point, depending on your screen resolution and eyesight).

See also Tip 106, on page 147, which describes how to alter the CPU speed on the fly, and Tip 150, on page 185, which explains how to monitor CPU temperatures.

241 See Whenever Caps Lock Is Active

Some say that Caps Lock is one of the most useless keys on the keyboard. It's certainly more of a pain than a help when hit by accident, particularly on some keyboards that lack the usual LED lights to show it's active (such as battery-powered models). You can turn off Caps Lock by following Tip 90, on page 135, but another solution is to use Synaptic to install lock-keys-applet, which will simply warn you if Caps Lock has been activated. Once installed, right-click a blank spot on the panel, click Add to panel, and then select Lock Keys from the list. Now, whenever Caps Lock is hit, you'll have a visible notification.

Lock Keys also shows whether the numeric keypad button is active (it should be, unless you like the keypad being a clone of the cursor keys), as well as the Scroll Lock key, which isn't used much nowadays. By right-clicking the applet's icon and selecting Preferences, you can control which keys are shown in the display.

242 Make Files and Folders Entirely Private

Ubuntu is set up so that if one user creates a file, all other users have read-only access to it (in other words, file permissions of -rw-r--r-- and folder permissions of drwxr-xr-x). To make any files or folders you create accessible only by yourself (-rw------ and drwx------), open your .profile file in Gedit (gedit ~/.profile), and remove the hash alongside umask=022. Then change the entire line to read umask=077 (that's *zero*, seven, seven). Save the file, and log out and back in again.

You can also alter the permissions on folders and files you've already created. To protect filename.doc, for example, you would type chmod go-rw filename.doc. This will remove (-) read and write (rw) permissions from members of your group (g) and others not in your group (o). To change permissions on a folder and everything in it, you could type something like chmod -R go-rwx Documents/, which will change your Documents folder—and all files/folders within it—so that you can access only them.

Be sure to resist the temptation to change permissions on your entire /home folder. Various pieces of software store configuration files there and sometimes run with unique ownerships, so changing permissions could cause real problems. Many folders holding personal information, such as your Firefox browsing history, already have restrictive permissions set so that only you can access them.

Should you want to return to the old file ownership rules, simply edit your .profile file once again, and reinsert the hash (#) before the umask line. Then save the file, and log out and back in again.

243 | Get Quick Access to Stuff You're Working On

If you're working on a particular project, it's likely that there will be a handful of files that you'll access on a regular basis. Yet it seems strange that no operating system ever takes this into account. Some operating systems will give quick access to recently accessed files, but none (to my knowledge) will tell you which are the most popular.

Until such a feature arrives, you might like to take a look at TopShelf, which can help organize your workflow. It's a simple panel applet that lets you create organized shortcuts to files on which you're currently working. Then all you need to do whenever you boot your computer is click the TopShelf icon and double-click the relevant file entry from its list. TopShelf doesn't actually copy the files. It just creates shortcuts and then organizes them in one easily accessible location. It's simple but useful.

The program can be installed by using Synaptic to search for topshelf. Once it's installed, right-click a blank spot on the panel. Select Add to panel and then TopShelf from the list.

Click its icon, and then click and drag any files you want TopShelf to organize for you onto the TopShelf window. Remember that you're creating only a shortcut—the actual file isn't copied. From then on, you can simply click the TopShelf icon and double-click the file's icon to open it. Folders can be added too. To remove a file or folder from the list, just highlight it only, and click the Remove button.

244 Insert Command-Line Output and Files into the Clipboard

Wouldn't it be useful to quickly pump an entire configuration file, or the output of a terminal command, into the clipboard for pasting into a website forum's posting page or similar? Well, that's just what xclip is designed to do. It can be installed via Synaptic.

Once installed, you can redirect text files into xclip so that they become the clipboard contents:

```
$ xclip < /etc/fstab
```

...which will add the contents of the /etc/fstab configuration file to the clipboard, or you can pipe the output of a command into it:

```
$ dmesg|xclip
```

...which will place the output of the dmesg command in the clipboard (dmesg shows system log output and can be useful when diagnosing problems).

There is one proviso. The piped output/files are placed in the *selection buffer* clipboard, which is distinct from the standard cut/copy and paste clipboard accessible from the Edit menu of most applications. xclip's output can be pasted by positioning the cursor in the relevant spot and clicking the middle mouse button (this means pressing the scroll wheel, if your mouse has one; if not, click both the left and right mouse buttons simultaneously).

In theory, the use of the -selection command option with xclip should allow the user to add to the primary clipboard, but this doesn't appear to work, perhaps because of the way the Ubuntu desktop is configured. To be honest, I see this as less of a bug and more as a feature—xclip will leave any existing clipboard contents untouched.

If you're in the process of asking for help on a forum, as mentioned earlier, see also Tip 312, on page 355, which describes how to record your onscreen actions for posting on a forum.

245   Have a Cow Talk to You   ☐

Do you see anywhere in this book that said the tips actually had to be useful? Me neither (well, I might have hinted at it in the introduction). With this in mind, use Synaptic to search for and install cowsay. Once it's installed, open a terminal, and type the following:

```
$ cowsay "Ubuntu Kung Fu"
```

You can have the cow say a single word or an entire phrase. Cows aren't the only things that can talk. If you look in /usr/share/cowsay/cows/, you'll find other models that can be made to talk. Just specify the model using the -f command option (without the .cow extension). For example, to have Tux (the Linux mascot) appear instead, type the following:

```
$ cowsay -f tux "Ubuntu Kung Fu"
```

For a little fun, add one of these commands to the end of your .bashrc file (to edit the file, type gedit ~/.bashrc). Then you'll see it every time you open a terminal window or log in at a virtual console.

You could even combine this tip with Tip 183, on page 212, to have your quotation of the day come out of the mouth of a cow. Just add the following line to your .bashrc line (adding any cowsay command options you want after the command):

```
signify|cowsay
```

If you like having things talk to you, see also Tip 13, on page 61, which describes how to use the Ubuntu built-in speech synthesizer.

246   Get Notified When New Mail Arrives   ☐

If Evolution is running, it will pop up a message telling you when new mail has arrived. However, what if it's not running? After all, you might not choose to keep Evolution running all the time.

The solution is gnubiff, a GNOME applet that is able to periodically check mailboxes and report when there are new messages. It's actually a modern version of biff, an old and venerable program that does much the same thing at the command line.

gnubiff can be installed using Synaptic by searching for gnubiff. Once it's installed, right-click a blank spot on the panel, select Add to panel from the menu that appears, and select gnubiff from the list.

To configure it for your email account, right-click the applet's icon, and select Preferences. Then, with the Mailboxes tab selected, click mailbox 1 in the Mailboxes list, and click the Properties button. Assuming your email provider uses POP3 email (it probably will), select Pop from the Type drop-down list. The dialog box will then change to accommodate new information fields, which you should fill in as usual. You'll need to supply your mail server's POP3 address in the Address field. If the server uses encryption, click the Details drop-down list, and select the type from the Authentication drop-down list (if in doubt, try SSL). Then click the OK button.

To disable Evolution's own email alert, start Evolution, and click Edit → Plugins. In the dialog box that appears, look down the list on the left side for Mail Notification. Then remove the check from alongside. Quit Evolution, and then start it again, if desired.

See also Tip 296, on page 336, which describes how to enact a desktop notifier for Gmail accounts.

247	Increase Output "Remembered" by GNOME Terminal

By default, GNOME Terminal "remembers" 500 lines of output, which you can then scroll through. That's a lot, but you'll be surprised at how quickly you'll burn through it in a typical session. Just one long file listing (ls -la) of my home folder took 59 lines, for example. To increase the number of lines remembered, click Edit → Current Profile in an open terminal window, and then click the Scrolling tab. Then increase either the Scrollback figure or the kilobytes figure—the two are related, and if one increases, so does the other.

Even at 500 lines, 318KB is used when all 500 lines are inputted, and that's a significant chunk of the system memory. The trick is, as always, to balance functionality with memory demands. Personally, I think a value of 1,000 lines (636KB) is good on a system with 1GB or more of memory.

248 Use Ubuntu's Version of Microsoft Paint

□

I've worked in several offices where people have made heavy use of Microsoft Paint, not only to alleviate the boredom of a long day but also to sketch quick diagrams (such as maps) that were then faxed to others. Under Ubuntu you can use GIMP for sketching things, but it's a sledgehammer to crack a nut when it comes to simple diagrams.

Ubuntu's equivalent to Microsoft Paint is GNU Paint, and it can be installed using Synaptic (search for the gpaint package). Once installed, it can be found on the Applications → Graphics menu, and operation is almost the same as the Windows program. GNU Paint is a fork of the older but perhaps more feature-full XPaint, which is also available in Synaptic (search for the xpaint package; once installed, you'll find it also on the Applications → Graphics menu). However, Xpaint lacks integration with the GNOME desktop. For example, it utilizes menu buttons that you access by clicking and holding, rather than simply hovering your mouse over them.

If you're just looking for a package for kids to play around with, try installing the tuxpaint package. Once installed, this can be found on the Applications → Education menu.

249 Have OpenOffice.org Save in Microsoft Office Format by Default

□

Like it or loathe it, Microsoft's file formats dominate the world of office work. .doc, .xls, and .ppt are the *lingua franca* of most workplaces.

OpenOffice.org is fully conversant with these file formats and can open/save them, but it defaults to its own file format for saving new documents. It can then be a pain to keep having to manually select Microsoft Office format.

To make the OpenOffice.org programs default to Microsoft Office file formats when saving, open OpenOffice.org Writer (Applications → Office → OpenOffice.org Word Processor), and then click Tools → Options. On the left side of the dialog box that appears, expand the Load/Save heading by double-clicking it, and click then General, which will appear beneath it. In the Always Save As drop-down list at the bottom right of the dialog box, select Microsoft Word 97/2000/XP. Then, in the Document Type drop-down list, select Spreadsheet, and once again click the Always Save As drop-down list, this time selecting Microsoft Excel 97/2000/XP. Repeat again, this time selecting Presentation and selecting Microsoft PowerPoint 97/2000/XP. Once done, click the OK button.

See also Tip 121, on page 158, which describes how to boost Open-Office.org's support for newer Microsoft Office file formats, and Tip 308, on page 351, which explains how to avoid formatting incompatibilities when outputting Office file-format documents.

☐ | **250** | Password-Protect and Encrypt Files

Any file or folder within Ubuntu can be encrypted so that it can be decrypted only by using a passphrase. What actually happens is that an encrypted version of the file or folder is created that requires a passphrase to unlock it. The original file or folder must then be deleted by the user. Whenever you want to edit or view the file after this, you must double-click the encrypted file to extract a decrypted copy. Then, if you update the file in any way, you must reencrypt it.

This isn't the most user-friendly solution for protecting files and is best used with files that you want to archive and access occasionally. A better solution of protecting files you regularly access is described in Tip 145, on page 178.

Some setup work is necessary before the files or folders can be encrypted, and you must generate a personal *key pair*, as described in

Tip 172, on page 200, which explains how to encrypt and sign emails (in fact, essentially the same technique and underlying technology is used here).

Files encrypted using the method outlined in this tip aren't particularly "portable," which is to say this isn't a system designed to let you copy files to another machine and decrypt them. For that to happen, you would have to export your key pair, which represents a security risk. Nevertheless, how to do this is explained later in this tip.

Bear in mind that if you follow these instructions to encrypt files and then forget your passphrase, any files you encrypted are effectively lost forever. There is no "back door" and no way of cracking the system—the method of encryption used is extremely thorough.

First we look at creating a key pair and then look at how to encrypt/decrypt files or folders.

Creating a Key Pair

Follow these steps to create a key pair, which is necessary before you can encrypt/password-protect any files (note that you can skip these steps if you've already created a key pair by following the instructions in Tip 172, on page 200):

1. Click Applications → Accessories → Passwords and Encryption Keys to start the Seahorse application, which is used to manage all encryption keys within Ubuntu.

2. In the program window that appears, click the New button. In the dialog box that appears, select PGP Key, and click the Continue button.

3. In the dialog box that appears, fill in the Full Name and Email Address fields (you can leave the Comment field blank). To be frank, the email field is used only if you later publish the public component of the key pair for email encryption purposes. If you don't intend to do this, then it doesn't matter what you type. Note that you must type both a forename and surname into the Full Name text field.

4. In the Advanced key options drop-down list, you can choose a different type of encryption, although the default choice of DSA Elgamal and 2048 bits is considered extremely secure and also flexible enough to meet most needs. Once done, click the Create button.

Figure 3.40: ENCRYPTING A FILE (SEE TIP 250)

5. After this, you'll be prompted for a passphrase. Essentially, this is the password you will need to decrypt files. It's important you make the passphrase something hard to guess but also memorable enough so you don't forget it. The passphrase can include letters, numbers, symbols, and space characters.

6. After this, the key will be generated. Depending on the speed of your computer, this could take up to an hour. Once it's done, quit the Seahorse application.

Encrypting/Decrypting Files or Folders

Once the key pair has been created, encrypting a file or folder is as simple as right-clicking it and selecting Encrypt. In the dialog box that appears, put a check alongside the key you created, and then click OK, as shown in Figure 3.40.

If you've selected to encrypt a folder, you'll be asked whether you want to encrypt each file separately or automatically create a zip archive that will then be encrypted. The latter is the best option in most cases.

If you password-protected a file, once the encrypting process is complete, you should find yourself with a new version of the file that has a .pgp extension. You can then delete the old file. If you encrypted a folder, you should find two files have been created—the protected .pgp version and a .zip archive of the original folder. That archive, along with the original folder itself, can then be deleted.

For security reasons, the unencrypted versions should be permanently deleted, rather than just sent to the trash. To learn how to securely erase files, see Tip 113, on page 151. Before destroying the old file, however, you might want to first test-run decrypting the file.

To do so, just double-click the .pgp file, and then type your passphrase when prompted. The original file will then reappear. In the case of a folder, the .zip archive will appear, and you can then double-click it to extract the contents.

Decrypting Files on Another Computer

As mentioned in the introduction to this tip, this isn't a system designed to create portable encrypted files. To decrypt files on another computer, you need to export your key pair and then import it on the other computer. Anybody in possession of your key pair file along with any encrypted files will be able to decrypt them, so this represents a security risk. However, sometimes it might be necessary to decrypt files on another machine. Here are the necessary steps:

1. On the computer that created the encrypted file(s), start Seahorse (Applications → Accessories → Passwords and Encryption Keys), and then right-click your personal key (the one created in the previous steps). Select Properties from the menu that appears.

2. In the dialog box that appears, click the Details tab, and click the Export button alongside the Export Complete Key heading. Save the file to the desktop. You will find a new file has been created with an .asc extension. This is your key pair in text format.

3. Copy the .asc file to a USB key stick or floppy disk, and take it over to the second computer. Still on the second computer, start Seahorse (Applications → Accessories → Passwords and Encryption Keys), and click the Import button. Navigate to your key file, and click Open. This will import the key. After this, close Seahorse. You can then double-click any encrypted files to decrypt them.

4. If the other computer doesn't have Seahorse installed—perhaps if it's a different version of Linux or maybe an older version of Ubuntu—copy the key file to the desktop, and then type the following into a terminal window (these instructions assume gpg is installed, which is very likely):

```
$ gpg --import "/home/username/Desktop/key file.asc"
```

Obviously, you should replace key file.asc with the name of the .asc file and replace username with your username. Then, to decrypt a file, type the following:

```
$ gpg filename.pgp
```

Again, you should replace filename.pgp with the name of the file you want to decrypt. You'll be prompted for your passphrase, so type it. After this, the original file will be restored in the same location as the .pgp file.

Note that you must ensure the internal PC clock is set correctly and shows the current time before exporting/importing keys. For various technical reasons, Seahorse and the gpg command cannot import a key if the time on the PC appears to be *before* the key file appears to have been created. Of course, this means that if the computer that created the key file had the wrong time, you will have real problems importing the key. The solution is to set your PC's clock to a time and date in the future. Then import the key, and return the PC's clock to the present time.

To have your computer always know the correct time, follow the steps in Tip 26, on page 72, which explains how to synchronize Ubuntu to Internet time servers.

251 Add Notes to Any File/Folder

Any file or folder under Ubuntu can have notes attached to it. This might be considered a solution waiting for a problem in some people's eyes, but it's a cool feature nonetheless. To add a note to a file or folder, right-click it, and then select Properties from the menu that appears. Then click the Notes tab in the dialog box that appears, and type what you want. Click Close when you've finished. After this, the file or folder icon will have a note emblem in one of its corners (probably the top right).

252 Encrypt Files So That Only the Recipient Can Open Them ☐

Passing a confidential file (or files) to others is fraught with dangers. You can email it to them, but what if the email is intercepted in transit? You can pass them it to them on a USB key stick, floppy disk, or CD-R disc, but what happens if you lose the disk or stick or it gets stolen?

The solution is to encrypt the files using the key pair system. Once this is done, only the recipient will be able to decrypt the file. Nobody else will, even the person who originally encrypted it or anybody who intercepts the file.

For it to work, the recipient will need to have their own key pair and have shared the public key with you. They will also need to be running Ubuntu or have GPG installed (most versions of Linux come with GPG installed nowadays).

For more details on key pairs and importing the public key of another person, see Tip 172, on page 200. You should also take a look at Tip 250, on page 280, because that tip describes almost exactly the same thing as described here—the only difference is that you are encrypting a file/folder for another person to decrypt, rather than yourself. To perhaps state the obvious, this tip differs in that you shouldn't delete the original file after encryption is complete—*only the recipient will be able to decrypt the file*. You won't be able to, even though you encrypted it.

Assuming you've imported the recipient's key (click Key → Import in Seahorse if it's provided as a file), simply right-click the file in question, and select Encrypt. Then, in the dialog box that appears, put a check alongside their details, and click the OK button. You will then create a new file with a .pgp extension, which is the encrypted version of the file and which you can then pass to the other person. Any existing file extension will remain in place, and the new .pgp extension will be added to the end.

Some email server scanners automatically remove files with two file extensions; to get around this, place the new .pgp into a ZIP file (even if it was a ZIP file prior to encryption!). You can do this by right-clicking it and selecting Create Archive. Then remove the .pgp component of the new ZIP file's filename (for example, file.pgp.zip would become file.zip). After this, the recipient will have to unzip and then decrypt the file; this shouldn't pose any problems for them, and it should be obvious to them what to do.

253 See Your File-Browsing History

Nautilus includes a little-known feature that will track folders you view, just like a web browser tracks the sites you visit. This can be useful when performing system maintenance, especially if, like me, you tend to forget where you've just located that all-important file.

To activate it, click the Places drop-down list above the left pane, and select History. The history view places the most recently visited folders at the top of the list.

254 Define Your Own Menu Shortcut Keys

As with Windows, most menus in Ubuntu show the keyboard shortcut of a particular function alongside it. For example, the File menu of Nautilus points out that Ctrl+N will open a new window.

You can redefine these shortcuts on the fly by simply hovering the mouse cursor over the menu option and pressing the new keyboard combination. However, first you need to activate this particular Ubuntu option. To do so, right-click the desktop, and select Change Desktop Background. Then click the Interface tab in the window that appears, and put a check alongside Editable menu shortcut keys. Then close the program window.

The changes will take effect immediately, so try it. Start your favorite application, highlight the mouse cursor over the menu option you want to change, and hit the new combination. You'll see that the menu instantly reflects the changes. To remove any keyboard shortcut, just hit the ⌈Backspace⌉ key (not the ⌈Delete⌉ key—that will cause ⌈Delete⌉ to be the new shortcut).

If you define a keyboard that's already in use in that application, it will be "stolen" from that particular function, and that function will no longer have a keyboard shortcut.

Note that this affects only GNOME applications, such as Nautilus, GNOME Terminal, and Gedit. It won't work with non-GNOME applications like OpenOffice.org and Firefox.

255 Always Know Your IP Address

You can find out your IP address in a number of ways. For example, right-click NetworkManager, select Connection Information in the menu that appears, and look for IP Address in the list. At the command line you can type ifconfig and look for the Inet addr line (assuming your computer isn't using IPv6, the new networking addressing system currently used in only a handful of academic and corporate institutions).

But you might come across a limitation if you're behind a NAT router. It's very likely to be the case that you're behind one of these if you use a broadband modem/router or use Ubuntu in an office environment. In that case, you'll see only the *private network* address—usually something like 192.168.1.45. These are *nonroutable*, which means they mean nothing to anybody else on the Internet. They're just for use on a local network. If you're trying to make an Internet phone call using some programs or connecting to a gaming server, then knowing your actual—rather than private—IP address can be useful so that others can connect.

The solution is Giplet, which you can install using Synaptic (search for and install giplet). Once installed, right-click a blank spot on the panel, select Add to panel, and then select Giplet from the list. By default, you'll see your private IP address, so right-click the icon, click Preferences, and ensure the Get IP from Website button is selected. This will ensure your external IP address is displayed.

☐ **256** See the Size of Files/Folders on the Desktop

Wouldn't it be handy to have the size of files written underneath their names on the desktop? No problem! Open a Nautilus window, and click Edit → Preferences. Then click the Display tab, and change the three drop-down lists under Icon Captions to read Size, Date Modified, and Type (or, indeed, the latter two can be anything you want from the drop-down list provided the first drop-down list reads Size). The changes will take effect immediately. Unfortunately, the side effect of this is that all file icons will now have their size listed under them in Nautilus windows. Then again, this is no bad thing.

For further desktop organization tricks, see Tip 104, on page 146, which describes how to stop the icons being aligned, and Tip 173, on page 204, which explains how to add the familiar desktop icons for system functions, such as Trash or My Computer.

☐ **257** View Technical Details of Any Multimedia File

If you right-click an audio or video file, click Properties, and then click the Audio/Video tab in the dialog box that appears, you'll see the technical details of the file, such as the bit rate for audio files or the resolution of a video file. Note that this will work only if you have the correct codecs installed—codecs are automatically installed upon demand, but to learn how to manually install all the codecs you could ever need, see Tip 65, on page 114.

258 | Convert PDFs and Images to Flash Slideshows

☐

Although PDFs have become the de facto document transfer format across the Internet, there are still lots of computer users who haven't heard of them. Unfortunately, they are also the kind of people who don't understand how to install new software, so getting them to install Acrobat Reader is often asking too much.

In such a situation, you could try converting the file to a Flash animation. Virtually all Windows computers come with Flash preinstalled.

To do this conversion under Ubuntu, use Synaptic to install the swftools package. This is a series of command-line programs designed to manipulate or create Flash files.

When typed into a terminal window, the following will convert chapter.pdf into a Flash file:

```
$ pdf2swf -t chapter.pdf
```

This will output chapter.swf, which can then be loaded into Firefox for viewing, although note that the Totem movie player associates with .swf files, so you specifically opt to open it in Firefox by right-clicking it and selecting from the Open With menu, rather than just double-clicking the file. The -t command option turns off automatic scrolling through the pages of the file. To turn pages, the reader must right-click the presentation and select Forward or Back. To avoid this inconvenience, you can combine the new Flash file with a simple pager, provided by the swftools team. The following uses the swfcombine tool to create a new Flash file called paged_file.swf, using chapter.swf as a base. The new Flash file incorporates two arrows at the top of the document to move backward and forward:

```
$ swfcombine -o paged_file.swf /usr/share/swftools/swfs/simple_viewer ↩
.swf viewport=chapter.swf
```

Obviously, you should replace chapter.swf with the name of the file you created earlier.

To create a slideshow from JPEG photos, use the jpeg2swf command. The following will output slideshow.swf from the specified JPEG images:

```
$ jpeg2swf -r 0.1 -o slideshow.swf photo1.jpg photo2.jpg photo3.jpg ↩
photo4.jpg
```

You can specify as many images you want, although this works best if the images are all the same resolution. The -r command option sets the frames per second, which in this case means the pause between pictures—put simply, a value of 0.1 means that one picture appears onscreen for ten seconds (this effectively sets the frame rate at one frame per second divided by 0.1, which is 10 seconds; for a value of 20 seconds, you'd need to set 0.05—1/0.05=20 seconds).

If your images are in .gif or .png format, then use gif2swf and png2swf, respectively.

There's no reason why you can't include the pager tool, as used with the earlier PDF conversion, to let the user scroll through the images. The following will add the pager and output a file called paged_slideshow.swf, using the slideshow.swf file created earlier as a base:

```
$ swfcombine -o paged_slideshow.swf /usr/share/swftools/swfs/simple ↩
_viewer.swf viewport=slideshow.swf
```

For information on how to simply create an HTML slideshow of images, see Tip 126, on page 161.

259 Create an Alias to Save Typing Long Commands

Several tips in this book—such as Tip 208, on page 233, which explains how to view images in a folder as a slideshow—involve typing a chain of commands at the prompt. If your memory is as bad as mine, you may find it hard to recall the precise order of commands (or even the command itself).

The solution is to create a bash alias. This lets you create a homemade single-word command that, when typed into a terminal window or virtual console, invokes another command, or a stream of commands, if need be.

Let's take as an example the aforementioned tip—Tip 208, on page 233. The command needed to view all the images in a folder as a slideshow is eog -f *.{jpg,tif,bmp,gif,png}. It would be nicer, and easier, to just switch to the folder and type slideshow. To make this possible, open your .bashrc file in Gedit (type gedit ~/.bashrc into a terminal window), and add the following new line at the bottom:

```
alias slideshow="eog -f *.{jpg,tif,bmp,gif,png}"
```

In other words, the new command you want to create comes first, after which you list the command (in quotation marks because it includes spaces).

Open a new terminal window to see whether your new command works by typing slideshow in a folder full of images.

You can have as many aliases as you want listed in the .bashrc file. Just type each on a new line. Before creating a new alias, ensure that the command you intend to use isn't already in use—a surprising amount of seemingly innocuous words are already in use as commands. You can do this by simply typing whereis followed by the command. To check to see whether slideshow is in use, I'd type whereis slideshow. If I received a listing of a folder, then I'd know the command was in use. If I see just the command with nothing after it, then I know it's not in use.

If all you want to do is create personalized shortcuts to already installed applications, see Tip 239, on page 272.

260	Send Genuine Smileys in Your Emails	

Are you a fan of emoticons, the little pictures of smiley, unhappy, or confused faces that help convey emotions in online correspondence? Although they're never more than a few keystrokes away, Evolution can enhance the effect by automatically inserting actual pictures of smileys into your emails in place of the usual :), ;), and so on. The recipient will then see these pictures alongside your text.

To configure the emoticons, click Edit → Preferences in Evolution, and then select Composer Preferences. Then check Automatically insert emoticon images. Obviously, if you haven't already, you should also check the box alongside Format messages in HTML, because plain-text images cannot have images inserted into them.[40] After this, the smiley images will be inserted automatically whenever you type a smiley combination.

For more Evolution tricks, see Tip 42, on page 90; Tip 156, on page 189; Tip 158, on page 190; Tip 172, on page 200; Tip 246, on page 277; and Tip 7, on page 54.

261 Add an "Open in terminal" Option to Nautilus's Right-Click Menu

Have you ever been browsing through the Ubuntu file system using Nautilus and wanted to open a terminal window where you ended up? Just use Synaptic to install nautilus-open-terminal. Then log out and back in again. In the future, you can right-click a blank space in a particular folder and select Open in terminal to open a terminal window automatically in that folder, or you can right-click a folder itself and click the option.

262 Make Windows Bootable If Things Go Wrong During Ubuntu Installation

Sometimes resizing the Windows partition during the installation of Ubuntu can make it unbootable. You'll know whether this is the case because Windows will appear to boot but will just sit there forever, with the boot-time progress bar scrolling. You'll need to run chkdsk from within Windows to fix it, but how do you do this if Windows won't boot (even into Safe Mode)?

---

40. There isn't a great deal of tolerance in the wider Linux world for HTML email. It's considered an aberration. As a rule, Linux people prefer plain-text emails and get annoyed with anybody who disagrees. However, they usually don't mind smileys typed as text.

You'll need to use the Windows Recovery Console. Boot from the Windows installation CD/DVD, and at the menu, hit r to enter the Recovery Console. Select your Windows partition when prompted, and enter your administrator password when prompted (just hit Enter if you didn't set an administrator password). Then, at the command prompt, type chkdsk C: /r (assuming C: is the drive on which you have Windows installed). Once it's completed, type exit to reboot the computer.

You can also try repairing the Windows file system from within Ubuntu: see Tip 38, on page 87.

263 Edit the Name and Artist Information of MP3 Files

Most MP3 files contain ID3 tag information, which usually indicates the artist, song name, and album, amongst other things. Unfortunately, some of this information can be wrong. RhythmBox features the ability to change it, but you have to right-click the track in question and select Properties, which can be long-winded if you have lots of files to edit.

To edit the track information quickly and efficiently, consider using exfalso, which can be installed using Synaptic (search for and install the exfalso package). Once installed, it can be found on the Applications → Sound & Video menu. Simply select the folder the track(s) is in on the left and then the track itself, and double-click each entry on the right to edit the ID3 information. Click the Add button to add entirely new information, if you think you need to do so.

If your problem is the inverse of this—the ID3 tag information is correct but the filenames are wrong—use Synaptic to install mp3rename. This is a command-line program that, as its name suggests, renames files based on their ID3 tag information. Either specify a file for it to work on (mp3rename filename.mp3) or switch into the relevant folder and type mp3rename * to rename all MP3 files. Remember that if you do this and RhythmBox has previously cataloged the files, you'll have to make it reindex. To do this, click Music → Import Folder within RhythmBox, and select the folder containing the MP3 files.

☐

264 Never Touch the Mouse While Using Ubuntu (Well, Almost)

GNOME Do is an exciting piece of software that lets you start programs, play music, browse to websites, create emails, and much more, all without taking your hands off the keyboard. It does this by opening a kind of search box into which you simply type what you're interested in. To start Firefox, you'd simply type firefox, for example. GNOME Do will likely almost instantly recognize what you want, so before you've even typed fir, it will suggest that you want to run Firefox. All you need do then is hit Enter. Similarly, by typing a URL such as http://www.ubuntukungfu.org, Firefox will open with the URL. To start an email, you'd simply type the name of your contact (they will have to be in your email address book, of course). To add an MP3 to RhythmBox's playlist, type its title.

In order to install GNOME Do, use Synaptic to install both gnome-do and gnome-do-plugins. Once installed, a little extra configuration work is necessary to make it start on login: click System → Preferences → Sessions, and then click the Startup Programs tab. Click the Add button, and in the dialog box that appears, type GNOME Do in the Name field and gnome-do --quiet in the Command field (note that there are two dashes before quiet). Leave the Comment field empty, and then click OK. Then the Close button in the parent dialog box. After this, log out and back in.

You can open the GNOME Do search box by hitting Windows +spacebar.

GNOME Do is a very powerful piece of software. To learn more about what it can do, visit the website of its maker: http://do.davebsd.com.

For an almost completely mouse-free email-reading and web-browsing experience, see Tip 7, on page 54.

265 Alter Image Viewer's Zoom Speed

☐

You might have already noticed that, if you roll the mouse wheel while viewing an image in Eye of GNOME (GNOME's default image viewer), you'll zoom in and out of the image. You can alter the rate of zoom by firing up gconf-editor and heading over to /apps/eog/view. Then change the value in the zoom_multiplier key. The figure is the zoom in/out percentage divided by 100—the default value of (circa) 0.05 is 5%. This means that each "click" of the mouse wheel zooms in 5%. A value of 0.01 makes for smoother zooming (1%), although you'll need to spin the mouse wheel quite a lot to make much progress! A value of 0.1 or even 0.2 (10 and 20%) makes for faster zooming.

If you'd like to turn off zooming with the mouse wheel and make the wheel simply scroll the window as in any other application, open gconf-editor, head over to /apps/eog/view, and remove the check from alongside scroll_wheel_zoom. The changes will take effect immediately, so open an image by double-clicking it, and see what happens!

266 Install Skype

☐

Skype is software used to make phone or video calls, either to other computing devices or to actual phones. It's proprietary software but free of charge. To install it under Ubuntu, the best plan is to add the Skype repository so that you can then install it via Synaptic. If any updates of the software are released, as they are frequently, they'll be suggested for installation using the Update Manager tool.

To add the Skype repository, click System → Administration → Software Sources, and then ensure the Third-Party Software tab is selected. Click the Add button, and in the APT Line text field, type the following:

```
deb http://download.skype.com/linux/repos/debian/ stable non-free
```

Click the Add Source button, then click the Close button, and agree to reloading the list of packages when prompted. Open Synaptic, and use it to install the skype package. Once installed, you'll find the program on the Internet menu. To have Skype start on login, click System → Preferences → Sessions, and click the Add button. In the dialog box that appears, type Skype in the Name field and skype in the Command field. Leave the Comment field empty, then click OK, and finally click the Close button in the parent dialog box.

To change configuration options, click the small Skype icon at the bottom left and select Options. See also Tip 96, on page 141, which describes how to ensure others can hear you if you run into audio problems.

If you run into problems with Skype's audio output, use Synaptic to install the nas package. Then restart the computer.

267 Arrange Output into Columns

This is a handy hint if you have to read through system configuration files. Virtually all configuration files have some attempt at layout within them to make for easier reading, usually in the form of spaces between the various configuration options. The problem is that these become eroded by the constant editing of the file. When used at the prompt, the column command is able to spot these attempts at layout and use them to arrange the data into columns. It's best demonstrated by a before-and-after example, so open a terminal window, and type the following:

```
$ cat /etc/fstab
```

Used in this way, the cat command simply displays the contents of a file. You'll see that /etc/fstab is a pretty messy file.

Now run it through the column command by piping the output of the previous command, as follows:

```
$ cat /etc/fstab|column -t
```

The -t command option tells column to figure out the layout using the spaces within the file.

What you'll see is a file that's better formatted. It should be easier to make out the data within the file. It probably won't be perfect, because column isn't very intelligent. But it'll probably be an improvement.

268 View Images Without a Graphical Environment

☐

The issue of how to view graphics at the command line is a thorny one. Theoretically, should you find yourself without a GUI, it should be possible to install and use simple image-viewing programs that use the *framebuffer*. This is where the image data is written straight into the memory of the graphics card, without any need for complexities such as actual graphics drivers. However, Ubuntu prohibits the use of the framebuffer because it can cause problems with the hibernation power-saving mode.

A solution, one that has a measure of entertainment value, is to convert the image to lots of letters and numbers. When viewed from a distance, or through squinted eyes, the contents of the photo can just about be made out. It's far from ideal, for sure, but can be surprisingly useful and is often entertaining to boot.

Start by using Synaptic to install the aview and imagemagick packages. Then switch to a virtual console, log in, and type the following:

```
$ asciiview filename.jpg
```

Obviously, you should replace filename.jpg with the name of your file. The file can be any image format.

You can zoom into the picture using the plus and minus keys and move around it using the cursor keys. A good tip is that repeatedly zooming in and out somehow causes the image to be easier to comprehend. When you've finished, hit q.

269 Synchronize Files Between a Laptop and Desktop PC

☐

If you have two computers, you might want to synchronize data between the two. For example, if you have a laptop, you might want to transfer the files in your Documents folder to the main PC (and vice versa). You could do this manually by creating a network share (see Tip 28, on

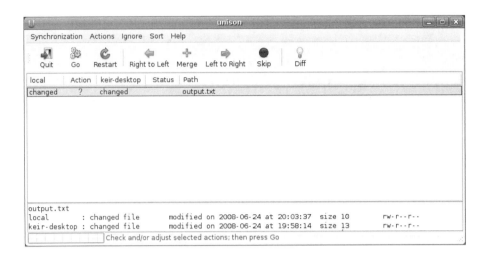

Figure 3.41: RESOLVING A FILE CLASH IN UNISON (SEE TIP 269)

page 73 for details), but it's much better to do it automatically, with just a single click.

There are a variety of ways of synchronizing files under Ubuntu, and indeed, this is the kind of task that Linux excels in. However, perhaps the most fuss-free method is to use a program called Unison (or, actually, Unison GTK, which adds a graphical front end to the Unison command-line program; throughout I refer to the whole thing as Unison for simplicity). Unison uses built-in Linux tools to sync files but hides everything behind a friendly user interface.

The following are the steps required to sync the Documents folders on two separate computers using Unison. Before following these steps, follow the instructions in Tip 26, on page 72, which explains how to ensure Ubuntu always has the correct time. Follow the steps on both computers. This is essential because synchronization will fail otherwise.

These instructions make reference to a desktop PC and laptop computer but could be any two computers capable of running Ubuntu (or indeed any computer with Linux installed that can run Unison):

1. On the desktop PC, use Synaptic to install the unison-gtk package. Meanwhile, on the laptop, use Synaptic to install the openssh-server and unison-gtk packages. As you might have guessed, Unison uses

SSH in the background to provide the file transfer conduit. If you want to learn more about SSH, see Tip 190, on page 218.

2. Once installed on the desktop PC, Unison can be found on the Applications → Accessories menu. When it starts, a wizard will walk you through creating an initial profile. The first step is to enter the folder on the desktop PC that you want to synchronize. Click the Browse button, and then locate your Documents folder. Click OK to close the file-browsing dialog box and OK again to move onto the next step of the wizard in Unison.

3. In the next step, you must tell Unison which folder you want to synchronize with on the laptop. In the Directory text field, type Documents again. There's no need to precede it with /home/username because Unison will automatically log into the laptop's /home/username folder each time it synchronizes.

4. Click the SSH radio button. You'll now need to find the IP address of the laptop. This can be done by moving over to it, right-clicking its NetworkManager icon, and selecting Connection Information. Then look in the dialog box that appears for the line that reads IP Address. Type what you see (four numbers separated by dots) into the Host text field back on the desktop PC.

5. In the User text field, still on the desktop PC, type the login name you use on the laptop. Then click the OK button.

6. You'll immediately be told that the laptop computer is being contacted. Then a dialog box will pop up telling you that the "authenticity of host can't be established." This is fine. Just type yes to continue, and hit OK.

7. You'll then be prompted for the login password on the laptop. Type it, and then click OK.

8. After this, you'll see a scary-looking warning dialog box saying that "no archives were found for these roots." Don't worry. This appears because this is the first time you've synchronized. Once you click OK, Unison will detect the files both on the desktop PC and on the laptop (it's worth pointing out that you won't see any sign of Unison running on the laptop, and you won't have to do anything on the laptop—Unison runs automatically in the background).

9. After a few minutes, the program window on the desktop PC will indicate the file differences between the two folders. The Path heading will show the file in question, and under the Action heading will be the "direction of travel," indicated by an arrow—if the arrow points left, the file will be transferred *to* the desktop PC from the

laptop. If it points right, the file will be transferred *from* the desktop PC to the laptop. If you don't want to synchronize a particular file or folder, select it, and click the Skip button on the toolbar. However, assuming you're happy with everything, click the Go button on the toolbar. The files will then be copied across. When Unison has finished (look at the status bar in the bottom left of the Unison window and the Status heading in the list of files), you can close the program window.

And that's all there is to it. After this, you should run Unison on the desktop PC every time you want to sync the Documents folders on the two computers, such as when you get home from work. When Unison starts, just select default from the list.

Note that Unison always updates older files when synchronizing. For example, if you started a file on your desktop PC, transferred it to your laptop using Unison, and edited it while out and about, Unison would automatically overwrite the older file on the desktop PC with the updated version. This makes sense, of course. If the situation arises that the file gets updated on both machines between synchronizations, a question mark will appear alongside the file when you come to synchronize—for an example, see Figure 3.41, on page 298—and it won't get automatically copied across. You'll then have to manually intervene to decide which to overwrite—the copy on the desktop PC or the copy on the laptop. Click the Right to Left toolbar button to overwrite the file on the desktop PC or the Left to Right button to overwrite the file on the laptop. Of course, it might be simpler just to manually copy the file across in this case—because SSH is providing the connection Unison uses to transfer files, you can use Nautilus to browse the files on the remote computer via an SFTP connection. To learn how, see the closing paragraphs of Tip 190, on page 218.

You can create additional profiles to sync other folders too—just click the Create New Profile button in Unison's startup program window, type a name for the profile when prompted, and then double-click its entry in the list to start working through the wizard again. I find it useful to synchronize the Desktop folder on both machines because I tend to temporarily store a lot of files there. Don't choose to sync your entire /home folder—hidden files are copied across too by Unison, and hidden files within your /home folder contain program configuration files unique to each computer. Upon synchronization there would be some almighty file clashes, and the likelihood of the login accounts on both systems getting damaged beyond repair because of mangled configuration files is high.

It's worth noting that you don't necessarily have to sync between two computers. You can also sync between a folder on a removable storage device and one on the computer's hard disk, or even just another folder on the same computer. Just select the Local radio button in the previous step when you choose SSH, and fill in the details appropriately.

270 Rename Files Quickly

Ubuntu doesn't allow the "slow double-click" used on some operating system to rename files. The best solution for quick renaming is to select the file/folder in question and hit F2. Then type the new filename. By default, only the actual filename is selected for renaming and not the file extension. To select this too before typing, quickly tap Ctrl+a.

To rename lots of files at once, see Tip 230, on page 261.

271 Have sudo Insult You

This is a strange tip that reflects the *Monty Python* style of humor that pervades Linux. To see mild and humorous insults whenever you get your sudo/gksu password wrong, open a terminal, and type sudo visudo. Then navigate to the end of the line that begins Defaults, and type a. This will switch to INSERT mode, so type a comma and then the word insults. For an example of how the file looked after editing on my test PC, see Figure 3.42, on the next page.

After this, don't hit Enter, but instead hit Esc, and type :wq to save the file and quit the text editor. The changes will take effect immediately, so try preceding a command with sudo and deliberately get your password wrong to see what happens (first you will have to kill the sudo grace period: sudo -K). Note that if you make a mistake editing the previous file, just hit Esc and type :q! to quit without saving. Then make another attempt.

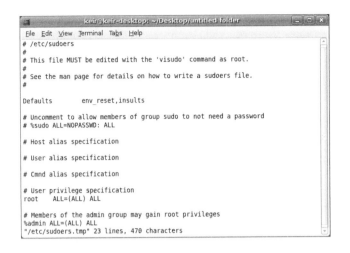

```
                keir@keir-desktop: ~/Desktop/untitled folder
File  Edit  View  Terminal  Tabs  Help
# /etc/sudoers
#
# This file MUST be edited with the 'visudo' command as root.
#
# See the man page for details on how to write a sudoers file.
#

Defaults        env_reset,insults

# Uncomment to allow members of group sudo to not need a password
# %sudo ALL=NOPASSWD: ALL

# Host alias specification

# User alias specification

# Cmnd alias specification

# User privilege specification
root    ALL=(ALL) ALL

# Members of the admin group may gain root privileges
%admin ALL=(ALL) ALL
"/etc/sudoers.tmp" 23 lines, 470 characters
```

Figure 3.42: EDITING THE SUDO CONFIG FILE (SEE TIP 271)

272 Make Nautilus Display "Traditional" File Permissions

If you right-click a file, select Properties, and click the Permissions tab, Nautilus will show the permissions of the file in a series of three drop-down lists. To be honest, although designed to be simple, these sometimes confuse me, and I long for the more arcane but recognizable -rwx-r--r-- style of permissions listing.

I was therefore very happy when I discovered this tweak. Start gconf-editor, head over to /apps/nautilus/preferences, and put a check alongside show_advanced_permissions. The changes take effect immediately. Any new Nautilus Properties dialog boxes that are opened will now show a series of simple checkboxes for permissions (once the Permissions tab is selected, of course), as well as a Text view section, listing traditional-style file permissions that would appear at the command line. For an example, see Figure 3.43, on the facing page.

For tips describing how to alter how Nautilus displays files and file information, see Tip 85, on page 132; Tip 104, on page 146; Tip 165, on page 194; and Tip 132, on page 165.

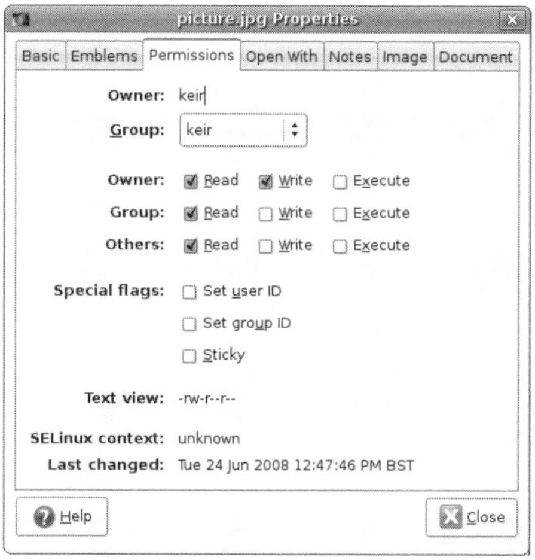

Figure 3.43: SWITCHING TO A TRADITIONAL PERMISSIONS VIEW (SEE TIP 272)

273 See the GNOME Fish

This is a nice little hidden feature of GNOME. Hit $\boxed{\text{Alt}}$+$\boxed{\text{F2}}$, and type free the fish into the text field. Then click Run. Wait a second or two, and you'll see a fish swim across the screen. It's a lady fish, and she's called Wanda. Yes, really. She even has her own fan site (http://jrong.tripod. com/wanda.html), and you'll have probably realized by now that she's most likely named after the eponymous hero of the movie *A Fish Called Wanda.*

To get rid of her, just click her. But she'll be back.... To *really* get rid of her, you'll have to log out and back in again or open a terminal window and type killall gnome-panel.

She also plays a mean game of Space Invaders, except the invaders are cows with five legs. Yes, really. To play the game, once again hit $\boxed{\text{Alt}}$+$\boxed{\text{F2}}$, and type gegls from outer space (note that that's "gegls" with an *l*, and not "gegis"). To move Wanda left or right, use the cursor keys. To fire, hit the spacebar. To regain your sanity, lie in a darkened room for thirty minutes.

You can put Wanda in a tank and have her contained on the desktop by right-clicking a blank spot on the panel, selecting Add to panel, and selecting Fish from the list. If you click her tank, you'll see a pithy or witty motto.

☐ | **274** | ## Use Desktop Widgets

The fashion amongst desktop operating systems is to utilize desktop widgets. These are small programs that float on the desktop and provide specific but useful functionality, such as telling the time or showing the weather. Mac OS X has included them since version 10.4 in the form of its Dashboard component, while Windows Vista introduced them upon release in the form of the desktop sidebar.

As you might expect, Ubuntu offers its own variation on this theme in the form of Screenlets. This needs Ubuntu's desktop effects to work—for more information, see Tip 74, on page 120.

To install Screenlets, use Synaptic to search for and install the screen-lets package. While Synaptic is open, also search for and install the compizconfig-settings-manager package. This is needed because, before running Screenlets, you first need to enable the "widget layer" visual effect. To do this once the software is installed, click System → Prefer-ences → Advanced Desktop Effects Settings, and in the program win-dow that appears, put a check in the box alongside Widget Layer, under the Desktop heading.

Then close that program, and start Screenlets by clicking System → Preferences → Screenlets. Note that Screenlets will automatically start each time you log in, and when you click the icon in the notification area, the Screenlets configuration panel will open.

When the program first starts, you might see a warning about how there is "no existing autostart directory." Click the Yes button to create one. After this, to add a Screenlet to your desktop, just select it in the list, check the Auto start on login box at the bottom right of the program window, and then click the Launch/Add button. The Screenlet will be placed somewhere on your screen (probably the top left), but you can then drag it to wherever you want, as shown in Figure 3.44, on the facing page. Right-clicking each Screenlet will let you configure it.

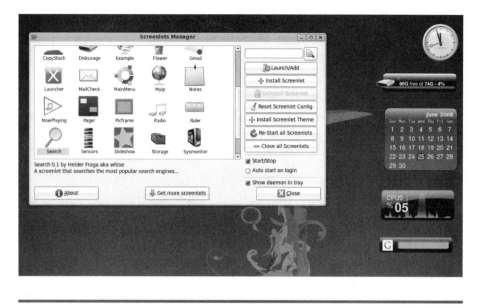

Figure 3.44: ADDING SCREENLETS TO THE DESKTOP (SEE TIP 274)

Instead of having Screenlets floating on the desktop (or in addition to), you can create a setup like Mac OS X, where the widgets are on a floating layer that appears whenever you hit F9. To add a widget to the floating layer, add it to the desktop as described earlier, and then right-click it and select Window → Widget.

Many more Screenlets are available in addition to those provided out of the box. To download them, visit http://www.screenlets.org. Look for the Downloads heading, and click an entry beneath the Third-party Screenlets link. To install a new screenlet, download it to your desktop (don't unpack it if it's an archive!), open the Screenlets configuration program (System → Preferences → Screenlets, or just click the Screenlets notification area icon), and click the Install Screenlet button. Then select the download using the file browser, and select it from the list of Screenlets in the main program window once it's been added to the main collection. After this, add it to the desktop as described earlier. You can delete the file you downloaded once it's installed.

For more tips on adding desktop bling, see Tip 21, on page 67; Tip 79, on page 127; Tip 147, on page 183; Tip 199, on page 227; Tip 74, on page 120; Tip 274, on the facing page; and Tip 289, on page 328.

275   Read E-books

E-books are, as the name suggests, electronic versions of books. Many classics of literature have been converted to e-book format and can be downloaded from sites such as Project Gutenberg (http://www.gutenberg.org). Additionally, some contemporary authors and publishers release their work as e-books.

To read any e-books that are in plain/rich-text format, FictionBook, HTML, Plucker, or Windows Help formats, use Synaptic to install FB-Reader (search for the fbreader package). Note that FBReader isn't able to read e-books in PDF format—for that, Ubuntu's default PDF viewer can be used. Nor can it read e-books that are protected by Digital Rights Management, such as some Mobipocket files (although standard Mobipocket books should work OK).

Once installed, you'll find FBReader on the Applications → Office menu. Any e-books you download will have to be imported into FBReader's library before you can read them, and to do this, click the Add eBook to Library toolbar button—it's the third icon from the left on the toolbar, and you can hover the mouse cursor over each icon to see a tooltip explaining what the icon does. Then navigate to the file. You may need to fill in author and title details when prompted, depending on the e-books format.

To choose between the e-books in your library in the future, click the first icon on the toolbar.

Once the e-books has been opened, use the Page Up and Page Down keys to page through the document. A progress bar at the bottom of the screen will show your progress through the entire text.

276   Make (Almost) Any Wifi Card Work with Ubuntu

Ubuntu's wifi support has gotten steadily better over the years, and with Ubuntu 8.04 (Hardy Heron) it's safe to say that the majority of wifi devices will work fine. However, if you find that yours doesn't (you'll know because it will be like no wifi hardware is installed), help is at hand in the form of Ndiswrapper.

This lets you use Windows XP wifi drivers under Ubuntu. As you can imagine, it's something of a hack and doesn't always work, although in most cases the results are very good.

The following steps walk you through what's needed to get XP wifi drivers working under Ubuntu. The guide is split into three sections: identifying your wifi card make and model, sourcing the Windows driver and extracting the driver file components, and finally installing the Windows XP driver files.

Identifying the Wifi Card Hardware

To source the correct driver for your wifi hardware, it's necessary to find out its make and model. However, you *don't* need the make and model listed on the box or in the specification list. You must find out what company actually manufactured the hardware, which will probably be different from the company that sold it (particularly with more inexpensive hardware). You must also find out the PCI ID number, which is how operating systems like Ubuntu and Windows refer to the card on a technical level.

1. Open a terminal window, and type the following:

   ```
   $ lspci -vv -nn|less -i
   ```

   This will list the hardware on your system connected through the PCI bus (which is practically all of it). The command options specified cause lspci to return more information (-vv) and cause the vital PCI ID numbers to be returned too (-nn).

2. Hit the forward slash (/) to search, and type wireless. Then hit Enter. If you find no result, hit forward slash again, and search for wlan. If you still get no results, try searching for 802.11. These are the common terms used to describe wifi hardware. When you get a match, use the up/down cursor keys to scroll so you see the entire entry for that device (each entry is separated from the others in the list by a blank line). Make a note of the make and model name listed on the *first* line.

3. After this, look at the end of the same line for a pattern of numbers and letters that look like [168c:0013]—four digits, a colon, and then four more digits (the digits are hexadecimal, if knowing that helps you identify them). Write these down too. For an example taken

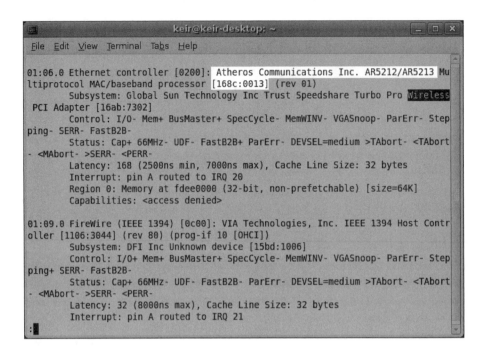

Figure 3.45: IDENTIFYING A WIFI CARD'S NAME, MODEL NUMBER, AND PCI ID (SEE TIP 276)

from my test PC with the relevant parts of the entry in the listing highlighted, see Figure 3.45. Be careful not to get the details mixed up with the Subsystem line.

Sourcing the Windows XP Driver

Finding the Windows XP driver isn't too difficult. The easiest way of doing it is to head over the Ndiswrapper website and browse its database of cards, which links to the download sites of drivers known to work. Of course, you'll need to do this using a computer that can get online (assuming your Ubuntu computer is currently unable to for lack of wifi drivers), and the easiest way of doing this is simply to boot into your Windows partition.

Once you've found the correct driver file, you must extract the components you need. The following instructions describe how all of this is done:

1. Use a web browser to head over to http://ndiswrapper.sourceforge.net. Once there, click the Documents/Wiki link on the left, and then click

the link that reads List of cards known to work. On the following page, click the entry in the alphabetical list that refers to the first letter of the manufacturer details you discovered earlier.

2. In the listing page that appears, search using the PCI ID number you noted earlier. Note that you shouldn't include the square brackets surrounding the numbers and letters. The details from my test PC were [168c:0013], so I searched for 168c:0013.

3. It's likely more than one entry in the list will match, so you should then check the details listed in the Card: and Chipset: components of the website listing against the manufacturer and model details you wrote down earlier. Try to get the best match possible. Some entries in the Ndiswrapper website list might even refer to the make and model of computer the wifi card is used in. Once you find a match, click the link provided to download the driver. Avoid any drivers marked as x86_64 in the list—these are designed to work on 64-bit versions of Linux (unless you have the 64-bit version of Ubuntu installed, of course, although this is unlikely unless you specifically opted to).

4. Once you have the driver file, you must extract the necessary driver components from it. To be frank, this is easier done using Windows rather than Ubuntu, so if you don't already have Windows up and running, copy the driver installation file to your Windows desktop and then boot into Windows. Once Windows has started, download a program called Universal Extractor from http://legroom.net/software/uniextract. This is a clever open source program that's able to extract files from just about any archive file, including Windows setup executable files (.exe). Once it's downloaded and installed, right-click the Windows XP driver file, and select UniExtract to Subdir. This will create a new folder containing the individual driver files.

5. The files you want will probably be in a folder named WinXP, WindowsXP, or similar. If you've ever installed hardware drivers in Windows, this will sound familiar, although the folder might be called ndis5x or similar. In the folder, look for .inf files. If you're in luck, there will be only one, and you can skip straight to the last step in this section. If there's more than one, then you'll need to search through each until you find the correct one.

6. Open the first .inf file in Windows Notepad by double-clicking it. Click Edit → Find, and search for the *first* part of PCI ID you noted

earlier. For example, the whole PCI ID number on my test PC was 168c:0013, so I searched for 168c. If you find no match, close the file, and move onto the next .inf file. If you do find a match, look further along that particular line, and look for the second part of the PCI ID. It will probably be next to the word DEV_. If you find a match, then congratulations! You've found the .inf file you need.

7. Copy the .inf file to a new folder, along with any .sys and .bin files you find in the driver folder (you may not find .bin files). Any other files can be ignored. You now have all you need to install the XP driver under Ubuntu, but don't reboot just yet. First you'll need to grab some package files from the Ubuntu repositories.

Installing the XP Driver Files

As mentioned, installing the XP drivers is easy, but first you'll need to download and install the Ndiswrapper configuration software (the actual Ndiswrapper system software is already installed out of the box on Ubuntu). The following steps are all you need to do to install the driver:

1. Type the following addresses in the address bar of your browser. Each will cause a file to be downloaded:

   ```
   http://us.archive.ubuntu.com/ubuntu/pool/main/n/ndiswrapper/ ↩
   ndiswrapper-utils-1.9_1.50-1ubuntu1_i386.deb
   ```

   ```
   http://us.archive.ubuntu.com/ubuntu/pool/main/n/ndiswrapper/ ↩
   ndiswrapper-common_1.50-1ubuntu1_all.deb
   ```

   ```
   http://us.archive.ubuntu.com/ubuntu/pool/main/n/ndisgtk/ndisgtk ↩
   _0.8.3-1_i386.deb
   ```

2. Reboot into Ubuntu, and copy the XP driver files to the desktop, plus the three system software packages you downloaded. Open a terminal window, and type the following to install the software:

   ```
   $ sudo dpkg -i ~/Desktop/ndis*.deb
   ```

3. Once installation has finished, click System → Administration → Wireless Network Drivers. Once the program window opens, click the Install New Driver button.

4. A dialog box will appear prompting for the location of the .inf file. Click the Location drop-down list to open a file-browsing window, and navigate to the .inf file. Then click the Install button.

5. In the Wireless Network Drivers program window, you will now see your wireless hardware listed on the left of the window. Beneath

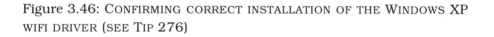

Figure 3.46: CONFIRMING CORRECT INSTALLATION OF THE WINDOWS XP WIFI DRIVER (SEE TIP 276)

it should be listed the words Hardware present: yes, as shown in Figure 3.46. If you see Hardware present: no, you have an incompatible driver. Select the hardware in the list, and click Remove Driver. Then repeat the previous steps to download an alternative driver.

After this, your wifi hardware will be immediately available for configuration using NetworkManager at the top right of the desktop. You can close the Wireless Network Drivers window and delete the driver and package files from the desktop.

277 Connect to the Remote Desktop of a Windows Vista Computer

If you have any problems connecting to a Windows Vista computer's remote desktop using Terminal Server Client (Applications → Internet), you might have to tweak a setting or two on the Vista computer.

Try the following things:

- Ensure the Vista username you're using to log in has a password. Passwordless accounts won't work when it comes to remote desktop access. (This is true of Windows XP computers too.)

- On the Windows computer, click the Start button, and then right-click Computer. Click Properties, and in the window that appears, click the Remote Settings link on the left side. In the dialog box that appears, click Allow Connections from Computers Running Any Version of Remote Desktop (Less Secure). Then click Apply. Note that these instructions apply only to the Business and Ultimate editions of Vista; Home Premium and Home Basic editions lack this degree of control.

278 Use Ubuntu on Your Games Console

If you're a fan of gaming, then you might be interested to learn that, with some effort, Ubuntu can be installed on the latest range of games consoles, such as Microsoft Xbox 360, Sony PlayStation 3, and even the Nintendo DS Lite handheld console. All of this is strictly unofficial, of course, and supported by "homebrew" communities who enjoying hacking hardware and software. As such, it brings with it the possibility of damage to the existing console software if you don't know exactly what you're doing.

Running Ubuntu on consoles is usually done more for fun and educational value rather than actual utility, although a handful of users have reportedly turned their games console into streaming media servers. Unfortunately, using consoles in this way is something the manufacturers dislike and frequently update the system hardware to make the task impossible (at least until somebody figures out how to bypass it!).

There isn't space here to describe the often extremely lengthy steps of how to install Ubuntu on the consoles. Instead, you should visit https://help.ubuntu.com/community/PlayStation_3 to learn how to install it onto a PS3, or you should visit http://forums.xbox-scene.com/index.php?showtopic=595543 to learn how to install it onto an Xbox 360. To install Ubuntu on the Nintendo DS Lite, visit http://dslinux.org. It's worth noting that Google lists many guides written by other community members that can often be worth trying.

279 Use a "Legal" MP3 Codec

Even though Ubuntu will install multimedia playback codecs upon demand, the actual software it installs resides in a legally gray area. Much of what the software implements is protected by patents in countries that allow software to be patented, such as the United States of America (currently European Union countries do not allow software patenting).

Nobody is entirely sure of the implications of software patenting on open source codec software, as used under Ubuntu. If it's an issue at all, it'll likely affect those creating and distributing the codecs, rather than those who download and use them.

But if you simply don't like the idea of using the codecs but still want MP3 playback, you can install the Fluendo MP3 codec. Just use Synaptic to search for and install the gstreamer0.10-fluendo-mp3 package. Once it's installed, MP3 playback should work straightaway in Totem and RhythmBox.

Fluendo is a multimedia software company that, in an egalitarian spirit, licensed MP3 patents for the use by all the Linux community. The only issue is that the codec is one-way only—it will decode only and can't be used to encode MP3 tracks. However, I strongly advise you to use Ubuntu's built-in Ogg Vorbis encoding for the future ripping of music tracks. Ubuntu is set up automatically to use this. It is similar to MP3 in both audio quality and file size results.

See also Tip 65, on page 114, to learn how to install all the codecs you'll ever need, although these may suffer from the issues mentioned earlier.

280 Use Look-a-Likes of the Microsoft Fonts

Tip 170, on page 197, explains how to install the popular Microsoft Windows fonts on your system. Yet if you feel the whole point of installing Ubuntu is to get away from Microsoft products of any kind, you might not want to do this.

The solution is to install the Liberation fonts, created by Linux vendor Red Hat to be metrically identical to Microsoft's fonts. In other words, the three fonts offered—replacements for Arial, Times New Roman, and Courier—are the same size as the Microsoft fonts and so can be used as swap-in replacements without any disruption to websites or office documents.

Just use Synaptic to search for and install the ttf-liberation package. Once it's installed, you might choose to configure Firefox to use the fonts as defaults. Click Edit → Preferences, select the Content icon, and click the Advanced button alongside the Fonts & Colors heading. Then, in the dialog box that appears, select Liberation Serif in the Serif drop-down list, Liberation Sans in the Sans-serif drop-down list, and Liberation Mono in the Monospace drop-down list. In the Proportional drop-down list, you might choose to change it to read Sans Serif—this will cause a sans serif font to be used with sites like http://slashdot.org or BBC News (http://news.bbc.co.uk), something you might have been used to under Windows.

Once done, click OK and then the Close button in the Preferences dialog box. Then browse to a website to test your new settings.

☐ ## 281 Play Old MS-DOS Games

This tip should appeal to anybody who grew up in the 1980s and 1990s, arguably the period of classic gaming. It involves the use of DOSBox, a program that emulates DOS inside a virtual computer. However, unlike DOS days of old, there's no need to spend hours installing drivers or extended-memory managers—everything is set up for you.

Start by using Synaptic to install the dosbox package. Once installed, you need to create a virtual hard disk, so create an empty folder in your /home folder and call it something like dosbox_c. After this, start DOS-Box by clicking its link on the Applications → Games menu, and mount your new hard disk by typing the following at the DOSBox prompt:

```
mount C dosbox_c
```

Then you'll need to switch into the folder in the usual DOS method by typing this:

```
C:
```

Figure 3.47: PLAYING OLD GAMES USING DOSBOX (SEE TIP 281)

Then all you need do is raid the attic for all those DOS games you stored there back in 1995. Alternatively, you could search Google for *abandon-ware*—old computer software that has been released into the public domain. A particularly good site is http://www.abandonia.com. Once you have downloaded a game, copy it into your dosbox_c folder, and then use DOSBox to either run its installer or, more likely, just run the executable to start playing the game. For an example game played on my test PC, see Figure 3.47.

Note that you might need to quit and then restart DOSBox for it to see the contents of the mounted folder after files have been copied there.

If you find you really like your reintroduction to DOS, see Tip 177, on page 207, which describes how to run an old but freely available version of Microsoft Word under DOSBox.

282 | Install Google Applications

As with Windows and Macintosh, Google has released a series of down-loadable applications for Linux: Google Earth, Picasa, and Google Desktop. Google Earth allows you to spin around the globe looking at satellite photographs and planning routes between locations. Picasa lets you catalog and tweak photographs on your hard disk and then upload them to online photo albums provided as part of your Google account.

Google Desktop lets you organize and search your files, as well as quickly search your Gmail account (rather like Tracker, the built-in Ubuntu search tool, as discussed in Tip 77, on page 123, although Tracker will not search your Gmail unless it has been downloaded using Evolution).

Both Google Desktop and Picasa can be downloaded by adding Google's APT repository to your system. However, for reasons best known to Google's engineers, Google Earth can't be installed this way and must be installed manually.

Installing Google Desktop and Picassa

The following instructions explain how to add the Google APT repository, install Google Desktop and Picasa, and configure them afterward:

1. Start by adding Google's APT repository to your Ubuntu setup. This will let you install the applications using Synaptic and also receive regular updates in a fuss-free way. Click System → Administration → Software Sources, and then click the Third-Party Software tab. Click the Add button, and then type the following:

   ```
   deb http://dl.google.com/linux/deb/ stable non-free
   ```

2. Still in the Software Sources application, click the Authentication tab. Then open a terminal window, and type the following to download the Google APT GPG key, which will authenticate any Google packages you install:

   ```
   $ wget https://dl-ssl.google.com/linux/linux_signing_key.pub
   ```

   In the Software Sources program window, click the Import Key File button. Then navigate to and select the file you downloaded—it will be saved in your /home folder and be called linux_signing_key.pub. Once you're done, click the Close button in the Software Sources program window. Agree to reload the list of applications.

3. After this, you can use Synaptic to install the Google packages. Here are their package names:

   Google Desktop Search: google-desktop-linux
   Picasa: picasa

   If installing Picasa, it is also a good idea to install the Microsoft fonts, as described in Tip 170, on page 197. This is because the program is actually a modified Windows program made to work using the Wine program (for more information about Wine, see Tip 216, on page 240; note that the Wine components are "built in" to Picasa, so they are not visible to the user).

4. Once installed, Picasa can be started by clicking Applications → Other → Picasa. Before running it, click Applications → Other → Picasa Font Settings. Click the Menu Font tab, and change the Menu Font Size setting to 13. This will ensure Picasa's menus are readable and not in too-small a font. Then quit the application, and start Picasa. To sign into your web albums, click the link at the top right of the program window.

5. Google Desktop will be added to the Applications → Google Desktop menu. Once started, it will add a new icon to your notification area that, when clicked, will open the Google Desktop search window. To have Google Desktop search your Gmail too, right-click the icon, select Preferences, and then click the Gmail tab in the browser window that appears. Check the Index and search email in my Gmail account box, and then provide your login details when prompted.

Note that Google Desktop first needs to index your files and emails for searching to be successful. To see how far it has progressed, right-click the notification area icon, select Index, and then click Index Status.

Google Desktop will start automatically upon login following its initial activation.

Installing Google Earth

Google Earth for Linux must be downloaded and installed manually. This isn't difficult—just follow these instructions:

1. Follow the instructions in Tip 170, on page 197, and install the Windows fonts. This is useful because Google Earth is actually an adapted Windows program made to work under Wine, and as such it looks and functions better with typical Windows fonts. For more information about Wine, see Tip 216, on page 240; note that the Wine components are "built into" Google Earth and aren't visible to the user.

2. Google Earth requires your computer to be using 3D drivers for best performance. Click System → Hardware Drivers to check that

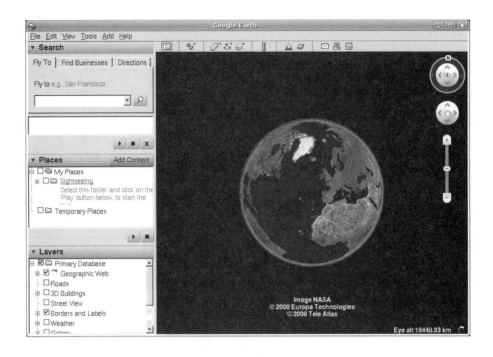

Figure 3.48: Google Earth (see Tip 282)

this is the case for your PC, and if necessary, choose to enable 3D drivers (users of computers containing recent Intel and some ATI graphics chips do not need proprietary drivers).

3. Browse to http://earth.google.com, and opt to download the installation file. Once the file has downloaded, you can install it by opening a terminal window and typing the following (this assumes the file has been downloaded to your desktop):

```
$ chmod +x ~/Desktop/GoogleEarthLinux.bin
$ ~/Desktop/GoogleEarthLinux.bin
```

When the installer dialog box appears, click inside the Install Path text field, and put a period before google-earth. On my test PC, this meant the line reads /home/keir/.google-earth. Then click the Begin Install button.

After this, you can start Google Earth by double-clicking its desktop icon. For an example of Google Earth running on my test PC, see Figure 3.48.

There's no Linux version of the handy Gmail Notifier program, the system tray application that can inform you of new Gmail messages. However, there is a community-created alternative that's perhaps even better: see Tip 296, on page 336.

283 Install MS Comic Sans–Style Fonts ☐

MS Comic Sans is the "handwriting" font offered under Microsoft Windows and is supposed to be based on handwriting used in comic speech bubbles. It has to be said that there are possibly more people who dislike it than actually like it, but Comic Sans lovers might have already spotted that Ubuntu has only one handwriting font out of the box (Purisa).

Luckily, some excellent handwriting fonts are just a download away via Synaptic—use it to search for and install the ttf-fifthhorseman-dkg-handwriting, ttf-sjfonts, and ttf-breip packages. The fonts to be installed are called Delphine, Steve, Breip, and DkgHandwriting. Additionally, you might be interested in the ttf-dustin package, which includes a handful of fonts, one of which—Domestic Manners—has a similar "marker pen" feel to MS Comic Sans.

284 Use Alternative Office Applications ☐

The office suite provided with Ubuntu, OpenOffice.org, is certainly comprehensive. However, it's not the only set of office applications available for Ubuntu. Here are some alternatives you might like to try—all are just a download away via Synaptic.

- Abiword: Abiword is a word processor that ties in tightly with the GNOME desktop look and feel. It understands most common document file formats, including Microsoft Word, and supports all the common ease-of-use features you might be used to, such as live spell checking, WYSIWYG page formatting, font previews, mail merge, and more. As is typical with open source applications, a plug-in structure is utilized, meaning that function add-ins are

Figure 3.49: ABIWORD WORD PROCESSOR

available—for more details of the plug-ins that are available, see http://www.abisource.com/wiki/PluginMatrix.

Abiword can be installed by using Synaptic to search for and install the abiword-gnome package. You should also add in the useful abiword-plugins package, which automatically installs a handful of the more useful plug-ins, including a thesaurus tool (most of the plug-ins, once installed, can be found on the Tools menu). Once installed, you'll find Abiword on the Applications → Office menu. For an example taken from my test PC, see Figure 3.49.

- Gnumeric: In many ways Gnumeric is the spreadsheet equivalent of Abiword, being closely tied in to the GNOME look and feel (which is where the name comes from; it's pronounced with the same hard *G* as "GNOME"). It too features excellent file format support, being able to read the pervasive Microsoft Excel spreadsheet type (although, unfortunately, it doesn't understand Visual Basic macros; for that you'll need to use OpenOffice.org). However, most of the useful mathematical functions from Excel are included, and Gnumeric also features a plug-in structure, so its usability can be expanded. Gnumeric also claims to be more accurate than its competitors—apparently, a recent report found that Gnumeric was even more accurate than Excel when it came to statistical analysis! See the Gnumeric website for more information: http://www.gnome.org/projects/gnumeric.

Gnumeric can be installed by using Synaptic to search for and install the gnumeric package. Once installed, it can be found on the Applications → Office menu.

- Koffice: It's probably fair to call Koffice the KDE Desktop Project's equivalent of OpenOffice.org, but that isn't to say that it's a clone. It's a completely separate project and in many ways exceeds the boundaries set by OpenOffice.org. Included in the Koffice suite are a word processor (KWord), a spreadsheet (KSpread), a presentations package (KPresenter: notice a naming theme here?), a database application (Kexi), a flowcharting application like Microsoft Visio (Kivio), a drawing application (Karbon14), a bitmap image editor (Krita), and a project management tool (KPlato). Phew! And I haven't mentioned several support applications, such as KChart, which is a graphing and charting tool.

All the applications are designed to work under KDE, but they operate fine under the GNOME desktop of Ubuntu, although their look and feel is sufficiently different to be a little off-putting at first. Additionally, some applications take a rather unorthodox approach to usability. KWord, for example, is based around the concept of frames, like Adobe FrameMaker. However, each of the applications includes just about every function you would expect, and each understands the relevant Microsoft Office file format. It's well worth spending some time to explore their features.

To install Koffice, use Synaptic to search for and install the koffice package. Note that a lot of support packages will be added and the total size of download is large. Once the suite has been installed, the applications can be found on the Applications → Office menu.

☐ **285** ## Have the Firefox Robot Talk to You

Open a Firefox window, and type about:robots in the address bar to see the Firefox 3 Easter egg. Do you know which book the third line of the text that pops up is taken from? Here's a hint: meditate on 42.

☐ **286** ## Back Up Your Data

If they aren't already, regular backups should be part of your routine. The fact is that computers are fallible and hard disks break. Humans are also fallible, and tired minds mean we don't always watch what we type or click.

Backing up is one task that Linux is particularly good at, and a wealth of command-line tools are available. For this tip we're going to look at a GUI tool called Simple Backup, which automates the procedure of backing up but uses the traditional backup tools. It produces the standard Linux backup file type: compressed tar archives.

But what kind of data should you back up? Data on your system falls into three broad categories: program data, configuration data, and personal data. It's reasoned that backing up all three is inefficient, because that would mean backing up the entire hard disk. Even if you have the storage capacity, this simply takes too long. Therefore, people usually back up configuration and personal data. If a disaster strikes, the operating system can be reinstalled from CD, and once the configuration files are restored from the backup, it should work just like it did.

Part of the technique of backing up is to copy the backup archives you create to a secure location. Backup files should certainly be copied off the hard disk that contains the original data as soon as possible after creation. Good choices for safe storage of the backup are rewritable DVD discs or a separate hard disk that connects via a USB connection. Some higher-capacity USB memory sticks can also be used.

In order to install Simple Backup, use Synaptic to search for and install sbackup. Once installed, two new entries will be found on the System

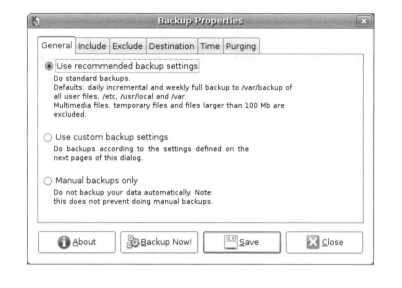

Figure 3.50: SIMPLE BACKUP CONFIG (SEE TIP 286)

→ Administration menu: Simple Backup Config and Simple Backup Restore. As you might expect, Simple Backup Config is used to create or amend the backup job, while Simple Backup Restore is used after the disaster has occurred to restore the files.

Creating and Scheduling a Backup Job

Start by clicking System → Administration → Simple Backup Config. In the program window that appears, you'll have three choices: Use recommended backup settings, Use custom backup settings, and Manual backups only. For an example, see Figure 3.50.

Automated Backups

The first option configures Ubuntu to run an automated backup job every day, in the background and shortly after the computer has booted for the first time. Vital configuration files along with all the data within users' /home folders are backed up, although audio and video files as well as any file exceeding 100MB are ignored to avoid the backup archive becoming too large.

Once an initial backup has been taken, the daily backup pass creates incremental backups, meaning that only altered files are backed up. This makes all subsequent backup passes much faster.

If all of this sounds like what you want, then select the Use recommended backup settings option, and click the Save button. Then click the Backup Now! button to create the first backup. And that's all you need do. You can immediately close the Simple Backup window because the actual backup job runs entirely in the background. The downside of this is that you have no progress display, but generally speaking, it's best to wait about an hour for the backup to complete. You can check on the backup job from the command line by typing the following:

```
$ ps aux|grep tar
```

This checks for the tar archiving program amongst the currently running processes. Look for the command in the output—it will probably run across several lines and begin tar -czS -c / -no-recursion.... If the command is not listed in the output (ignore grep tar in the output), then the command has finished.

The backup folder containing the actual backup archive and necessary directory files will be placed in the /var/backup folder (*not* /var/backups!). It will have a .ful extension. You can copy this folder to wherever you want (for example, a DVD-RW disc, depending on size).

Subsequent incremental and much smaller backup folders will be saved to the same location every day (these will have .inc extensions), although every seven days a completely new backup will be taken, which will result in a new main backup .ful folder. Old backup files are automatically deleted after thirty days. Each backup file is named after the day's date. Note that you should copy the incremental backup files to your chosen storage media along with the main backup file—incremental files are useless without the main backup file.

Configuring Backup Jobs

If you want to tweak the backup job, click the Use custom backup settings button. Then click the tabs to change the options. The backup is entirely configurable, but here are some particular options you might like to change:

- Back up all types and sizes of file: If you intend to store the eventual backup archives on an external hard disk, there's no reason why you shouldn't back up all the files in your /home folder, including multimedia files, which tend to make the eventual backup archive very large. To allow this to happen, click the Exclude tab, click the Max Size subtab on the left of the program window, and remove the check alongside Do not backup files bigger than. Additionally, click the File Types subtab, and remove all the entries in the list by highlighting them and clicking the Remove button.

- Changing the backup file location: By default, the backup files are saved to /var/backup (*not*/var/backups!), but you might choose to save them directly to an external hard disk or a network share. To do this, click the Destination tab, and select Use custom local backup directory. Then click the file browse drop-down list, and select the location.

- Changing the backup time: By default, the backup will occur each day shortly after your computer has booted for the first time. To change it so that the backup occurs hourly, weekly, or monthly, click the Time tab, and select the relevant option from the Do Back-ups drop-down list. To set a specific time when the backup should occur—maybe 1:30 p.m. while you're at lunch, for example—click the Precisely button, and set the time in the Hour and Minute boxes. If you select Weekly or Monthly in the Do Backups drop-down list, you'll also be able to select from the Day of month or Day of week list.

Once done, click the Save button and then the Backup Now button to create the initial backup.

Restoring a Backup

If the worst happens and you need to restore any number of files from the backup, click System → Administration → Simple Backup Restore. If the very worst happens and you had to reinstall Ubuntu from scratch, then ensure you re-create the same username for yourself—this will avoid problems with file ownerships and restored file locations. Then follow these steps to restore the data:

1. The first step is to select the location of the backup archives. Select the Use Custom radio button, and click the folder icon to open a file browse dialog box so you can navigate to where the backup is stored. It's important not to specify the backup folder itself— just the folder that it's in. For example, if the backup folder were stored on your desktop, you should enter /home/username/desktop as the location (replacing username with your username). Once done, click the Apply button. This will cause Simple Backup to scan the archives.

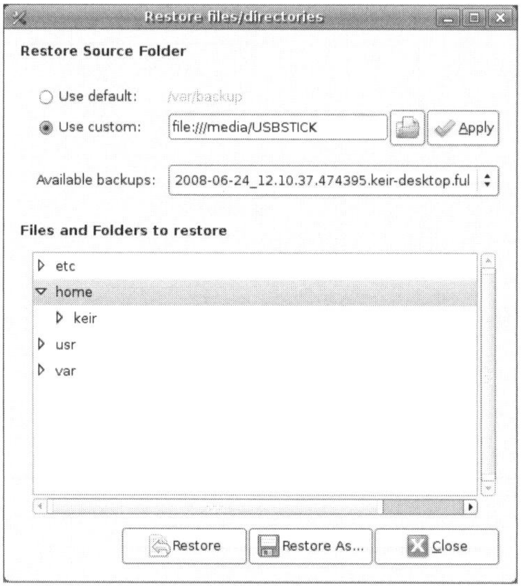

Figure 3.51: SIMPLE BACKUP RESTORE (SEE TIP 286)

2. Click the Available Backups drop-down list to choose a backup from which to restore—they are sorted by the dates they were made.

3. Once the backup has been selected, the files that the backup archive contains will be displayed after the Files and Folders to restore heading, as shown in Figure 3.51. Each folder will have a small triangle to its left, which you can click to expand the folder and show its contents.

4. After you've found the file(s) or folders you want to restore, highlight them, and then click the Restore button. To restore system configuration settings, you should select to restore /etc, /usr, and /var. Beware: this will rewrite the files and folders to their original locations. Files or folders already there with matching filenames will be overwritten! If you want to restore any files to a different location, click the Restore As button, and then choose a folder.

287 Use the Ubuntu Install CD as a General-Purpose Partitioning Tool ☐

The Ubuntu install CD includes Gparted, a powerful partitioning tool that can create, delete, and also resize partitions. It's there to aid Ubuntu installations, but there's no reason why that's all it should ever do. It doesn't just work with Linux partition types—it can create, delete, and resize most Windows and Macintosh partition types. Considering that this kind of functionality costs a lot of money in the form of commercial products like Norton PartitionMagic, the Ubuntu install CD should have a place in any PC repairperson's kit—even if they don't use Ubuntu!

To use the Gparted, boot from the Ubuntu install CD, select Try Ubuntu from the boot menu, and when the desktop appears, click System → Administration → Partition Editor. The best thing is that, while the repairman is waiting for the partitioning to finish, he can use Ubuntu to browse the Web or play games on the Applications → Games menu! Even PartitionMagic doesn't offer that!

Once the live distro mode is up and running, software can be installed, just like on a "real" Ubuntu installation. If you really are in the business of fixing Windows computers, you might be interested in installing the ntfsprogs package, which, amongst other things, can help fix NTFS file systems. See Tip 38, on page 87.

288 Give Old Macintosh Computers a New Lease on Life ☐

When Apple introduced OS X, lots of less powerful computers were left out in the cold, unable to cope with the high hardware requirements. This is still the case today, because newer releases of OS X simply refuse to work on even quite recently manufactured computers.

But there's no need to turn them into doorstops just yet. Ubuntu is available in a PowerPC remix that will run on computers containing G3,

G4, and G5 chips. However, the very latest releases of Ubuntu aren't officially supported, meaning that future security updates aren't guaranteed. The previous long-term support release, 6.06 Dapper Drake, is supported on PowerPC until June 2009.

PowerPC versions of Ubuntu can be downloaded from http://cdimage. ubuntu.com/ports/releases/—just select the version number you're interested in and then click the release link. Then select the Mac (PowerPC) and IBM-PPC (POWER5) desktop CD link. For instructions on how to install Ubuntu on older Macs, including a handful of caveats to watch out for, visit https://wiki.ubuntu.com/PowerPC.

289 Use Absolutely Any Picture as an Icon

Any image file can be used as a file/folder/launcher icon—even JPEG images straight off of your digital camera. Just right-click the file/ folder/launcher, select Properties, and click the icon preview at the top left of the dialog box that appears. Then browse to the image. Don't forget that desktop icons can also be resized (see Tip 79, on page 127), allowing you to create quarter desktop-sized icons of your partner's face, which, when double-clicked, launch the terminal program. Should you want to....

290 Install the GNOME Wallpapers

The GNOME Project supplies the desktop technology used by Ubuntu, and the default installation of GNOME includes several very pretty wallpapers that sadly aren't included with Ubuntu. However, you can get them by using Synaptic to search for and install the gnome-backgrounds package. Once installed, just right-click the desktop as usual, and select Change Desktop Background. The new wallpapers will be included in the list.

291 Zoom In for More Info in Nautilus

Did you know that the more you zoom in to an icon in a Nautilus file-browsing window, the more file or folder information becomes visible? Try it! Ensure icon view is active, and click the zoom control on the toolbar. You'll see that new text is added to the label beneath each showing how many files a folder contains or a file's size. To zoom in using the main keyboard, hit `Ctrl`+`=`. To zoom out, press `Ctrl`+`-`. To zoom in/out using the numeric keypad, if your computer has one, use `Ctrl`+`+` and `Ctrl`+`-`.[41]

To change what information is revealed, click Edit → Preferences, and click the Display tab in the dialog box that appears. Then choose from the drop-down lists. Note that although two file detail items can be displayed at Nautilus's default zoom level, Nautilus is configured to show only one by default.

292 Play MP3/Ogg Files at the Command Line

So, you've tweaked Ubuntu into a state of disrepair. Any hope of a GUI is a pipe dream, at least for the moment. While you hack away fixing things, wouldn't it be nice to have some music to console you at the console?

Just switch to an unused virtual console, log in, and type sudo apt-get install vlc. VLC is the GUI media playback application mentioned in Tip 231, on page 263, but it can also run with a text-mode interface—just start it with the -I ncurses command option (note that's a capital *I*, not *L*). For example, to play back filename.mp3, I would type vlc -I ncurses

---

41. I should point out for the pedants amongst the readership that I misstate the "zoom-in" keyboard shortcut. The required keyboard combination is actually `Ctrl`+`+`. Of course, the `=` key doubles up as both = and +, depending on whether the `Shift` key is pressed. Nautilus is just considerate enough to realize that you mean `Ctrl`+`+` when you actually hit `Ctrl`+`=`.

filename.mp3. Multiple files can be specified one after the other, thus creating a playlist, or a wildcard can be used to play back all files in a particular folder (that is, vlc -I ncurses ~/Music/*.mp3). Use a and z to alter the volume.

Once the music starts playing, switch to the original console to continue enacting repairs (and maybe see Tip 30, on page 76, which explains how to install a text-mode web browser, which is useful for looking up solutions!). See Tip 76, on page 122, to see how to alter the master volume of the audio system at the command line—this might be necessary if playback is too quiet.

293 Optimize Ubuntu's Performance

If you're using Ubuntu on an older computer, you might find that performance is not what you'd like. The best solution is always to expand the system if possible, and more memory will make the biggest difference. However, if that's not possible, then you might want to try prelinking. This makes for faster program start times by linking library files and executables for better memory usage. However, it doesn't work with all programs, and larger programs in particular seem to benefit the most. In fact, you may not see much improvement, and a handful of users have even reported that some applications won't start after prelinking. However, it's trivial to remove prelinking, so you might as well give it a try.

To enable prelinking, start by using Synaptic to search for and install the prelink package. Once installed, open a terminal window, and open the prelink configuration file in Gedit:

```
$ gksu gedit /etc/default/prelink
```

Look for the line that reads PRELINKING=unknown, and change it to read PRELINKING=yes. Then save the file and close Gedit.

Prelinking is now activated, and a prelinking pass of your system's executable files will run in the background periodically, but it's a good idea to create an initial prelinking pass of the system. To do this, type the following into a terminal window:

```
$ sudo prelink -a
```

It will take some time to complete, and you'll see a lot of output, but don't worry about it. Once complete, try starting some of the larger applications on your system—OpenOffice.org Writer, for example, or Firefox—to see whether there's any improvement in start times.

Should prelinking cause problems, type the following to remove it from your executable files:

```
$ sudo prelink -ua
```

Then uninstall the prelink package using Synaptic.

294 Tweak Ubuntu into Oblivion

Some people are born with the desire to poke around inside their operating system's deepest settings. If you're one of them, then take a look at Ubuntu Tweak, a program created by an Ubuntu community member. It brings to the surface usually hidden GNOME desktop settings to allow for true customization.

To install it, click System → Administration → Software Sources, then the Third-Party Software tab, and then the Add button. Then type the following into the dialog box:

```
deb http://ppa.launchpad.net/tualatrix/ubuntu hardy main
```

Click the Add Source button, and agree to refresh the list of software when prompted. After this, close Software Sources, and use Synaptic to search for and install the ubuntu-tweak and compizconfig-settings-manager packages. Once installed, Ubuntu Tweak can be found on the Applications → System Tools menu.

The tweaks are split up into six categories: Applications, Startup, Desktop, Personal, System, and Security, and the details are as follows (for an example of the interface, see Figure 3.52, on the next page):

- Applications: This section lets you install and remove some of the most popular Ubuntu software, including adding a handful of third-party APT repositories to add useful third-party applications. It's well worth investigating the lists of software provided because they filter out much of the dross available in the package archives.

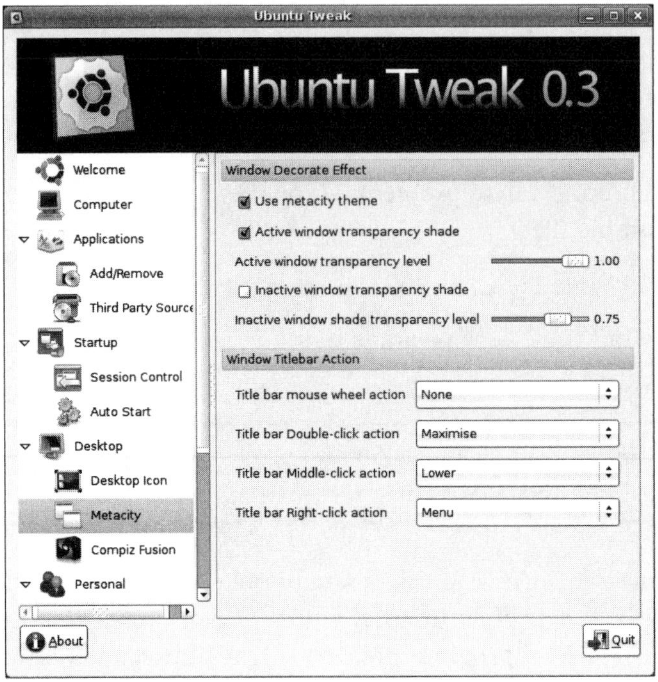

Figure 3.52: UBUNTU TWEAK (SEE TIP 294)

- **Startup:** Here you can control what happens when the Ubuntu desktop appears, such as what programs automatically run or whether the splash screen appears. Much of the same functionality can be accessed using the System → Preferences → Sessions program.

- **Desktop:** This option gives control over the desktop and windows appearance/operation, such as whether desktop icons appear or what happens when you double-click the title bars of windows. You can also configure some of the desktop effects' functions (select the Compiz Fusion option), and unlike CompizConfig Settings Manager, as described in Tip 74, on page 120, everything is kept very simple, and only the most pertinent options are offered for tweaking.

- **Personal:** This is something of a grab bag of options related to your user account that don't fit elsewhere. You can alter the location of your document folders, for example, or add some template documents to the right-click Create Document menu.

- System: Here you can change options relating to how the GNOME desktop used by Ubuntu functions, including the Nautilus file manager and also some specific power management settings.

- Security: This option lets you "lock down" some features of the Ubuntu desktop, such as stopping people from hitting Alt + F2 to run arbitrary programs. If you've followed Tip 50, on page 102, which explains how to "child-proof" Ubuntu, this could be very useful.

295 Do Just About Anything to a File by Right-Clicking It

In a default Ubuntu setup, right-clicking a file offers the opportunity to open it with an application or delete it, rename it, and so on. Wouldn't it be useful if you could add your own right-click option that performed a specific action on the file? For example, if you right-clicked a Microsoft Word or OpenOffice.org document, how about if a Print document option appeared? If you right-click an image, how about if an option appeared to shrink the image or sharpen it?

All of this is possible using the Nautilus Actions add-in. As its name suggests, this lets you add options to the right-click menu that perform certain actions on particular types files. It's simple to create your own action, but hundreds of ready-made scripts are available and can be imported easily.

To install Nautilus Actions, use Synaptic to search for and install the aptly-named nautilus-actions. Once installed, the configuration program can be found on the System → Preferences menu.

Creating a Configuration from Scratch

Let's take as an example adding a Print document option that will appear whenever a word processing document is right-clicked. This takes advantage of the fact that OpenOffice.org Writer can be used from the command line to print any document by using the -p command option, without actually starting the program in editing mode—for example, oowriter -p filename.doc.

Here are the necessary steps (these steps can, of course, be adapted for any type of file and/or action):

1. Start by running the Nautilus Actions Configuration program, which can be found on the System → Preferences menu. When the program window appears, click the Add button.

2. In the Label field of the dialog box that appears, type Print document. This is the text that will actually appear on the right-click menu and can be anything you want. You can add some text to the Tooltip menu too—this will appear if the mouse is hovered over the menu option. However, it isn't essential. You can also select a suitable icon from the Icon drop-down list. This will appear alongside the new entry on the menu, but, again, it isn't essential.

3. In the Path field, type /usr/bin/oowriter. Most programs you use every day can be found in /usr/bin, and it's necessary to provide the path to the program along with its command-line filename. If you are in any doubt as to where an application "lives," open a terminal window, and type whereis command, replacing command with the name of the command in question.

4. In the Parameters text field, specify any command options that are needed, along with the filename and path. For our particular example, we need to type -p and then %d/%f, so the line reads -p %d/%f. %d and %f are Nautilus Actions shorthand—%d refers to the path of the file that has been right-clicked, and %f refers to the filename itself. The slash in the middle separates the two, just like at the command line. As you type, an example of the command that will be executed appears at the bottom of the dialog box. This is effectively what you would type at the command line to run the same command, so you can check to ensure it makes sense.

5. Click the Conditions tab. Here we can ensure that the new Print document option appears only whenever we right-click word processing document files, and not any others. We do this by specifying file extensions in the Filenames text field—several extensions can be entered, but they must be separated by a semicolon (;). Most word processing documents you're likely to encounter will be .doc, .sxw, .rtf, or .odt files. If you know you will encounter others—for example, WordPerfect documents (which use the .wpd file extension)—then add the relevant file extension. Precede each file extension by a wildcard (an asterisk). For an example, see Figure 3.53, on the facing page. Once done, click OK. Click the Close button on the main Nautilus Actions configuration window.

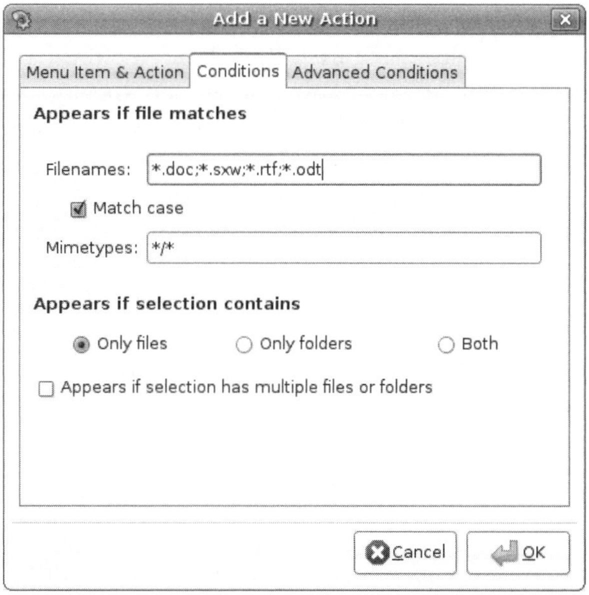

Figure 3.53: NAUTILUS ACTIONS CONFIGURATION (SEE TIP 295)

After this, you can test your new action by right-clicking a word processing document and selecting the new option—it will appear about two thirds of the way down the menu. Also try right-clicking other files that aren't word processing files, and note how the option doesn't appear. If the menu option doesn't appear when it should, try logging out and then back in again.

Note that if you find it annoying that the OpenOffice.org splash screen appears even when just printing a file automatically, see Tip 197, on page 226, for details of how to turn it off.

Importing Configurations Made by Others

By visiting http://www.grumz.net/index.php?q=configlist, you can download Nautilus Actions *schemas* (effectively configuration files) for just about any task you might want to do to any kind of file. To download a schemas file, click the header in the list, and then click the schemas link to download.

Be sure to read the schemas description to see whether any particular software is needed. For example, schemas that manipulate images will almost certainly need the ImageMagick software installed, so use

Google to search for it. Schemas that manipulate video files will probably need the ffmpeg software installed. Bear in mind that the notes alongside each schema are probably not written specifically for Ubuntu users, so don't name specific packages you will need. You might well have to use common sense when searching through Synaptic's package archive.

Once the schemas have downloaded, open Nautilus Actions Configuration (System → Preferences menu), and click the Import/Export button. Then click the button to the right of the File to Import text field, and browse to the schemas file. Click the OK button, then the Close button in the Nautilus Actions parent window. The new menu option will appear immediately, although you might have to log in and out again to see the icon (if applicable) appear alongside its entry in the list.

296 Get Notified of New Gmail Messages

Part of the usefulness of Google's Gmail service is provided by the Notifier programs for Windows and Mac OS X that tell you about new messages from the system tray area. Sadly, Google doesn't currently produce a Linux version, but no worry—just use Synaptic to download the community-created checkgmail package.

Once installed, you'll need to make the program start on bootup, so click System → Preferences → Sessions, click the Add button, and then, in the dialog box that appears, type checkgmail in both the Name and Command fields. Leave the Comment field empty, and click the OK button. Then close all programs, and log out and back in again.

As soon as the desktop appears, a dialog box will pop up asking you to input your Gmail details. You'll see this only once. Fill in your username and password in the relevant text boxes. If you don't want to be prompted for your password each time you log in, click the Save Password box, but bear in mind that password is saved as a text file that any user of the system can access, so this is considered insecure. There's no need to change any of checkgmail's other details, so click the OK button.

After this, a new Gmail icon will be added to the notification area. It will change from gray to red to indicate new mail, and a small window will scroll down to tell you who the sender is. If there's more than one message, the senders will be listed in order in the scroll-down window. You can then hover the mouse over the icon to see previews of the messages, and you can select any of them to open them in Firefox (or just click the icon itself to view your inbox). To create a new mail, right-click the icon, and select Compose mail.

If you'd like to be notified of emails in non-Gmail accounts, see Tip 246, on page 277. To search your Gmail messages from the desktop, consider installing Google Desktop—see Tip 282, on page 315.

297 OCR Scanned Text

Optical character recognition (OCR) is the process of turning printed text into electronic text. Utilizing it under Ubuntu is a breeze, as follows:

1. Start by using Synaptic to search for and install gocr. This is optical character recognition software that integrates into XSane, Ubuntu's scanner program. Once installed, it doesn't create an Applications menu entry.

2. Instead, gocr is accessed through XSane, so start the program (Applications → Graphics → XSane Image Scanner). Before scanning, you must choose settings conducive to good OCR, so, on the main XSane control panel, set the image type drop-down list to Gray and the resolution drop-down list to 300. These two drop-downs aren't labeled but can be found roughly in the middle of the XSane configuration window, as shown in Figure 3.54, on the following page.

3. In the XSane Preview window, click the Acquire Preview button. This will run a preview scan. In the resulting image, drag the selecting bounding box in the Preview window from the edges of the image in order to tightly define the text area that you want to scan. Ensure you crop out as much surrounding area as possible, as this will help avoid errors in the OCR output.

4. Back in the main XSane control panel window, click on the Scan button.

5. Once the scan is complete and the image viewer window appears, rotate the image so it's the right way up using the relevant toolbar buttons (if necessary). Then click File → OCR → Save As Text. A dialog box will then pop up asking you for the name of the file

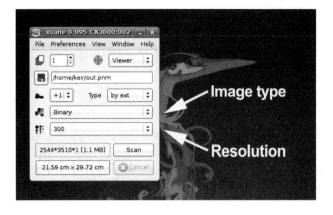

Figure 3.54: CHANGING THE RESOLUTION AND COLOR SETTINGS OF THE OCR SCAN (SEE TIP 297)

you'd like to create. After you click the Save button, the OCR process will start and might take some time to complete, depending on the complexity of the scanned page. Alas, no progress display is provided, although the image viewer window will remain grayed out and unresponsive until the OCR process has completed.

Once the OCR process has completed, take a look at the output file. It's unlikely this will be perfect, and you should definitely check it against the original source to correct errors. I noticed that apostrophes seem to cause problems with the character recognition. You might even want to try scanning again, this time perhaps altering the brightness and contrast settings in the main XSane control panel window before scanning.

Perhaps it goes without saying that less complex documents tend to OCR better. Thus, straight text on a page is likely to produce a better result than complex magazine layouts involving pictures, colored backgrounds, and different fonts/sizes. If you have to scan such documents, it might be worth scanning parts of the page piece by piece by selecting each column or block of text in the image scan preview window, scanning it separately, and running an OCR pass on it.

298 Use Ubuntu's Movie Player to Watch YouTube Movies

☐

Like many open source applications, Totem utilizes a plug-in structure, meaning that its functionality can be expanded by add-in modules. Several are supplied out of the box, including a YouTube browser. This lets you search for and play back YouTube videos within Totem. However, none of the plug-ins are activated.

To activate the YouTube plug-in, start Totem (Applications → Sound & Video → Movie Player), click Edit → Plugins, and put a check alongside YouTube Browser in the list. Click the Close button, and then in the main Totem program window select YouTube from the drop-down list called Properties at the top right. After this, a search box will appear, in which you can search for videos on YouTube. Double-click any entries in the Search Results field to play them in Totem.

You might need to follow the instructions in Tip 65, on page 114, to ensure all the multimedia codecs are installed prior to playback in order to watch YouTube videos in Totem; for some reason, codec installation for YouTube videos isn't automatic as it is for other video file formats.

299 Turn Your Desktop into Your /home Folder

☐

Do you use your desktop as a dumping ground for files and pretty much ignore your actual /home folder, which is where you *should* store things? If so, you might be interested in this tweak, which effectively makes Ubuntu use your /home folder for the desktop, instead of the actual /home/username/Desktop folder. Anything saved to the desktop, such as files/folders dropped there, will be placed in your /home folder. Additionally, anything in your /home folder will appear on the desktop.

To try this, start gconf-editor, navigate to /apps/nautilus/preferences, and put a check alongside desktop_is_home_dir. Then log out and back in again.

Remember that the contents of your desktop haven't vanished. They're still in the Desktop folder in your /home folder.

☐

300 Avoid Programs Quitting When the Terminal Is Closed

You might have noticed that, whenever you run a program from a terminal window, it quits when the terminal window is closed (there are some exceptions to this, such as the Firefox web browser, but it's generally the case). There are a handful of ways around this. Perhaps the easiest is to precede the command with nohup. For example, to run Gedit, you might type nohup gedit. Try this now. Then close the terminal window, and see what happens (or, actually, what doesn't happen).

The reason Gedit doesn't quit is that nohup tells the new program to ignore any future "hangup signals," which is to say Gedit is told ignore requests to terminate that are sent to it when the terminal quits.

See also Tip 207, on page 232, which describes how to use the screen command to create a command-line login that's independent of any terminal window.

☐

301 Allow Terminal Server Client to Access VNC Desktops

In Ubuntu 8.04 Hardy Heron, the Remote Desktop Viewer software on the Applications → Internet menu is used to access VNC-based remote desktops. This is a new addition to Ubuntu's software lineup, and I found it a little clunky. It also refused to connect to my MacBook's shared desktop.

The Terminal Server Client program (Applications → Internet) was used for this up until the 8.04 release and is rather more established than Remote Desktop Viewer. However, out of the box in 8.04 it lacks support for such connections—the VNC option on the Protocol menu is grayed out. This is easily fixed—just use Synaptic to search for and install xtightvncviewer. Then restart Terminal Server Client if you have it open. VNC will now appear as an option under the Protocol drop-down list.

302 Search All of Ubuntu's "Supported" Software

☐

One of the fun things about Ubuntu is the sheer volume of software available, and it can be both entertaining and productive to spend a few minutes (or hours) taking a look through what's available. Ideally, you want to install the officially supported software because the other software available might not be updated. You can make Synaptic sort by supported software by clicking the second column heading in the package view, but it's a little slow when operating this way.

A better method is to use the Add/Remove program on the Applications menu. By selecting Supported applications in the Show drop-down list, the list of packages will filter to show only officially supported software. As a bonus, you can then click the Popularity heading in the list to sort by popularity, as voted by Ubuntu users who participate in the package survey. This should then display particularly useful applications.

To install a software package, click the checkbox alongside it in the list, and then click the Apply Changes button.

303 Install Windows on a Computer That Has Ubuntu on It

☐

The Ubuntu installer is fully capable of squeezing Ubuntu onto a computer that has Windows on it. What about the other way around? What if Ubuntu is the only operating system that's installed and you want to install Windows alongside it?

Here is how it's done—these steps tell you how to make space for Windows, install it,[42] and then repair the boot loader so that Ubuntu can once again boot. The steps involve repartitioning your disk, which

---

42. It isn't usually possible to install Windows on an Ubuntu PC using a "restore" CD/DVD, as is supplied by some computer manufacturers; these usually wipe the entire hard disk and start afresh, or they restore a backup partition hidden on the disk. Because of this, these instructions (in Tip 303) require an original Windows XP or Vista installation CD/DVD disc (these discs are sometimes called *retail* discs).

brings with it a degree of risk, so it's vital that you back up essential data before carrying them out and also that you check and double-check each option, because an errant click could be disastrous:

1. Boot from your Ubuntu installation CD/DVD, and select the Try Ubuntu... option from the Ubuntu installer boot menu. Once Ubuntu is up and running, click System → Administration → Partition Editor. This will start the Gparted partitioning tool.

2. Right-click the Ubuntu partition (it will be the largest in Gparted's display), and click Resize/Move. In the dialog box that appears, click and drag the right edge of the partition so that the Ubuntu partition shrinks to make space for Windows.[43] You should consider about 3–4GB the minimum for Windows XP, depending on your needs, although Vista will likely require at least 15GB, depending on the version you're installing—check the product documentation's "Minimum Requirements" section. Once a size has been set, click the Resize/Move button. Then click the Apply button in the main Gparted window. Once resizing is complete, you should see that Gparted now indicates an "unallocated" area in the middle to the right of the disk display, similar to that shown in Figure 3.55, on the next page.

3. If you intend to install Windows XP, reboot the computer using your Windows installation CD, and install Windows as you would normally, on a blank hard disk, but with one caveat—select Unpartitioned Space when prompted where on the disk you want to install Windows. Be careful when you select it again after creating the partition—it will probably be identified as Partition 3 (New (Raw)). You'll be warned the other operating system on the disk must be marked inactive. This is fine.

4. If you intend to install Windows Vista, reboot the computer using your Vista installation DVD. When the installer dialog box comes up, select your language, and then follow the steps as usual, including clicking the Install Now button. Don't worry—you'll be prompted about which disk/partition to use later, and nothing will be installed immediately. Eventually you'll be offered a Custom (Advanced) option. Select it, and then, in the list of disks and

---

43. If you see an error message while resizing the partition (in Tip 303, on the preceding page), right-click the partition after clearing the error message dialog box, and click Check. Once the check is complete, shut down your computer. Then boot using the Ubuntu install disk, and try resizing again, as described in the tip. This time it should complete successfully.

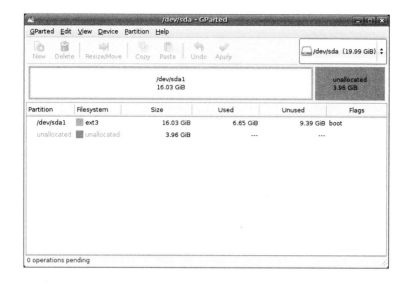

Figure 3.55: RESIZING THE UBUNTU PARTITION TO MAKE SPACE FOR WINDOWS

partitions, select your new "unallocated space," and click the Drive options (advanced) option. Click New and then Apply. Once that's done, hit Shift+F10 to open a DOS box, and type the following:

```
X:\Sources> diskpart
X:\Sources> select disk 0
X:\Sources> select partition 3
X:\Sources> active
X:\Sources> exit
X:\Sources> exit
```

Then, in the original installation dialog box, once again ensure your new Windows partition is selected, and click the Format button. Then click the Next button, and complete the installation in the usual way.

5. Once the Windows installation has completely finished and the Windows desktop appears, reboot from your Ubuntu installation disk. You'll now need to restore the Ubuntu boot loader (you'll no longer be able to boot your Ubuntu installation on the hard disk, should you try, but don't worry—it's still there!). Select the Try Ubuntu... option on the menu. Once the Ubuntu desktop appears, open a terminal window (Applications → Accessories → Terminal).

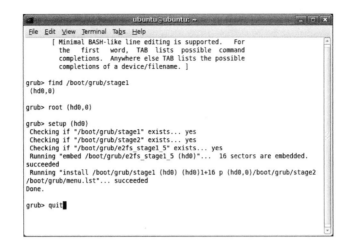

Figure 3.56: RESTORING THE UBUNTU BOOT LOADER (SEE TIP 303)

Then type the following:

```
$ sudo grub
grub> find /boot/grub/stage1
```

You will see something like (hd0,0). Using this information, type the following (for an example, see Figure 3.56):

```
grub> root (hd0,0)
grub> setup (hd0)
grub> quit
```

If applicable, replace (hd0,0) with the details that you discovered earlier.

6. Reboot the computer. The Ubuntu boot menu will be back, but you now need to add an entry for Windows. Boot Ubuntu as usual, and once the desktop appears, open a terminal window. Type gksu gedit /boot/grub/menu.lst. At the bottom of the file, after the line that reads ### END DEBIAN AUTOMAGIC KERNELS LIST, type the following (this assumes that, as described earlier, you created the Windows partition in the middle of the disk, in between the Ubuntu main and swap partitions):

```
title Boot into Windows
rootnoverify (hd0,1)
makeactive
chainloader +1
```

7. You'll also need to change two lines at the top of the file—put a hash before the line that reads hiddenmenu on its own so that it now reads #hiddenmenu. Then change the line that reads timeout 3 to read timeout 10 (the number of spaces between timeout and the number don't matter). Then save the file and reboot. You should find that there's now a Windows entry on the boot menu.

304 Turn Your Computer into a Egg Timer

Nice and simple, this one. Just install timer-applet using Synaptic. Once it's installed, right-click a blank spot on the panel, and select Add to panel. Then select Timer from the list. Click the applet that appears on the panel (it will look roughly like a cook's kitchen timer), and then set three minutes in the Minutes text field for the perfect boiled egg (or any other time in the Hours, Minutes, or Seconds fields, in fact—it does more than time boiling eggs). To pause the countdown, for any reason, just click the timer.

If all you want to do is count down how long it takes for a cup of tea to brew, see Tip 307, on page 351.

305 Create a Portable USB Stick Installation of Ubuntu

This is a handy hack that lets you install Ubuntu to a USB stick so you can use it on just about any computer (provided the computer concerned can boot from USB—computers younger than about three years old should be fine). This is ideal for situations where using a computer's permanent operating system might pose a security risk, such as in Internet cafés. You can even use it on computers that lack a hard disk.

Unfortunately, there are a number of caveats. Running Ubuntu from a USB stick is slow because of read/write speeds that are a fraction of those of standard hard disks (write speeds in particular). Additionally, you'll need a large USB key stick to make this work properly—at least

4GB—and the Ubuntu 8.04.1 install CD, or later, because there's a bug in the original 8.04 install CD that stops the new OS from booting correctly once installed.[44] See Tip 31, on page 77, to learn how to get an Ubuntu installation on smaller USB sticks, although a handful of compromises are necessary in that case.

Here are the steps involved to install Ubuntu on a USB key stick:

1. If possible, disconnect any hard disks in your computer while you carry out the installation onto the USB stick. This stops Ubuntu's setup routine from incorrectly referring to the USB key stick during boot menu configuration. Disconnecting the hard disk(s) can be done by opening up your computer and temporarily removing the data cable connected to the hard disk drive. If your drive is SATA, bear in mind that the smaller of the two cable connections is the data one—to see where the data cables connect on SATA and older EIDE hard disks, take a look at Figure 3.57, on the next page.

   If you have a notebook computer, it might be possible to temporarily remove the hard disk—consult the manual, where removing the disk might be described under the section describing how to upgrade it. You'll be able to reconnect the disks after the installation has finished.

   However, if you can't disconnect the hard disks, don't worry too much—it just adds a little complexity to the issue, and you'll have to perform a handful of extra steps later (and also whenever a system upgrade brings a new kernel file).

2. Other than the previous step, installing Ubuntu on a USB key stick doesn't differ much from installing it on any kind of storage device. Ensure the stick is inserted, and start by booting from the Ubuntu CD, selecting Install Ubuntu from the boot menu.

3. When Ubuntu starts, work through the questions and prompts until you reach the partitioning stage. Then select Guided – use entire disk, and click the radio button alongside your USB key stick. You should be able to identify it by brand and model, as well as by

---

44. The bug with the original Ubuntu 8.04 install CD causes the desktop to hang after you log in when installing on a USB key stick. If you have no choice but to use the original install CD, the bug can be fixed by booting from the USB stick after installation and then switching to a virtual console before logging in. Kill the X server (sudo killall gdm), empty the /tmp folder (sudo rm -rf /tmp/*), and manually start X (startx). Once the desktop appears, configure your network connection, and update online. This will install new system software that fixes the bug.

Figure 3.57: DATA CABLE CONNECTION POINTS ON TYPICAL HARD DISKS (SEE TIP 305)

its capacity, which will be a lot less than the hard disks installed in your computer (or it might simply be identified as USB DISK). If you've disconnected your hard disks for the duration of the installation, then there will be only one option here. Once done, click the Forward button.

4. Again, follow through the installation procedure, creating your new user account when prompted, until you reach the Ready to install summary screen. If you've disconnected your hard disks, then simply click the Install button to start the installation. If the hard disks are still connected, click the Advanced button. In the dialog box that appears, click the drop-down list under the Device for boot loader installation heading, and again look for the entry referring to your USB key stick. However, select the entry *beneath* it in the list—it will be identical to the entry for the key stick but

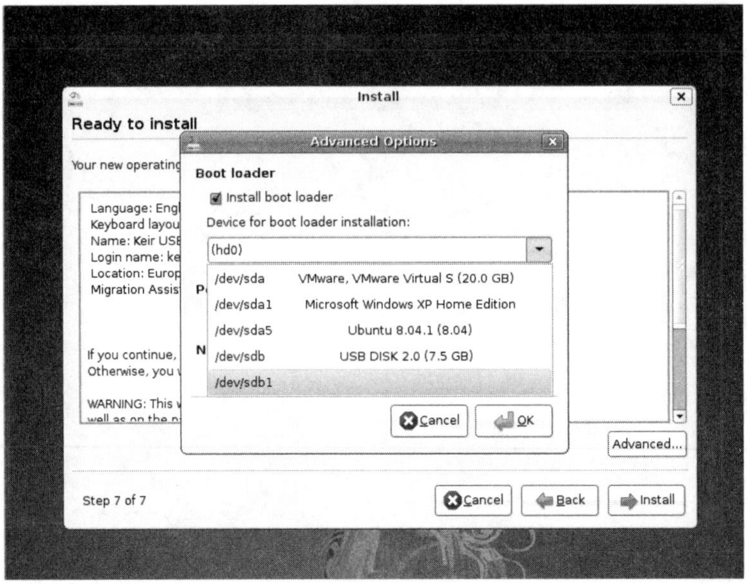

Figure 3.58: SELECTING THE RIGHT DEVICE TO INSTALL THE BOOT LOADER (SEE TIP 305)

will have a 1 after it (in other words, the first partition on the memory stick). For example, on my computer, the memory stick was identified as /dev/sdb Easy Disk (7.5GB), and I therefore selected the entry under this—/dev/sdb1. For an example, see Figure 3.58. Once done, click the OK button and then the Install button in the parent dialog box.

5. If you installed Ubuntu without the hard disks connected, once the installation has finished, you can now shut down the computer, reconnect the drives, and then boot the computer from the USB stick to test everything. Don't forget that some computers have to be manually configured to boot from USB—this can normally be done by hitting the [Esc] during initial self-testing to see a boot device menu or by changing a setting in the computer's BIOS setup screen.

6. If you installed Ubuntu to a USB disk with the hard disks connected, one more step is necessary before you can boot from the USB stick. Reboot the computer using the Ubuntu installation CD, and select the Try Ubuntu option. Once the desktop appears, click

the USB stick's entry on the Places menu to ensure it's mounted and that its files are available—you should be able to identify it on the Places menu by its size.

7. You now need to ensure that the USB stick's boot menu correctly refers to the USB key drive, and this involves editing the boot menu file. You will need to repeat this step whenever Update Manager installs a new kernel update because the update process will rewrite the boot menu. Open a terminal window, and type the following to open the menu.lst file on the USB key stick:

```
$ gksu gedit /media/disk/boot/grub/menu.lst
```

Look for the line that reads ## ## End Default Options ##, and look almost immediately underneath for a line beneath it for the first line that reads root (hd1,0) (or similar—the first number might be different on your computer if you have more than one hard disk installed). Change it to read root (hd0,0). Although not essential, you might want to change the two other identical lines in the boot menu entries beneath so they say the same thing (that is, root (hd0,0)). These refer to the Ubuntu rescue boot option and memtest86+. You might also want to delete *everything* that appears beneath the line that reads ### END DEBIAN AUTOMAGIC KERNELS LIST so that it then becomes the last line, because these are effectively useless boot menu entries added by the Ubuntu installer that refer specifically to the PC configuration used to create the USB Ubuntu installation. Once done, save the file, and close Gedit.

After this, you should be able to reboot from the USB key stick. Again, keep in mind that some computers have to be manually configured to boot from USB—this can normally be done by hitting the Esc during initial self-testing to see a boot device menu or by changing a setting in the computer's BIOS setup screen.

306 Enhance the Copy and Paste Clipboard

□

Perhaps surprisingly, the GNOME desktop clipboard—as supplied with Ubuntu—is rather basic. You can copy and paste only single items at a time. Keeping a clipboard history—where several items can be held in the clipboard at one time—can sometimes be useful and is one of those features that, once tried, is hard to give up. Luckily, the KDE desktop project comes to the rescue with Klipper, a desktop applet that also works under GNOME.[45]

To install it, use Synaptic to search for and install klipper. Be sure to select the version of Klipper that's officially supported by the Ubuntu project—you can tell whether this is the case because there will be an Ubuntu logo alongside its entry in Synaptic's list of packages.

Once installed, you'll need to make Klipper start when you log in, so click System → Preferences → Sessions. In the program window that appears, ensure the Startup Programs tab is selected, and click the Add button. In both the Name and Command fields, type klipper. Leave the Comment field empty. Then hit OK, and log out and then back in. You should now find the Klipper icon in the notification area.

Using Klipper is simplicity itself. It records any text that is copied/cut into the clipboard, along with any text that is selected by clicking and dragging. You can then select from its history of cuttings by clicking the icon, which will insert that cutting into the clipboard so you can paste it as usual by clicking Edit → Paste within an application. Klipper remembers the cut/copy history even after reboots. You can boost Klipboard's memory beyond the default seven entries by right-clicking it and selecting Configure Klipper. Then click and drag the Clipboard history size slider.

To turn off the perhaps less-than-useful facility of recording click-and-drag selections to the clipboard, open Klipper's configuration options, as described earlier, and put a check in Ignore selection. This can avoid several seemingly blank entries being added to Klipper's history list. When configuring Klipper, bear in mind that many of its options and program features apply only when the KDE desktop is being used. However, the core functionality works fine in the GNOME desktop.

See also Tip 244, on page 276, which explains how to utilize the cut and paste functions at the command line.

---

45. There is a Klipper-like project for the GNOME desktop—Glipper. Unfortunately, it didn't function correctly with Ubuntu 8.04 in my tests, and selected text was added incorrectly so that the history list became prematurely full. Feel free to try Glipper, however—the package is called glipper, and once installed, you can start the background demon by typing /usr/lib/glipper/glipper. Then right-click a panel to add the Glipper applet (it's referred to in the applet list as Clipboard manager). If you intend to keep using Glipper, add it to your startup items, as described in Tip 306, on the previous page. Bear in mind that Klipper and Glipper can't work alongside each other.

307 Be Told When Your Tea Has Brewed ☐

It's said that the Boston Tea Party is responsible for the fact that America, unlike many parts of the world, doesn't have a taste for hot tea. Compare that to England or China, for example, where tea is drunk by the gallon. Had the Boston Tea Party not happened, then I'm sure that the Teatime applet—which can be installed by searching Synaptic for the teatime and gstreamer0.10-plugins-ugly packages—would be a standard feature of Ubuntu. Put simply, it times how long tea should be left to brew and informs you when that time is up.

Once the package is installed, right-click a blank spot on the panel, click Add to panel, and select Teatime from the list. Then right-click the icon to select the tea you're brewing—Assam, Darjeeling, and green tea are available, amongst others. This will start the timer, and when the tea is ready, you'll be told courtesy of a spinning teacup in the center of the screen. Click the teacup to get rid of it. Then drink your tea—but not too quickly, or you'll burn your lips.

308 Avoid Bad Formatting When Viewing OpenOffice.org Files on Windows ☐

OpenOffice.org is pretty good at exporting files in Microsoft Office format, but there might still be one or two occasions when what you created in Ubuntu just doesn't translate well when opened in Microsoft Office. Provided the document doesn't need to be further edited by the recipient, the solution is to save it as a PDF, in which case its formatting will remain fully intact. The recipient can then print it out at their end, if need be.

To save as a PDF, just click File → Export as PDF within any OpenOffice.org application. Alternatively, if that doesn't produce optimum results, try printing to Ubuntu's PDF printer—click File → Print, and select PDF from the printer selection drop-down list.

But what about OpenOffice.org Impress presentations that include moving images and maybe even sound? In that case, you should choose to export the presentation as a Macromedia Flash file—click File → Export, and then select the option from the File type fold-down menu. The recipient will then have to drag and drop the file onto the browser window to open it (assuming they have Flash Player installed, and most Windows computers do); note that RealPlayer, regardless of operating system, has a habit of associating with the .swf file extension used by Flash files but doesn't seem to be able to play back the files properly. You will have to provide specific information for the recipient of the file regarding how to view it in a browser.

☐

309 Fix USB Key Sticks That Wrongly Report They're Full

Have you ever tried to copy files to a USB key stick (or other removable storage device, such as a memory card) and received an error message to say that the disk is full even though the total file size of the files is nowhere near the USB key stick's limit? The probable cause is the invisible .Trash folder that Nautilus creates on a USB key stick each time you delete something on it. This fills up with old files each time you delete something on the USB stick.

The quickest solution is just to unmount the USB stick by right-clicking it and selecting Unmount Volume. You should then be prompted if you want to empty the trash on the device. Click the Empty Deleted Items button and then pull the USB stick out of your computer and reinsert it again to remount it.

If this doesn't work or if you don't see the prompt asking whether you want to empty the trash, you can delete the hidden trash folder using a handful of terminal commands. Start by reinserting the USB stick so it's mounted again. USB key sticks are usually mounted in the /media folder, in a folder named after their label. For example, the USB key stick on my test computer is called KINGSTON, so I opened a terminal window and issued the following command to change into the relevant folder: cd /media/KINGSTON.

Use the ls -a command to reveal hidden files, and then use the rm -rf to remove any file called .Trash, or a variation of this.

On my test system the folder was called .Trash-1000, so I typed the following to delete it:

```
$ sudo rm -rf .Trash-1000
```

In actual fact, assuming you're using the USB stick simply to store files, it might be wise to delete all other hidden files and/or folders (those with a period in front of them). Ubuntu isn't alone in saving hidden files to the disk for the purposes of trash (and more)—Macintosh OS X does too.

To stop the disk from getting full in this way in the future, follow Tip 228, on page 260, which describes how to add a Delete entry to the right-click menu that bypasses the trash facility. Unfortunately, currently it is not possible to disable Ubuntu's trash function.

310 Use Ubuntu's Built-in Download Manager

Downloading big files that take a long time to arrive, such as new Ubuntu installation ISO images, can be fraught with difficulties. You'll need to have a perfect connection for the duration of the download (not always possible with wifi), and the remote server may sometimes drop the connection. Restarting from scratch to download a 670MB file when 669MB of it has arrived fine can be a very frustrating experience!

The solution is wget, Ubuntu's built-in command-line download manager. It runs at the command line, and all you need do is specify the complete URL for the download file, including the http:// or ftp:// components, as applicable. For example, at the time of writing, the Ubuntu 8.04.1 release can be found at http://releases.ubuntu.com/hardy/ubuntu-8.04.1-desktop-i386.iso, so to download this I would type the following into a terminal window:

```
$ wget http://releases.ubuntu.com/hardy/ubuntu-8.04.1-desktop-i386.iso
```

As the download progresses, you'll see a percentage figure progress display, along with figures showing how much has been downloaded and the speed of the transfer. If wget loses the connection for any reason, it'll automatically try again and attempt to resume where it left off. If you want to quit the download, type [Ctrl]+[c]. Don't forget to clear up the partially downloaded file.

Because large downloads can take a long time, you might want to use nohup with wget to avoid wget quitting when the terminal window that started it is closed. This will effectively invisibly download the file in the background and will persist even if you log out (to stop the download if needed, type killall wget into a terminal window/virtual console). See Tip 300, on page 340, for more information. Alternatively, you might consider using screen to start the wget download in a background command-line instance that you can switch in and out of in order to check progress—see Tip 207, on page 232, for more information.

You might also be interested in kget, which can be installed using Synaptic (search for the kget package; don't install the KDE4 version) and provides a GUI front end to wget. It's officially a component of the KDE desktop and is designed to work with the Konqueror web browser but works fine under the GNOME desktop and Firefox of Ubuntu. Once installed, you'll find it on the Internet menu. You can drag and drop download links to its program window to start them downloading or click Settings → Show Drop Target for a small window onto which you can drag and drop the download links, like with some Windows download managers. (Tip: Right-click the floating window's minimize/maximize buttons, and select Always On Top; this will stop it from falling behind other program windows.)

311 Avoid an F-Spot Startup Error

When you start F-Spot for the first time after a fresh installation, you'll be warned that "The folder contents could not be displayed." This happens because the Photos folder that F-Spot expects to find isn't present. It's a trivial error but one that can be alarming for newbies.

To fix the problem, just rename the Pictures folder to Photos on any new installation of Ubuntu. After this, F-Spot will start up without any gripes.

312 | Record Your Desktop

☐

Have you ever been chatting on a website forum and been totally unable to describe an action you've performed on Ubuntu? "Click the top bar— the gray thing at the top, you know. Then drag the icon. The blue icon. Drag it to the desktop..."

It can be hard describing in words what are simple procedures with a mouse. A solution is at hand, however. The Byzanz application lets you record your desktop, a window, or a defined area of the screen as a movie. The resulting file is an animated .gif and so is viewable in almost any web browser made over the past ten years. You could attach it to a forum posting if you're asking for help, for example. The only downside is that the resulting movie file can be large, depending on the area you've defined and the length of the movie. Full desktop recordings can easily come in at double-digit megabytes, in fact.

The package can be installed using Synaptic—search for byzanz. Once installed, right-click a blank spot on the top panel, and select Add to panel. Then select Desktop Recorder from the list. Note that Byzanz won't work correctly if desktop visual effects are enabled—to disable them, click System → Preferences → Appearance, and then click the Visual Effects tab. Then click the None radio button. When you've finished recording using Byzanz, repeat, and click the Normal, Extra, or Custom button, depending on your preference (you won't see the Custom option unless you've installed Simple Compiz Settings Manager, as described in Tip 74, on page 120).

Once the application's icon appears on the panel, click the small down arrow next to it to select to record the desktop, an area of it, or a particular window. When selecting to record an area of the desktop, the screen will turn black, and you should click and drag to define where you want to record (the screen turning black is an unfortunate bug, and you'll have to try to remember where on the desktop it is you want to record). If you select to record a program window, the mouse will turn to a crosshairs—just click the window you want to record.

After this, recording will start. The Byzanz icon will turn to a red circle to indicate this. When you've finished, click the red circle to stop recording. You'll then be prompted to save the movie file. Click Cancel to discard the movie.

Bear in mind that resulting movie .gif files will not play in Ubuntu's default image viewer, which will open when you double-click the file. You'll see nothing but the first frame. Instead, you must play them in Firefox to see the full animation. To do this, right-click the file, and select Open With → Open with "Firefox Web Browser."

☐ | **313** | **Take Screenshots in Any Format**

Have you ever wondered why many Linux desktop screenshots on websites or even within books seem to have GIMP running? It's not because the authors are inveterate image tweakers. It's because the GIMP includes a powerful screenshot tool. To use it, start the program, and click File → Acquire → Screenshot. Then make your selection of what you want to capture from the dialog box that appears—single program window, defined region, or entire screen. Particularly useful is the Delay function, listed under the previous options, which allows you to set a delay (in seconds) before the screenshot is taken.

Once taken, the screenshot will be opened as a GIMP image. You can choose to crop it, if necessary, or just click File → Save As to save it to disk. Remember that GIMP sets the image type automatically, based on the file extension you type. So, typing a filename of screenshot.bmp will automatically save the file in BMP format.

See also Tip 202, on page 229, to learn how to use Ubuntu's built-in screenshot tool. Note that this saves only in PNG format, however.

☐ | **314** | **Trace Network Routes**

If you're used to using the network diagnostic command traceroute, you might wonder where it's gone under Ubuntu. It's simply been replaced with tracepath, a similar tool that works in almost exactly the same way. See its man page for details.

315 Automatically Scroll PDF Files ☐

And now for the last tip in this monster of a book. If you're viewing a long PDF file (such as, say, *Ubuntu Kung Fu*, if you purchased it as a PDF file), then you can scroll automatically within the Evince PDF viewer by right-clicking and selecting Autoscroll from the menu that appears. Simply drag the mouse up or down to scroll through the pages. The closer the middle of the program window the mouse cursor gets, the slower the scrolling will be. Experiment with it. It takes a little while to get used to, but it can be very useful. Just click the left mouse button to cancel when you're done.

What do you mean I should have told you this tip right at the beginning, so it would have helped you when reading the PDF? I did say back in the introduction chapter that I don't necessarily recommend reading this book from the first tip onward. In fact, I believe I might have suggested staring at the back and working your way to the front....

Index

Web 2.0

Welcome to the Web, version 2.0. You need some help to tame the wild technologies out there. Start with *Prototype and script.aculo.us*, a book about two libraries that will make your JavaScript life much easier.

See how to reach the largest possible web audience with *The Accessible Web*.

Prototype and script.aculo.us

Tired of getting swamped in the nitty-gritty of cross-browser, Web 2.0–grade JavaScript? Get back in the game with Prototype and script.aculo.us, two extremely popular JavaScript libraries that make it a walk in the park. Be it Ajax, drag and drop, autocompletion, advanced visual effects, or many other great features, all you need is write one or two lines of script that look so good they could almost pass for Ruby code!

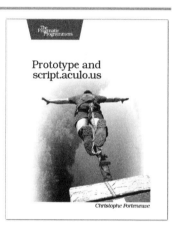

Prototype and script.aculo.us: You never knew JavaScript could do this!
Christophe Porteneuve
(330 pages) ISBN: 1-934356-01-8. $34.95
http://pragprog.com/titles/cppsu

The Accessible Web

The 2000 U.S. Census revealed that 12% of the population is severely disabled. Sometime in the next two decades, one in five Americans will be older than 65. Section 508 of the Americans with Disabilities Act requires your website to provide *equivalent access* to all potential users. But beyond the law, it is both good manners and good business to make your site accessible to everyone. This book shows you how to design sites that excel for all audiences.

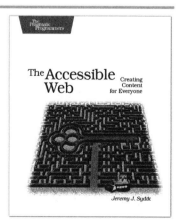

The Accessible Web
Jeremy Sydik
(304 pages) ISBN: 1-934356-02-6. $34.95
http://pragprog.com/titles/jsaccess

Getting It Done

Start with the habits of an agile developer and use the team practices of successful agile teams, and your project will fly over the finish line.

Practices of an Agile Developer

Agility is all about using feedback to respond to change. Learn how to apply the principles of agility throughout the software development process • establish and maintain an agile working environment • deliver what users really want • use personal agile techniques for better coding and debugging • use effective collaborative techniques for better teamwork • move to an agile approach

Practices of an Agile Developer: Working in the Real World
Venkat Subramaniam and Andy Hunt
(189 pages) ISBN: 0-9745140-8-X. $29.95
http://pragprog.com/titles/pad

Ship It!

Page after page of solid advice, all tried and tested in the real world. This book offers a collection of tips that show you what tools a successful team has to use, and how to use them well. You'll get quick, easy-to-follow advice on modern techniques and when they should be applied. **You need this book if:** • You're frustrated at lack of progress on your project. • You want to make yourself and your team more valuable. • You've looked at methodologies such as Extreme Programming (XP) and felt they were too, well, extreme. • You've looked at the Rational Unified Process (RUP) or CMM/I methods and cringed at the learning curve and costs. • **You need to get software out the door without excuses**

Ship It! A Practical Guide to Successful Software Projects
Jared Richardson and Will Gwaltney
(200 pages) ISBN: 0-9745140-4-7. $29.95
http://pragprog.com/titles/prj

Real World Tools

Learn real-world design and architecture for your project, and a very pragmatic editor for Mac OS X.

Release It!

Whether it's in Java, .NET, or Ruby on Rails, getting your application ready to ship is only half the battle. Did you design your system to survive a sudden rush of visitors from Digg or Slashdot? Or an influx of real-world customers from 100 different countries? Are you ready for a world filled with flaky networks, tangled databases, and impatient users?

If you're a developer and don't want to be on call at 3 a.m. for the rest of your life, this book will help.

Design and Deploy Production-Ready Software
Michael T. Nygard
(368 pages) ISBN: 0-9787392-1-3. $34.95
http://pragprog.com/titles/mnee

TextMate

If you're coding Ruby or Rails on a Mac, then you owe it to yourself to get the TextMate editor. And, once you're using TextMate, you owe it to yourself to pick up this book. It's packed with information that will help you automate all your editing tasks, saving you time to concentrate on the important stuff. Use snippets to insert boilerplate code and refactorings to move stuff around. Learn how to write your own extensions to customize it to the way you work.

TextMate: Power Editing for the Mac
James Edward Gray II
(200 pages) ISBN: 0-9787392-3-X. $29.95
http://pragprog.com/titles/textmate

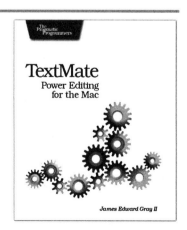

It All Starts Here

If you're programming in Ruby, you need the PickAxe Book: the definitive reference to the Ruby Programming language, now in the revised 3rd Edition for Ruby 1.9.

Programming Ruby (The Pickaxe)

The Pickaxe book, named for the tool on the cover, is the definitive reference to this highly-regarded language. • Up-to-date and expanded for Ruby version 1.9 • Complete documentation of all the built-in classes, modules, and methods • Complete descriptions of all standard libraries • Learn more about Ruby's web tools, unit testing, and programming philosophy

Programming Ruby: The Pragmatic Programmer's Guide, 3rd Edition
Dave Thomas with Chad Fowler and Andy Hunt
(900 pages) ISBN: 978-1-9343560-8-1. $49.95
http://pragprog.com/titles/ruby3

Agile Web Development with Rails

Rails is a full-stack, open-source web framework, with integrated support for unit, functional, and integration testing. It enforces good design principles, consistency of code across your team (and across your organization), and proper release management. This is the newly updated Second Edition, which goes beyond the Jolt-award winning first edition with new material on:

• Migrations • RJS templates • Respond_to
• Integration Tests • Additional ActiveRecord features • Another year's worth of Rails best practices

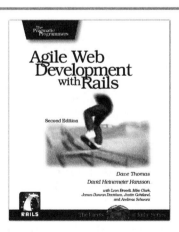

Agile Web Development with Rails: Second Edition
Dave Thomas and David Heinemeier Hansson with Leon Breedt, Mike Clark, James Duncan Davidson, Justin Gehtland, and Andreas Schwarz
(750 pages) ISBN: 0-9776166-3-0. $39.95
http://pragprog.com/titles/rails2

Get Groovy

Expand your horizons with Groovy, and tame the wild Java VM.

Programming Groovy

Programming Groovy will help you learn the necessary fundamentals of programming in Groovy. You'll see how to use Groovy to do advanced programming techniques, including meta programming, builders, unit testing with mock objects, processing XML, working with databases and creating your own domain-specific languages (DSLs).

Programming Groovy Dynamic Productivity for the Java Developer
Venkat Subramaniam
(320 pages) ISBN: 978-1-9343560-9-8. $34.95
http://pragprog.com/titles/vslg

Groovy Recipes

See how to speed up nearly every aspect of the development process using *Groovy Recipes*. Groovy makes mundane file management tasks like copying and renaming files trivial. Reading and writing XML has never been easier with XmlParsers and XmlBuilders. Breathe new life into arrays, maps, and lists with a number of convenience methods. Learn all about Grails, and go beyond HTML into the world of Web Services: REST, JSON, Atom, Podcasting, and much much more.

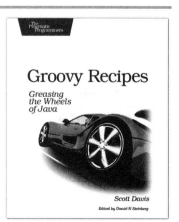

Groovy Recipes: Greasing the Wheels of Java
Scott Davis
(264 pages) ISBN: 978-0-9787392-9-4. $34.95
http://pragprog.com/titles/sdgrvr

Stuff You Need to Know

From massively concurrent systems to the basics of Ajax, we've got the stuff you need to know.

Programming Erlang

Learn how to write truly concurrent programs—programs that run on dozens or even hundreds of local and remote processors. See how to write high-reliability applications—even in the face of network and hardware failure—using the Erlang programming language.

Programming Erlang: Software for a Concurrent World
Joe Armstrong
(536 pages) ISBN: 1-934356-00-X. $36.95
http://pragprog.com/titles/jaerlang

Pragmatic Ajax

Ajax redefines the user experience for web applications, providing compelling user interfaces. Now you can dig deeper into Ajax itself as this book shows you how to make Ajax magic. Explore both the fundamental technologies and the emerging frameworks that make it easy.

From Google Maps to Ajaxified Java, .NET, and Ruby on Rails applications, this Pragmatic guide strips away the mystery and shows you the easy way to make Ajax work for you.

Pragmatic Ajax: A Web 2.0 Primer
Justin Gehtland, Ben Galbraith, Dion Almaer
(296 pages) ISBN: 0-9766940-8-5. $29.95
http://pragprog.com/titles/ajax

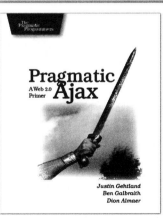

The Pragmatic Bookshelf

The Pragmatic Bookshelf features books written by developers for developers. The titles continue the well-known Pragmatic Programmer style and continue to garner awards and rave reviews. As development gets more and more difficult, the Pragmatic Programmers will be there with more titles and products to help you stay on top of your game.

Visit Us Online

Ubuntu Kung Fu's Home Page
http://pragprog.com/titles/ktuk
Source code from this book, errata, and other resources. Come give us feedback, too!

Register for Updates
http://pragprog.com/updates
Be notified when updates and new books become available.

Join the Community
http://pragprog.com/community
Read our weblogs, join our online discussions, participate in our mailing list, interact with our wiki, and benefit from the experience of other Pragmatic Programmers.

New and Noteworthy
http://pragprog.com/news
Check out the latest pragmatic developments in the news.

Save on the PDF

Save on the PDF version of this book. Owning the paper version of this book entitles you to purchase the PDF version at a terrific discount. The PDF is great for carrying around on your laptop. It's hyperlinked, has color, and is fully searchable.

Buy it now at pragprog.com/coupon.

Contact Us

Phone Orders:	1-800-699-PROG (+1 919 847 3884)
Online Orders:	www.pragprog.com/catalog
Customer Service:	orders@pragprog.com
Non-English Versions:	translations@pragprog.com
Pragmatic Teaching:	academic@pragprog.com
Author Proposals:	proposals@pragprog.com